D1043219

SCENES & MONOLOGS

From The Best New Plays

· · · · · · · · · · · ·

An anthology of new
dramatic writing from
professionally produced
American plays

EDITED BY

ROGER ELLIS

MERIWETHER PUBLISHING LTD.
Colorado Springs, Colorado

Meriwether Publishing Ltd., Publisher
P.O. Box 7710
Colorado Springs, CO 80933

Executive editor: Theodore O. Zapel
Typesetting: Sharon E. Garlock
Cover design: Tom Myers
Cover photography: Tom Myers / Theodore O. Zapel

Library of Congress Cataloging-in-Publication Data

Scenes & monologs from the best new plays: an anthology of new dramatic
    writing from professionally produced American plays / edited by
    Roger Ellis. — 1st ed.
      p.   cm.
    ISBN 0-916260-93-3
    1. Acting. 2. Monologs. 3. American drama—20th century.
I. Ellis, Roger, 1943 May 18- II. Title: Scenes and monologs from the
best new plays.
PN2080.S238   1992
812'.5408—dc20

                                          92-32989
                                            CIP

4   5   6   7   8   01   02   03   04

For Rose, Jeremy, and Alex

TABLE OF CONTENTS

SCENES FOR A MAN AND A WOMAN

MONOLOGS FOR WOMEN

NOTE: The numerals running vertically down the left margin of each page of dialog are for the convenience of the director. With these, he/she may easily direct attention to a specific passage.

INTRODUCTION

Focus of the Book

This book is a practical resource text for acting and directing students of all ages, and their coaches: middle through high school, university undergraduate and graduate, and professionals young and old. Its contents include a fair sampling of the most recent work of playwrights across the United States. Some of these authors are well known (Tina Howe, David Henry Hwang, Mark Medoff); while others have only begun to score an impact on their audiences (Claire Braz-Valentine, Charles Smith, Debbie Baley). But all of them have developed their scripts in the crucible of workshops, readings, and staged productions; and out of that body of work I've tried to select dramatically compelling and self-contained extracts for this anthology.

I think this book holds value for another group of people as well: for the general reader and beginning student of theatre it can provide a generous sampling, in one volume, of what many directors, producers, and audiences feel to be the most significant new plays being produced on the nation's regional stages today. Unlike classical works, both historical and modern, these dramas place their finger upon many of the major trends and conflicts which occupy our attention today. Hence, the gallery of characters contained in these pages offers readers an arresting and kaleidoscopic reflection of American society; and the literary styles one encounters here demonstrate the range and power of American writers who will continue to shape theatrical technique in the years to come.

Whether all the plays represented here will survive the test of time with a universal "historical passport" is, of course, anyone's guess. What *is* important is that they offer vital and compelling treatments of our social, artistic, and spiritual experience at this point in the twentieth century.

About the Anthology

Before presenting the plays themselves, however, a word is in order about the collection as a whole in order to guide or deter readers towards or away from this text. To begin with, all the ex-

1

tracts in this book are taken from American plays recently produced (within the past ten years), and plays that are not generally available to the reading public. They are, therefore, highly "original" in the sense that few people can claim to have read or seen them performed. I've made this editorial decision in order to carry out the scholarly "spadework" in bringing new scripts to light, an activity that most theatre people haven't the time or opportunity to do themselves.

Certainly one advantage of this focus is that it helps to publicize some of the wonderful, engaging, and creative work being done in the United States today — work which lies, for the most part, obscure on the dusty shelves of our regional theatres or in the musty files of New York agents because there simply just aren't enough theatres to produce it all. The sad fact is that once a writer's script has received its premiere nowadays — whether it's an adaptation of a classic like Frank Bessell's *Scarlet Letter* or an absurdist farce on 1-900 con artists like Stanley Rutherford's *Tables and Chairs* — the odds are heavily against its being done again.

Why is this? First of all because there are just too many new plays constantly being written and produced across the country for any one of them to occupy our attention for any length of time. An ironic situation perhaps, but one which certainly militates against new playwrights hungry for more productions of their scripts. A handful of plays each year reach the spotlight of national attention in L.A., New York, or Chicago. Perhaps another dozen or two are published by Theatre Communications Group as "plays in process," which are then circulated to TCG subscribers. And maybe twice or thrice as many have barely their titles and synopses reported in drama magazines or trade reviews. The vast majority, however, remain consigned to the dustbin of history, trapped, in a sense, within their regional birthplace instead of finding a freeway on-ramp to other stages across the nation.

I think this far-flung network of our regional theatre system (the vastness of the country itself) is a large part of the problem. Unlike theatre artists working in geographically more "tidy" nations like Britain, France, Italy, Germany, etc., it's practically impossible for the American theatre artist to learn about all the new work produced from Alaska to Miami, New York to San Diego. While Theatre Communications Group's attempt to publish the best work each year is certainly a wonderful resource, those editors must sadly pass by hundreds of fascinating, well-written pieces that can find another audience only with the greatest difficulty.

Limitations and Advantages

This is not, however, the place to lament the dearth of theatres willing and able to produce new scripts. More important for readers of this anthology is to understand that they hold in their hands 40 selections from 38 plays, the work of 31 contemporary American dramatists. And secondly, that this sampling contains characters from a broad range of ages. There are scenes here suitable for students at the secondary school level, a large number of selections for professionals 18-35, and several inclusions for senior actors of experience and maturity. My purpose in selecting such a wide range of material has been to offer readers a good sampling of American dramatic writing today, and also to offer drama coaches and students of *all* ages a resource text which should be valuable, helpful, and unique.

Finally, I need to point out that this anthology may not be suitable at all for those teacher-coaches who are convinced that character portrayal is impossible without the actor's understanding of the complete play. What you will find here are only excerpts with a bare plot synopsis preceding each — enough, I feel, to get the actor going. Only in a handful of examples will an actor be able to obtain copies of the entire script.

As a professional coach and actor, I understand very well the need to analyze the whole play in order to effectively present any single scene. I also feel, however, that too many acting coaches do their students a great disservice — and blind themselves to other rewards — by insisting that character portrayal and scene work can *only* be useful if the actor has the entire play in mind as background. Let me elaborate, because this is important.

We all understand and agree that one must analyze the whole play in order to enact a role effectively. The issue, however,

3

is rather: how can actors learn the value of imaginative, unique *choices* in their portrayals, which all plays require? Personally I feel that by hitting the actor with a scene totally out of its scripted context is an excellent way to train the actor to develop his or her own compelling, unique, and original choices. Actors then aren't burdened by any predigested ideas about how to play the character, nor inhibited by any emotional preconceptions about getting the character "right" (the kiss of death in performance); nor of over-intellectualizing one's performance with the baggage of complicated motivations, convoluted given circumstances, tangled relationships and the like. In short, acting only excerpts can yield the same advantages which actors and directors uncover when they do cold readings at auditions.

For those coaches and teachers who decry cold readings, I suggest they look elsewhere for resource material. But for those of us who glean amazing results from cold readings — inspiration for physicalization, originality in line interpretations, improvisational immediacy — this anthology can be extremely valuable. In fact, as a director I'm totally unconcerned with an actor's ability to interpret the character "properly" (whatever that means). On the contrary, that's what the rehearsal process is for after I've cast the person. What else are directors and coaches for?

In using these excerpts with actors what I've sought and found is the person's general suitability for the role (at an audition, for example); his or her ability to apply some basic *methods* of approaching a scene — any scene; and the actor's ability to invent choices and commit to them in the scene. Can this actor identify a strong relationship in the dramatic situation? Can he or she *commit to* ("believe in") that relationship from beginning to end as the scene is played? Can the actor use the language, the clues for physicalization, the beats in the text? Can actors, in short, arrest and hold my attention with those relationships they've created? These skills are critical in scene work as well as in auditions. Playing relationships, as Michael Shurtleff insists, is the basis of each and every scene the actor will ever play anywhere.

For those readers, however, who'd like to try to obtain a copy of the complete play, I've provided in the bibliography not just the customary list of credits with agents' addresses, but also

4

the authors' addresses (when the writer has no agent), and the publisher or magazine where published scripts may be found. Agents, of course, normally refuse to circulate perusal scripts except to potential producers (agents are not lending libraries); although a few may be willing to give you a copy if you send along funds to cover mailing and copying costs.

Selection Standards

Readers of this anthology are bound to ask the same question at some point: "Why is this scene included here?" So let me say a few words about the guidelines I've used in my selection process.

First of all, I've chosen only plays that have been produced or publicly read and workshopped in some way. While I know that good scripts abound which have never seen the light of *any* day, nonetheless one must begin somewhere; and I feel the crucible of public reception is the single most valuable litmus test of quality. Thus, selections included here may not be *great* (the term is debatable, and likely unimportant), but they are genuinely *actable*.

Secondly, all the selections here are *complete* in the sense that they have a beginning-middle-end which is playable by two actors. This implies, of course, that the scenes *develop* somehow and that the actor can and should play such development. Also, that the scenes are thematically self-contained: that is, they do contain a point and "imitate an action" in the Aristotelian sense. They are not muddy nor unfocused, even in cases where I've had to condense or edit a selection for one reason or another.

Finally, I've chosen these pieces because they are all fairly long; they give each actor in the scene some substantial "meat" to sink their imaginative teeth into. This is especially true of the six long monologs I've included at the end. I suggest that actors who feel some parts are unduly "short" should take Harold Pinter's advice and think again: "Don't count the number of lines," says Pinter, "count the heartbeats." Or to put it another way: "There are no small parts . . ." etc.

Overview of the Plays

It's probably inappropriate here to say much about the individual plays which make up this collection, since readers will have only excerpts of these writers' work. While actors, though, can dig more deeply into the *performance* values of these selections, perhaps *readers* might appreciate some editorial comments upon the highlights of what this anthology offers.

The *language* of these selections is probably a good point of departure. As an editor it's the words in a good script that first leap off the page to catch my eye, and in most of the selections here that's certainly been the case. The lyrical tenderness, for example, in Claire Braz-Valentine's *This One Thing I Do;* the sharp, terse, and realistic exchanges between men and women in Charles Smith's *Jelly Belly,* or in Alan Brody's *Five Scenes From Life;* the tongue-in-cheek satire in the scene between April and June in Richard Nelson's *Roots in Water* — highlights like these make this anthology a literary smorgasbord of styles, and I suggest that readers keep their ears attuned to these values.

A second point of interest is certainly the range of dramatic portraiture which readers will find in these pages. What is one to think, for example, of the foxy Chantel and the older naive Frank in Deborah Pryor's *Wetter Than Water?* How does one respond to the "reconsidered" Hester Prynne in Frank Bessell's adaptation of *The Scarlet Letter?* Or the zany characters Stanley Rutherford peoples the stage with in *Tables and Chairs?* These are characters who have stuck in my mind long after I've read or seen the plays, as I hope they may stick in yours even after a brief encounter in the pages to come.

There is also a vital strain of social criticism in American dramatic writing today which can only be partially suggested in the brief selections contained here. Christopher Davis' *A Peep Into the Twentieth Century* gives us penetrating new insight into the issue of capital punishment; Kevin Kling's *Lloyd's Prayer* warns us of the dangers of hypocritical and confused evangelists; and Tom Dulack's *Incommunicado* touches a sore nerve with all of us when he turns over the ground of artistic censorship in the case of the poet Ezra Pound.

And finally there are the "new" characters one will encounter here: types, people, and couples who've only in recent years been accorded some attention in our national culture. Perhaps the two Cuban women in Caridad Svitch's *Gleaning/Rebusca,* or Dell and Stuart's "bonding" in Stephen Metcalfe's hilarious and touching *White Man Dancing* are good examples of what I mean. Lavonne Mueller's *Little Victories* speculates upon the personal life of Susan B. Anthony; while David Henry Hwang's *Dance and the Railroad* reveals the culture of Asian-Americans in its painful clash with Western industrialized values. All these issues, however, are treated by these writers not simply as platforms for some form of political action, but instead as springboards for understanding more universal truths about human beings in relationships as widely different as life itself.

Remarks on the Staging

As I mentioned earlier, I've provided only a suggestion of the entire play's synopsis or theme in each of the selections that follow. I've also refrained in most cases from adding any editorial commentary in the form of stage directions or locale, except where the scripts themselves contain such instructions. I know that while some actors and teachers might appreciate more background information of this kind, I feel instead that ideas of this sort should properly come from the reader or the actor's own imagination.

Within this *general* limit, though, actors and coaches should bear in mind the following three points.

1. None of the selections should require more than ten minutes of playing time. While some are shorter than this, I've tried to adhere to the "10-minute rule" because I know that certain types of forensics and dramatic interpretation competitions often require pieces of this length.

2. The age ranges I've proposed at the top of each selection are meant to suggest *chronological* age. The emotional range of the actor, however, is another matter altogether, and may sometimes demand older performers in the roles.

7

3. None of these pieces may be performed for a public audience — aside from auditions, contests, or class presentations in educational theatre contexts — without arranging permissions and royalty fees with the agents or authors. I know that this frequently occurs, however, and that actors are always on the lookout for small two-character "shows" or monologs for a variety of performance situations. But people who pirate material in this way for profit, without permission, do the playwrights and the industry a great disservice. Think about it.

PUBLISHER'S NOTE TO TEACHERS OF DRAMA IN SECONDARY SCHOOLS:

The language, situations and conflicts of these play scenes are unedited from the playwright's original manuscript. If there are guidelines or restrictions within a school system regarding language or content, we recommend that the teacher evaluate each scene for suitability before readings.

Scenes for Two Men

WHITE MAN DANCING
by Stephen Metcalfe

Scene for two men, late twenties or early thirties.

This play was first professionally produced in 1990 at the Old Globe
Theater in San Diego. Stuart and Dell have been friends for years.
Stuart is a recently successful writer and Dell an out-of-work actor.
Dell has just moved in with Stuart after leaving his wife, Bonnie.
The scene is Stuart's New York apartment.

DELL: *(Reading)* **I am going to die someday. It is an absolute.
I wake at night and feel the shadow pressing down. The
incomprehensible, echoing foreverness of it. We end the
day as we begin the day. Alone.** *(Pause)* **Stuart, I just don't
know about this as an audition piece.**

STUART: **You're doing great.**

DELL: **I appreciate you offering to let me work with your
stuff. I appreciate it. But I kinda have the feeling that
when I walk in for an audition, people think I'm kind of
a negative guy to begin with. Don't ask me why but this
is true. And so this piece, while a very worthy piece, is
not the right piece for me.**

STUART: **You don't like the piece.**

DELL: **I'm not talking about the dramatic content of the
piece. The dramatic content of the piece is very full. It's
just . . . I mean, it moves me, Stuart, it really moves me.
It's just that it moves me to want to slit my wrists, that's
all.**

STUART: **Fine.**

DELL: **Stuart, come on, what's the story? I know you. I've
read all your work. You're a romantic guy, an optimist,
as it were, and that always comes through. You always
think well of things in this naive but enjoyable sort of
way. That's why you're doing so well writing movies.**

11

1 STUART: My plays seem to be getting away from happy
2   endings.
3 DELL: People love happy endings.
4 STUART: I seem to be getting away from happy endings.
5 ·   This is going to be my most successful play.
6 DELL: Well, good, I hope so.
7 STUART: Casting, however, will be of the utmost importance.
8   This play needs actors.
9 DELL: So few do.
10 STUART: Seriously. You could be one of those actors, Dell.
11   Having worked on this scene, you will have the inside
12   track — not to mention my favor.
13 DELL: A production of this play. Is it definite?
14 STUART: It's . . . semi-definite.
15 DELL: There's interest?
16 STUART: There's *apparent* interest.
17 DELL: Will this be in or out of town?
18 STUART: We don't know yet.
19 DELL: I don't want to miss pilot season.
20 STUART: It's a job, Dell.
21 DELL: I have first refusal on several national commercials.
22 STUART: We are talking a definite equity job.
23 DELL: The play needs work.
24 STUART: Of course it needs work. I have faith in you, have
25   faith in me.
26 DELL: What if Dustin Hoffman called you on the phone right
27   now, right this minute and said, Stuart, I want to do Dell's
28   part?
29 STUART: Dusty wants to do it?
30 DELL: My part.
31 STUART: Then you'd be out.
32 DELL: I knew it.
33 STUART: Dustin Hoffman's involvement with my play would
34   make my career and I'm supposed to pass on him for you?
35 DELL: Yes.

1   STUART: Why you . . .?

2   DELL: What?

3   STUART: You . . .

4   DELL: What?!

5   STUART: You actor!

6   DELL: *(Offended)* **Hey.**

7   STUART: Look, are you interested or not?

8   DELL: Seriously?

9   STUART: I am.

10 DELL: Stuart, no offense but look, your stuff always gets
11   done twice. The first time I usually do it for no audience
12   for free. The second time I pay twenty bucks for a ticket
13   so I can sit in the front row and mouth the words with
14   the guy on stage. I'm just trying to protect myself, that's
15   all.

16 STUART: I understand.

17 DELL: If the opportunity presents itself and I'm available,
18   I'll consider it.

19 STUART: I hear you.

20 DELL: It's not a statement I'm trying to make, it's a living. I
21   mean, I've got to look for a job tomorrow.

22 STUART: You mean . . . a *real* job?

23 DELL: Tuesday was my last unemployment check. Boy, I'm
24   going to miss unemployment. Every week I get to hang
25   out in a slow-moving line with a fair percentage of all
26   the other actors in New York.

27 STUART: The unemployment office should have an equity
28   deputy.

29 DELL: Being broke is like being impotent, Stuart. You know
30   it's not entirely your fault but still . . . you don't feel like
31   a man. *(Silence)*

32 STUART: Dell?

33 DELL: Huh?

34 STUART: You OK?

35 DELL: Probably not.

1   STUART: How long you think it's gonna be, Dell?

2   DELL: I don't know. I really don't know if Bonnie and I are

3   gonna work this thing out.

4   STUART: You still love her?

5   DELL: Right now real estate seems much more important

6   than my feelings. I'd like a place to live.

7   STUART: You're not imposing. I want you to know that. You

8   stay here as long as you want.

9   DELL: Till the end of September maybe.

10   STUART: As long as you want.

11   DELL: You need your privacy.

12   STUART: Come on. You know the worst thing about being a

13   writer? You're alone all the time. I'm looking forward to

14   your company. You stay as long as you want.

15   DELL: Buddies.

16   STUART: Unless, of course, Susan comes back.

17   DELL: Susan is thinking of moving back?

18   STUART: She might be.

19   DELL: You've talked?

20   STUART: Sort of.

21   DELL: What does that mean, sort of?

22   STUART: We talk. But it's like these days we're speaking

23   different languages.

24   DELL: She's . . . *implied* that she might be moving

25   back?

26   STUART: Well, I mean . . . not necessarily in *so many words*.

27   I mean, as I write I can't tell you how discouraging it's

28   been to realize what inept tools *words are*. But . . . sooner

29   or later I'm . . . confident. She will. Come back.

30   DELL: Why would you ever think this?

31   STUART: I read between the lines.

32   DELL: *(It ain't gonna happen.)* Stuart . . .

33   STUART: Yeah?

34   DELL: Look, Stuart . . .

35   STUART: Yeah? *(The phone rings.)*

1   DELL: If that's for me I'm not here.
2   STUART: *(On phone)* Hello? Hi, Bonnie — uh, Bon? Dell's not
3   here.
4   DELL: Give me the phone, Stuart.
5   STUART: Bon? Guess who just walked in?
6   DELL: *(Taking the phone)* Hi, Bon. I'm OK . . . it was OK. Aw,
7   Bonnie . . . No . . . Because I don't want to. Because I don't.
8   It didn't work last time, why should it now? Unmake the
9   appointment. Look, I gotta go . . . Because I'm busy. I'll
10   call you. I'll call you! *(He hangs up. Silence)* That
11   was . . . Bonnie.
12 STUART: Yeah.
13 DELL: She . . . wants us to see a marriage counselor.
14 STUART: You gonna?
15 DELL: We already tried it once.
16 STUART: It didn't help?
17 DELL: It sucked. Bonnie talked me into it. I mean, this guy,
18   he shares his waiting room with about twelve other
19   shrinks, right? So it's like a Greyhound station filled with
20   morose guys, distraught women and schizoid kids. Is
21   there something to read? No. "Smithsonian," "Scientific
22   American," crap like that, as if these guys want us all to
23   know how smart they are and we're not. We go in. The
24   counselor, he wears comfortable shoes, smokes a pipe
25   and smiles a lot and I don't trust him. I mean, I'm looking
26   at the walls to see if he got his degree at the University
27   of Central Casting. Bonnie, of course, loves him. She
28   thinks he's sensitive. Bonnie thinks anyone who agrees
29   with her is sensitive. She loves *it*. She complains for forty-
30   five minutes, cries for fifteen and then pays the guy a
31   hundred bucks and tells him it's been the most positive
32   experience of her entire life.
33 STUART: A hundred bucks?
34 DELL: Bonnie's old man took care of it.
35 STUART: You didn't talk at all?

1   DELL: The guy, he asks me to come back alone next time. So
2   I do. I sit there. He asks me if I want water.
3   STUART: For a hundred bucks it should at least be a coke.
4   DELL: The counselor, he says to me, he says, what's wrong,
5   Dell. It's like he thinks we're buddies and I'm going to
6   like, confide in him. What the fuck, I tell him, I don't
7   know. I'm unhappy. He nods as if he knows what I'm
8   talking about. Let's try to fix that, he says. Fine with me,
9   I say, give me the money Bonnie's dad's paying you and
10   I'll be a little happier by tomorrow. *(Pause)* He says I
11   obviously have a lot of anger in me. A lot of bottled-up
12   hostility. No shit, I mean, who doesn't? The guy is one
13   for one. And then, I kid you not, it's just what you expect,
14   he asks me about my parents. Do I like'm, do they like
15   me, do they get along? Like it's his business. *(STUART*
16   *moves to desk, takes out his checkbook.)*
17   STUART: You like your parents, Dell?
18   DELL: Not particularly. I love'm. Lately I just don't like'm.
19   They don't understand why I have a hard time talking
20   to'm on the phone.
21   STUART: Why do you?
22   DELL: ... They lied to me. All the time. Always pretending
23   everything was so great between'm. Never talking about
24   it when it wasn't. My mom running to the bedroom,
25   crying. My dad so pissed off he can't even see straight.
26   And then everybody acting like it didn't happen. My
27   parents gave me everything but honesty. *(STUART*
28   *scribbles a check, tears it off, hands it to DELL.)* What's this?
29   STUART: Three thousand. You pay me back when you can.
30   DELL: I'll pay you back when I can. *(Pause)* Stuart. Thank you.
31   STUART: Look, you should know.
32   DELL: What?
33   STUART: I would never take Dustin Hoffman over you. *(Pause)*
34   DELL: *(Happily, dramatically)* I am going to die someday! I
35   wake up at night and a shadow is sitting on my face. The

1   **incomprehensible, echoing something or otherness of it.**

2   **The day is done as the day is done. Ending. The aloneness**

3   **is . . . is . . . aloneable beyond beyondness.**

4   **STUART:**   **Never alone, Dell. We have each other.** *(They slap*

5   *hands.)*

6

7

8

9

10

11

12

13

14

15

16

17

18

19

20

21

22

23

24

25

26

27

28

29

30

31

32

33

34

35

1   # WHITE MAN DANCING
2   **by Stephen Metcalfe**
3
4   *Scene for two men, late twenties or early thirties.*
5
6   See the background note on this play in the preceding selection. In
7   this scene several months later, Stuart returns to the apartment after
8   attending a Lamaze session with Bonnie, who is eight months
9   pregnant. He has agreed to stand in for Dell who wants no part of
10   the Lamaze classes. The scene begins as Stuart enters the apartment,
11   whistling.
12
13   **DELL:**   Hey.
14   **STUART:**   What?
15   **DELL:**   *What?*
16   **STUART:**   What.
17   **DELL:**   I have been worried sick.
18   **STUART:**   Why?
19   **DELL:**   Why?
20   **STUART:**   Yeah. Why?
21   **DELL:**   You were supposed to be home hours ago.
22   **STUART:**   I was?
23   **DELL:**   Hey. No. No, you weren't. Forget it. I mean, I *am not*
24   an interested party here. You were not out with my wife
25   and, so to speak, potential child. Why? Jesus, Stuart.
26   **STUART:**   Zygote.
27   **DELL:**   What?
28   **STUART:**   That's what it is at first. I went to the library today.
29   I did research. Dell, did you know that at six weeks, give
30   or take a week, the zygote — or fetus if you prefer — is
31   about a quarter of an inch long. It has gills and a tail. Its
32   arms and legs are paddle-shaped buds. What do you think
33   of that?
34   **DELL:**   I think I need an air sickness bag.
35   **STUART:**   No. It's awesome.

1   DELL: Stuart, your enthusiasm is all well and good but this
2   Lamaze class was supposed to be done by 8:30.
3   STUART: It's not Lamaze actually, it's the Bradley method.
4   DELL: What, it takes longer? Where have you been?
5   STUART: Bonnie wanted to walk home. Moderate exercise
6   is important for an expectant mother.
7   DELL: And so you had to keep her company?
8   STUART: Of course I did, she's pregnant. *(Pause. DELL exhales*
9   *and lets whatever it is that's bothering him go.)*
10   DELL: OK. *(Pause)* I'm waiting.
11   STUART: What?
12   DELL: Everything you learn in these classes I want to know.
13   STUART: Actually the classes don't start until the third
14   trimester. Bonnie and I were just observing tonight.
15   DELL: I assume knowledge was passed?
16   STUART: Oh yeah, we learned a lot.
17   DELL: What you learned, I want to know. Did you take notes
18   like I asked?
19   STUART: I did.
20   DELL: Start at the beginning.
21   STUART: Everything?
22   DELL: Everything.
23   STUART: OK ... hold on ... *(Reads from his notes.)* The classes
24   you begin tonight are a husband-coached system of
25   natural childbirth.
26   DELL: Wait, wait, wait. You're not a husband.
27   STUART: I'm a stand-in.
28   DELL: You're not a husband.
29   STUART: Shall we put the emphasis on "coach"?
30   DELL: I can live with that. *(STUART underlines something in*
31   *his notes.)*
32   STUART: Fine. Coach. *(Again checks his notes.)* We will be
33   working towards the efficient handling of the stress that
34   accompanies labor and birth.
35   DELL: God knows I'm feeling it.

1   STUART: By "we" I was referring to Bonnie and myself.
2   *(Reads from his notes.)* The classes will cover relaxation,
3   physiology, nutrition, and parenting skills. It will also
4   help us to be a positive consumer of obstetric services,
5   emphasizing positive communication with the birth
6   attendant.
7   DELL: How much will it hurt?
8   STUART: What?
9   DELL: Let's cut to the chase, Stuart. I understand having a
10   baby is very painful.
11   STUART: The word "pain" was not mentioned. It was
12   referred to as "the sensations of labor." The women
13   present nodded matter-of-factly. They did not seem
14   concerned.
15   DELL: They will be. I've been doing research too. I
16   understand the sensations of labor are like
17   handclamping your upper lip in a vise and then trying
18   to pull it back over your head.
19   STUART: While some classes emphasize distraction as their
20   primary labor control technique, we will learn to trust
21   our bodies, emphasizing relaxed abdominal breathing
22   and relaxation through labor.
23   DELL: Breathing, huh?
24   STUART: The classes began their breathing tonight.
25   Cleansing breath. *(STUART inhales, exhales.)* Pattern
26   breath. *(Expels breath.)* Hee-hee-hee-hee-hee ...
27   DELL: Everyone did this?
28   STUART: Women and men. During the birthing process, it's
29   important for the labor coach to help the expectant
30   mother keep in rhythm with her breathing. We also get
31   to monitor contractions and remind the mother to empty
32   her bladder.
33   DELL: She'll forget?
34   STUART: We supply emotional and physical support.
35   DELL: Physical how?

1 STUART: This is great. Sit on the floor. *(DELL does. STUART*
2   *sits down behind him.)*
3 DELL: What are you doing?
4 STUART: C'mon, c'mon, relax. Lean back. Knees up. *(STUART*
5   *pulls DELL's knees back toward him. DELL's feet are yanked*
6   *up off the floor — his legs are spread.)* **There. Do you feel**
7   **nurtured and supported?**
8 DELL: I feel like a stranded beetle.
9 STUART: You're feeling vulnerable. Trust me. Breathe. *(They*
10   *do a cleansing breath. Then DELL does a pattern breath: hee-hee-*
11   *hee-hee-hee.)* **Good, good.**
12 DELL: What?
13 STUART: We give encouragement.
14 DELL: Puuuussshhhhhh.
15 STUART: We maintain a calm, relaxed atmosphere.
16 DELL: *(Softly)* **Push . . .**
17 STUART: We help time the contractions. Very important.
18   Miscalculate and Bonnie could end up giving birth in a
19   taxi cab. We remind the expectant mother to keep her
20   eyes on a fixed point. This helps us focus. *(STUART and*
21   *DELL put their eyes on a fixed point and focus. Suddenly:)*
22 DELL: Ah!
23 STUART: What?
24 DELL: I think I just got an empathic labor pain. At what fixed
25   point do we scream for drugs?
26 STUART: Come on. We are birthing the natural way.
27 DELL: Shouldn't we be doing this in a rice paddy?
28 STUART: Oh! Some of the women present? They were
29   talking about giving birth in a swimming pool filled with
30   warm, salty water.
31 DELL: That's natural?
32 STUART: Are you kidding? The baby comes out and swims
33   around like a polliwog. It breathes through the umbilical
34   cord. Bonnie loved it.
35 DELL: Oh, God.

21

1   STUART: You're there, Dell. You watch it happen. You see the
2   first breath, hear the first cry. Can you imagine how the
3   skin feels? You take this newborn human being and
4   holding it like the most fragile glass, you place it on its
5   mother's breast. *(Pause)* **Walking home with Bonnie after**
6   I realized something wonderful. The Upper West Side is
7   filled with pregnant women. Everywhere you look, you
8   see women with enormous bellies moving along the street
9   like lovely zeppelins. You know what else the Upper West
10   Side is filled with?
11   DELL: Panhandlers?
12   STUART: Babies. Everywhere there are babies. All you have
13   to do is take the time to look. And there are parents.
14   Adults so in love with their children, they're idiots.
15   Fathers holding kids on their shoulders cause they like
16   the way their ears get grabbed. Mothers making faces to
17   earn a giggle. This is the church, this is the steeple, open
18   the door and here are the — this stuff is all around us
19   and we never notice it. And it's so beautiful. Life is. And
20   we hardly ever see. We're so out of touch. *(The phone rings.*
21   *Self-conscious:)* If we had the right kind of pillows, of
22   course, I'd have arranged them for you in the nesting
23   position.
24   DELL: When the egg comes, do we take turns sitting on it?
25   Jesus, Stuart, answer the phone. *(STUART answers the*
26   *phone.)*
27   STUART: Hello? *(Pleased)* Hi. *(To DELL)* It's Bonnie.
28   DELL: I'm not home.
29   STUART: Dell's not here, Bon. *(Pause. To DELL, pleased:)* It's
30   OK, she's calling for me. *(Into phone)* How you doin', babe?
31   DELL: Babe? Bonnie is now "Babe"? My wife is "Babe"?
32   STUART: *(To DELL)* Poor kid, she's nauseous. Early this
33   evening she had an overwhelming yen for potato knishes.
34   DELL: Really? Maybe the baby's not mine. Maybe Bonnie
35   boned a Rabbi.

1   STUART: *(Into phone)* **Any vomiting? Uh-huh . . . Have any**
2   **soda crackers? You should eat some before bed. Aw . . .**
3   *(To DELL)* **She's crying.** *(DELL resignedly reaches out a hand*
4   *for the phone. STUART doesn't pay any attention.)* **What is it?**
5   **What's the matter, talk to me. No one loves you? A lot of**
6   **people love you. Me. I do.** *(He self-consciously mouths "not*
7   *really" to DELL.)* **Huh? You're not fat and gross.** *(To DELL)*
8   **Right now her self-image is vulnerable to negative**
9   **misgivings.** *(Into the phone)* **I want you to listen to me.**
10   **You're beautiful. Your eyes sparkle. Your skin is lustrous**
11   **with life. Your face is filled with it. Everyone who looks**
12   **at you sees.** *(To DELL)* **She's also susceptible to affirmative**
13   **conditioning.** *(DELL signals STUART. Into the phone:)* **Hold**
14   **on a second.** *(Covers the phone.)* **Yeah?**
15   DELL: **Is she gonna wanna talk to me or what?**
16   STUART: **You want me to ask?**
17   DELL: **No, I want you to register the question in your diary. I**
18   **have things to do, important things. I can't always be**
19   **dropping these things just because she happens to want**
20   **to talk to me.**
21   STUART: **Bon, wait —** *(To DELL)* **You're not here.**
22   DELL: **I just walked in.**
23   STUART: **Bon, guess who just walked in. You want to talk to**
24   **him?** *(To DELL)* **No.** *(STUART doesn't see that DELL takes it*
25   *like a slap in the face. DELL sits.)*
26   STUART: **Everything OK now? That's what I'm here for. See**
27   **you tomorrow. We'll go to F.A.O. Schwartz and look at**
28   **toys. Great. Bye.** *(He hangs up. He chuckles to himself.)* **Great**
29   **gal. We're really bonding.**
30
31
32
33
34
35

1 # THE CARNIVAL
2 ## by Chaim Potok
3

4 *Scene for two men in their teens.*
5

6 Alex and Michael are visiting a carnival, having secretly left their
7 summer boys' camp. They rush on-stage, emerging from a fast roller
8 coaster ride. Alex is holding a bloody handkerchief to his nose.
9

10 **ALEX: My God, I'm alive! Is there a blessing for surviving a**
11 **roller coaster ride? Thank you, God, for saving my life!**
12 **MICHAEL: That was a great ride!**
13 **ALEX: Michael, let's get out of this place.**
14 **MICHAEL: What are you talking about?**
15 **ALEX: I'm ready to go back.**
16 **MICHAEL: We just got here!**
17 **ALEX: That's the best time to leave.**
18 **MICHAEL: All we've done is take a roller coaster ride, and**
19 **you want to leave? Very funny. How do you feel?**
20 **ALEX: Grateful for the law of gravity. Why do you suppose**
21 **there's no blessing for gravity?**
22 **MICHAEL: Has the bleeding stopped?** *(ALEX looks at his*
23 *handkerchief.)*
24 **ALEX: We're lucky it was only my nose. Consider the supper**
25 **that still resides in my stomach.** *(He pockets the*
26 *handkerchief.)*
27 **MICHAEL: I've never heard of anyone getting a nosebleed**
28 **on a roller coaster.**
29 **ALEX: That was a crazy ride! Up and down, up and down.**
30 **What am I doing in this place? I'm only here because I'm**
31 **your friend, you realize that. I'm here because you**
32 **enticed me with promises of excitement and adventure.**
33 **So far I've lost half a pint of blood. What else do you have**
34 **in mind, Dr. Livingstone?**
35 **MICHAEL: Let's explore and see what there is.**

1   ALEX: I don't want to explore. I want to go back to the camp.
2   MICHAEL: Come on, Alex! It's too early to go back to the
3   camp.
4   ALEX: Look at this place, Michael! A carnival in Milltown,
5   New York. *Milltown!* A post office, a drug store, a
6   supermarket, a movie house, two gasoline stations, a
7   decaying flour mill, five saloons, not a single bookstore —
8   not one! — and lots of cows. Lots and lots of cows. What
9   are we doing here, Michael?
10   MICHAEL: It's summertime, Alex. It's playtime in America.
11   There's a season for everything. God gave us the summer
12   so we could relax and have fun.
13   ALEX: Michael, God didn't intend for us to ride on roller
14   coasters.
15   MICHAEL: I like roller coasters.
16   ALEX: Up and down, up and down. They can't be good for us,
17   Michael. They belong to another civilization, maybe near
18   a Roman vomitorium.
19   MICHAEL: Admit it, sourpuss, why don't you admit it? Deep
20   down inside you really liked it.
21   ALEX: It brought back memories.
22   MICHAEL: It did?
23   ALEX: Interesting memories.
24   MICHAEL: Of what?
25   ALEX: The low flat parts, you know, where the roller coaster
26   rolled along smooth and not too fast, that reminded me
27   of the trolley cars you kept talking me into hitching rides
28   on when we were kids. I hated those rides.
29   MICHAEL: What a grouch you are, Alex! You were a grouch
30   then, and you're a grouch now.
31   ALEX: And the high parts, where the car slowed down like
32   it was taking a deep breath just before a big plunge, the
33   high parts reminded me of the way we used to jump
34   across the spaces between the roofs of buildings. You
35   remember that, the spaces between the buildings? I'd

1   look down, I'd feel like vomiting. Six stories to the ground.

2   Six. Jump. God forbid, miss the roof, fall six *stories* —

3   *splat!*

4 MICHAEL: We never once missed!

5 ALEX: That's because God is kind sometimes and watches

6   over fools. I like smooth and flat, Michael, smooth and flat.

7 MICHAEL: All the time smooth and flat?

8 ALEX: All the time. I trust smooth and flat.

9 MICHAEL: Bor-ing, Alex! Bor-ing!

10 ALEX: I *want* boring. I *like* boring. I *worship* smooth and flat.

11   Between hitching rides on trolley cars and jumping

12   across roofs, we barely survived our childhood — and

13   now you take us on a roller coaster ride? You really *trust*

14   those things to stay on the rails?

15 MICHAEL: Alex, if I didn't trust them, I wouldn't ride them.

16   My father used to take me on them.

17 ALEX: He did? Really? And all these years I had the distinct

18   impression that your father loved you! Michael, there are

19   better ways to spend fifteen minutes of one's life. I'd

20   rather read Kafka.

21 MICHAEL: What fifteen minutes? It was three minutes.

22 ALEX: All right, three minutes. I'd rather read Kierkegaard.

23 MICHAEL: At the very most, five minutes.

24 ALEX: Fine, five minutes. I'd rather use five minutes the way

25   we once used it on the roof of your apartment house.

26   Remember? Looking into the window of what's-her-

27   name's bedroom . . .

28 MICHAEL: Who?

29 ALEX: What's her name?

30 MICHAEL: You mean, Marilyn Shapiro?

31 ALEX: Ah, Marilyn Shapiro . . .

32 MICHAEL: You still remember that? We were kids . . .

33 ALEX: I hope never to forget it. Five glorious minutes with

34   Marilyn Shapiro . . .

35 MICHAEL: Gorgeous Marilyn . . .

1 ALEX: Hea-ven-ly Marilyn . . . Thank you, God, for those five
2   minutes with Marilyn Shapiro. *(Pause. He is looking at the*
3   *sky.)* Look at it for a minute. It's like every star in the
4   universe is out tonight. Did you know our galaxy is a
5   hundred thousand light-years in diameter? *(MICHAEL*
6   *just looks at him.)* And the visible universe is ten billion
7   light-years? *(Pause)* Do you know the distance to the
8   Andromeda Galaxy?
9 MICHAEL: No.
10 ALEX: Almost four hundred and fifty thousand parsecs. Do
11   you know what that is in miles?
12 MICHAEL: No.
13 ALEX: Take the number ten and add eighteen zeroes. That's
14   how many miles it is. There are ten billion galaxies in
15   the universe. Ten billion galaxies.
16 MICHAEL: You want to try it again?
17 ALEX: Try what again? Marilyn Shapiro?
18 MICHAEL: The roller coaster.
19 ALEX: Michael, are you having problems? You know —
20   intimate problems? Are these excursions you talk me into
21   a kind of sublimation or repression or something? Two
22   years ago, a rodeo. Last year, a circus. This year, a
23   carnival . . . You remember the rodeo, with the horse that
24   went crazy from the heat and the noise, and they couldn't
25   stop it from jumping around? You remember the circus,
26   and the size of those elephant droppings? Goodyear
27   blimps! And now the carnival! Why do I keep letting you
28   talk me into these crazy excursions? It must be a
29   deficiency in my character. Michael, I'm your friend. You
30   can *trust* me. Don't ask me to go for another ride on that
31   metal monster. *Talk* to me instead. Tell me what your
32   problem is.
33 MICHAEL: Alex, sourpuss, I don't have a problem. All year
34   long all we see are books and books. Classrooms,
35   libraries, lecture halls. An occasional date, now and then

27

1   a movie. Am I right or am I right? Don't we deserve a

2   piece of the real world now and then?

3 ALEX: *This* is the real world? *This?* God, I should've taken

4   Ellen Goldstein into New York and seen a show or a movie

5   or something.

6 MICHAEL: Ellen Goldstein went with David Kaplan.

7 ALEX: I knew there was a reason I didn't take Ellen

8   Goldstein into New York.

9 MICHAEL: Let's walk around and explore.

10 ALEX: I'd rather be reading Dostoevsky.

11 MICHAEL: It looks like there are some good games.

12 ALEX: We're going to play the games?

13 MICHAEL: Sure, we're going to play the games. What else did

14   we come here for?

15 ALEX: *(As they walk off)* Look at this place! It's mobbed! Nine-

16   thirty at night and there are kids all over the place! They

17   even brought infants in baby carriages.

18 MICHAEL: America loves a carnival!

19

20

21

22

23

24

25

26

27

28

29

30

31

32

33

34

35

1 # ZARA SPOOK AND OTHER LURES
2 ## by Joan Ackermann-Blount
3
4 *Scene for two men, twenties or thirties.*
5
6 Talmadge and Mel are onshore while two women, Ramona and
7 Evelyn, are offshore in a rowboat fishing. The scene is the annual
8 ladies fishing contest. Talmadge is Evelyn's fiancé, while Mel is
9 Ramona's estranged husband. The scene is best played with the men
10 on the apron, using the audience as the lake where the women are
11 fishing.
12
13 **TALMADGE:** *(Running up and down the shore, shouting, waving*
14 *his arms)* **Evelyn! Evie! Get off the water! Lightning! It's**
15 **gonna rain, sweetheart, it's gonna pour! Evie, look up at**
16 **the sky! God forbid she should once in her life look up**
17 **at the sky. There's gonna be lightning! There is. It's**
18 **storming up! Evie! Go back to the marina! Oh God, please**
19 **make her go back. Get rid of your pole! Throw it out of**
20 **the boat, it acts as a lightning rod, give it to Teale! Why**
21 **did I ever get her that pole in the first place, why didn't**
22 **I just get her that home entertainment center for her**
23 **VCR I could have got it with my green stamps, go back**
24 **to the marina!** *(He runs and bumps into MEL, screams.)* **I'm**
25 **sorry. I didn't see you.**
26 **MEL:** *(Holding a rifle)* **What's your trouble, boy?**
27 **TALMADGE:** **Nothing. Just someone out there on the water.**
28 **MEL:** **There's someone out there on the water?**
29 **TALMADGE:** **Uh-humm.**
30 **MEL:** **Is that right?**
31 **TALMADGE:** **Uh-huh. They're fishing. She's fishing. There's**
32 **a tournament, a fishing tournament.**
33 **MEL:** *(Nods)* **Out on the water.**
34 **TALMADGE:** **Uh-huh.**
35 **MEL:** **How 'bout that.**

1   TALMADGE: Actually, my wife is out in it, in the tournament,
2   on the water, and I'm a little concerned.
3   MEL: Your wife? That gal you're with is your wife?
4   TALMADGE: Well, no, not really, not yet, she's just my girl-
5   friend now. Look, the little hairs on my arm are standing up.
6   MEL: They stand up every time you lie?
7   TALMADGE: They stand up when it's going to lightning. Have
8   lightning. Be lightning.
9   MEL: That's why you're concerned about her. Your girl-
10   friend.
11   TALMADGE: *(Tries to stay composed.)* Yes, I am. I am. Concerned.
12   *(Long pause)* Nice gun. *(Pause)* How 'bout those Oakland
13   Raiders, huh? Is that Joe Montana something else? *(No
14   response)* Well, I guess I better be going. Maybe I'll catch
15   her in the next canyon.
16   MEL: What's your hurry, boy? Can't get out of life alive.
17   TALMADGE: See, she's pregnant. She doesn't believe it yet but
18   she is. She is. Believe it.
19   MEL: You got her pregnant?
20   TALMADGE: Yeah.
21   MEL: You got her pregnant?
22   TALMADGE: Yup, I did. All by my lonesome. *(In low tones)* Nice
23   piece.
24   MEL: You lying again? *(Grabs him by the collar.)*
25   TALMADGE: No. Why does everybody get so upset about it?
26   It's a happy occasion. It's the life force.
27   MEL: You got my wife pregnant? *(Lifts up gun.)*
28   TALMADGE: Your wife? Oh no, not your wife. I wouldn't
29   dream of getting your wife pregnant. Look, could you
30   please fire your gun a couple of times to get her attention?
31   Evie! Evelyn!
32   MEL: *(Lets him go.)* Evelyn? Who's Evelyn?
33   TALMADGE: Evelyn, get off the water!
34   MEL: Aren't you with Ramona?
35   TALMADGE: Please get off the water! Oh, Jesus, I don't want

```
1        her to die.
2   MEL:   You picked Ramona up at the airport. I saw her get into
3        your car with you.
4   TALMADGE:   Evelyn! They're leaving. Goddammit it! That's
5        not the way to the marina! That's the complete opposite
6        direction. Look, they're going the complete wrong
7        direction. The other way! Evie, turn around! Turn
8        around, honey! Evie! *(Grabs MEL and starts crying*
9        *shamelessly.)* Oh, Jesus, I don't want her to die! Evie!
10  MEL:   *(Inadvertantly comforting him)* She'll be all right.
11  TALMADGE:   Every year someone dies on this lake from
12        lightning.
13  MEL:   No, they don't.
14  TALMADGE:   Yes, they do.
15  MEL:   Who told you that?
16  TALMADGE:   *(Still crying)* Ramona. She's a friend of my wife's.
17        I mean my girlfriend.
18  MEL:   You can't believe her.
19  TALMADGE:   *(Snivelling)* She's the world champion.
20  MEL:   You can't believe her.
21  TALMADGE:   Do you know her? You know Ramona? Does she
22        lie?
23  MEL:   Yeah, I know her. Look, pal, pull yourself together.
24        Storms come through here all the time, no one gets hurt.
25        Trust me, she'll be all right.
26  TALMADGE:   I'll try. I'll try to trust you. Are you from this
27        area? You know people don't get hit by lightning every
28        year?
29  MEL:   Yeah.
30  TALMADGE:   All right. Thank you so much. You're a sensitive
31        man.
32  MEL:   What did you call me?
33  TALMADGE:   Uh ... sorry, I didn't mean to offend you.
34        Someone as tough as you ... with a gun and all.
35  MEL:   You said I was sensitive.
```

1   TALMADGE: I did. My apologies. You aren't sensitive.
2   MEL: I'm not?
3   TALMADGE: Are you?
4   MEL: You said I was.
5   TALMADGE: Is that all right?
6   MEL: Yeah. It's all right.
7   TALMADGE: Good.
8   MEL: I am a sensitive man.
9   TALMADGE: You know, you really are. You just might be the
10   most sensitive man I've ever met.
11   MEL: Thank you. *(Looks at him, tears up, overwhelmed; pause.)*
12   You ever been to Mexico before?
13   TALMADGE: No.
14   MEL: How do you like it?
15   TALMADGE: *(Smiles, still ingratiating.)* I don't.
16   MEL: *(Hasn't heard.)* Uh-huh. *(Pause)*
17   TALMADGE: You didn't happen to see that TV show last
18   week where the woman was killed by a cement mixer?
19   The other woman who saved her boy, knocked him out
20   of the way, had a cerebral hemmorhage, got her brain
21   as a transplant? And then the husband came back?
22   MEL: No, I didn't catch that one.
23   TALMADGE: Mmm. I missed the end. I was just wondering
24   if the dead woman's personality came with her brain, or
25   if the woman with the body was who that person was.
26   *(Pause)* If the person was the brain or the body. If it was
27   the brain, I just wondered how the husband felt to come
28   home and find someone else in his wife.
29   MEL: In his wife?
30   TALMADGE: But maybe it wasn't. Maybe it was just his wife
31   who stayed in his wife; she just took over the new brain.
32   MEL: Hunh. *(Long pause)* You know, if I was to take a forked
33   willow branch and hold it over that water right now it
34   wouldn't budge.
35   TALMADGE: Really?

1   MEL: Only works on water underground.
2   TALMADGE: Huh.
3   MEL: Kind of like love. I tell people that, they don't
4   understand.
5   TALMADGE: How's that?
6   MEL: When first you fall in love you get this wide open
7   pretty view. Seems so easy. Before you know it that big
8   open view shrinks up. Next thing you can't see anything;
9   all you can feel are those underground currents, driving
10   you every which way, tearing up your insides.
11   TALMADGE: I see.
12   MEL: I knew you would. *(Long pause)*
13   TALMADGE: Here, let me give you one of my cards. *(Reaches in*
14   *wallet.)* I'm Talmadge Slay. I'm with Ryobi. We're a young
15   company but we're starting to make a mark with a new
16   product called "Catch and Release" — helps keep a fish
17   alive through a stressful situation.
18   MEL: *(Hands him the gun, for lack of anything else.)* Mel Graves.
19   *(They shake hands.)*
20   TALMADGE: Thank you very much. *(Pause. They both stare*
21   *at the lake.)*
22   MEL: Well, you take care now, Talmadge.
23   TALMADGE: You too, Mel.
24   MEL: Sorry 'bout your fiancée.
25   TALMADGE: *(Doesn't understand.)* That's all right. *(MEL exits;*
26   *TALMADGE stands holding gun down by his side, staring out*
27   *into the lake. Sits down.)*
28
29
30
31
32
33
34
35

1   # THE DANCE AND THE RAILROAD
2   **by David Henry Hwang**
3

4   *Scene for two men, late teens or early twenties.*
5

6   David Henry Hwang is one of the most vital artistic forces in Chinese-
7   American literature. In this play, Hwang depicts the values of two
8   Chinese immigrants working on the transcontinental railroad in 1867.
9   Lone has been in America for two years, and is a devoted admirer of the
10   Chinese opera. Each day after backbreaking labor on the railroad, he
11   leaves the company of his fellow workers in the camp and retreats to a
12   nearby mountaintop in order to practice opera dance steps. Ma, younger
13   than Lone and a new arrival, begs Lone to teach him the art form. He
14   wishes to return to China as a rich man, like the opera character Gwan
15   Gung. It would be helpful for the actors to know something about the
16   choreography in Chinese opera in order to carry out some of the physical
17   actions indicated in the script.
18

19   ### Scene Three
20

21   *(LONE and MA are doing physical exercises.)*
22   **MA:** How long will it be before I can play Gwan Gung?
23   **LONE:** How long before a dog can play the violin?
24   **MA:** Old Ah Hong — have you heard him play the violin?
25   **LONE:** Yes. Now, he should take his violin and give it to a dog.
26   **MA:** I think he sounds OK.
27   **LONE:** I think he caused that avalanche last winter.
28   **MA:** He used to play for weddings back home.
29   **LONE:** Ah Hong?
30   **MA:** That's what he said.
31   **LONE:** You probably heard wrong.
32   **MA:** No.
33   **LONE:** He probably said he played for funerals.
34   **MA:** He's been playing for the guys down at camp.
35   **LONE:** He should play for the white devils — that will end this

1   stupid strike.

2 MA: Yang told me for sure — it'll be over by tomorrow.

3 LONE: Eight days already. And Yang doesn't know anything.

4 MA: He said they're already down to an eight-hour day and

5   five-dollar raise at the bargaining sessions.

6 LONE: Yang eats too much opium.

7 MA: That doesn't mean he's wrong about this.

8 LONE: You can't trust him. One time — last year — he went

9   around camp looking in everyone's eyes and saying,

10   "Your nails are too long. They're hurting my eyes." This

11   went on for a week. Finally, all the men clipped their

12   nails, made a big pile, which they wrapped in leaves and

13   gave to him. Yang used the nails to season his food — he

14   put it in his soup, sprinkled it on his rice, and never said

15   a word about it again. Now tell me — are you going to

16   trust a man who eats other men's fingernails?

17 MA: Well, all I know is we won't go back to work until they

18   meet all our demands. Listen, teach me some Gwan Gung

19   steps.

20 LONE: I should have expected this. A boy who wants to have

21   twenty wives is the type who demands more than he can

22   handle.

23 MA: Just a few.

24 LONE: It takes years before an actor can play Gwan Gung.

25 MA: I can do it. I spend a lot of time watching the opera when

26   it comes around. Every time I see Gwan Gung, I say,

27   "Yeah. That's me. The god of fighters. The god of

28   adventurers. We have the same kind of spirit."

29 LONE: I tell you, if you work very hard, when you return to

30   China, you can perhaps be the Second Clown.

31 MA: Second Clown?

32 LONE: If you work hard.

33 MA: What's the Second Clown?

34 LONE: You can play the *p'ip'a*, and dance and jump all over.

35 MA: I'll buy them.

1   LONE: Excuse me?

2   MA: I'm going to be rich, remember? I'll buy a troupe and
3   force them to let me play Gwan Gung.

4   LONE: I hope you have enough money, then, to pay
5   audiences to sit through your show.

6   MA: You mean, I'm going to have to practice here every night
7   — and in return, all I can play is the Second Clown?

8   LONE: If you work hard.

9   MA: Am I that bad? Maybe I shouldn't even try to do this.
10   Maybe I should just go down.

11   LONE: It's not you. Everyone must earn the right to play
12   Gwan Gung. I entered opera school when I was ten years
13   old. My parents decided to sell me for ten years to this
14   opera company. I lived with eighty other boys and we
15   slept in bunks four beds high and hid our candy and rice
16   cakes from each other. After eight years, I was studying
17   to play Gwan Gung.

18   MA: Eight years?

19   LONE: I was one of the best in my class. One day, I was
20   summoned by my master, who told me I was to go home
21   for two days because my mother had fallen very ill and
22   was dying. When I arrived home, Mother was standing
23   at the door waiting, not sick at all. Her first words to me,
24   the son away for eight years, were, "You've been playing
25   while your village has starved. You must go to the Gold
26   Mountain and work."

27   MA: And you never returned to school?

28   LONE: I went from a room with eighty boys to a ship with
29   three hundred men. So, you see, it does not come easily
30   to play Gwan Gung.

31   MA: Did you want to play Gwan Gung?

32   LONE: What a foolish question!

33   MA: Well, you're better off this way.

34   LONE: What?

35   MA: Actors — they don't make much money. Here, you make

1   a bundle, then go back and be an actor again. Best of
2   both worlds.
3 LONE: "Best of both worlds."
4 MA: Yeah! *(LONE drops to the ground, begins imitating a duck,*
5   *waddling and quacking.)* Lone? What are you doing? *(LONE*
6   *quacks.)* You're a duck? *(LONE quacks.)* I can see that.
7   *(LONE quacks.)* It this an exercise? Am I supposed to do
8   this? *(LONE quacks.)* This is dumb. I never seen Gwan
9   Gung waddle. *(LONE quacks.)* OK. All right. I'll do it. *(MA*
10   *and LONE quack and waddle.)* You know, I never realized
11   before how uncomfortable a duck's life is. And you have
12   to listen to yourself quacking all day. Go crazy! *(LONE*
13   *stands up straight.)* Now, what was that all about?
14 LONE: No, no. Stay down there, duck.
15 MA: What's the —
16 LONE: *(Prompting)* Quack, quack, qauck.
17 MA: I don't —
18 LONE: Act your species!
19 MA: I'm not a duck!
20 LONE: Nothing worse than a duck that doesn't know his
21   place.
22 MA: All right. *(Mechanically)* Quack, quack.
23 LONE: More.
24 MA: Quack.
25 LONE: More!
26 MA: Quack, quack, quack! *(MA now continues quacking, as*
27   *LONE gives commands.)*
28 LONE: Louder! It's your mating call! Think of your twenty
29   duck wives! Good! Louder! Project! More! Don't slow
30   down! Put your tail feathers into it! They can't hear you!
31   *(MA is now quacking up a storm. LONE exits, unnoticed by MA.)*
32 MA: Quack! Quack! Quack! Quack. Quack . . . quack. *(He looks*
33   *around.)* Quack . . . quack . . . Lone? . . . Lone? *(He waddles*
34   *around the stage looking.)* Lone, where are you? Where'd
35   you go? *(He stops, scratches his left leg with his right foot.)*

1   **C'mon — stop playing around. What is this?** *(LONE enters*
2   *as a tiger, unseen by MA.)* **Look, let's call is a day, OK? I'm**
3   **getting hungry.** *(MA turns around, notices LONE right before*
4   *LONE is to bite him.)* **Aaaaah! Quack, quack, quack!** *(They*
5   *face off, in character as animals. Duck-MA is terrified.)*
6   LONE: **Grrrr!**
7   MA: *(As a cry for help)* **Quack, quack, quack!** *(LONE pounces on*
8   *MA. They struggle in character. MA is quacking madly, eyes*
9   *tightly closed. LONE stands up straight. MA continues to quack.)*
10   LONE: **Stand up.**
11   MA: *(Opening his eyes)* **Oh.**
12   LONE: **What are you?**
13   MA: **Huh?**
14   LONE: **A Chinaman or a duck?**
15   MA: **Huh? Gimmee a second to remember.**
16   LONE: **You like being a duck?**
17   MA: **My feet fell asleep.**
18   LONE: **You change forms so easily.**
19   MA: **You said to.**
20   LONE: **What else could you turn into?**
21   MA: **Well, you scared me — sneaking up like that.**
22   LONE: **Perhaps a rock. That would be useful. When the men**
23   **need to rest, they can sit on you.**
24   MA: **I got carried away.**
25   LONE: **Let's try . . . a locust. Can you become a locust?**
26   MA: **No. Let's cut this, OK?**
27   LONE: **Here. It's easy. You just have to know how to hop.**
28   MA: **You're not gonna get me —**
29   LONE: **Like this.** *(He demonstrates.)*
30   MA: **Forget it, Lone.**
31   LONE: **I'm a locust.** *(He begins jumping towards MA.)*
32   MA: **Hey! Get away!**
33   LONE: **I devour whole fields.**
34   MA: **Stop it.**
35   LONE: **I starve babies before they are born.**

1   MA: Hey, look, stop it!
2   LONE: I cause famines and destroy villages.
3   MA: I'm warning you! Get away!
4   LONE: What are you going to do? You can't kill a locust.
5   MA: You're not a locust.
6   LONE: You kill one, and another sits on your hand.
7   MA: Stop following me.
8   LONE: Locusts always trouble people. If not, we'd feel
9   useless. Now, if you became a locust too . . .
10   MA: I'm not going to become a locust.
11   LONE: Just stick your teeth out!
12   MA: I'm not gonna be a bug! It's stupid!
13   LONE: No man who's just been a duck has the right to call
14   anything stupid.
15   MA: I thought you were trying to teach me something.
16   LONE: I am. Go ahead.
17   MA: All right. There. That look right?
18   LONE: Your legs should be a little lower. Lower! There.
19   That's adequate. So how does it feel to be a locust? *(LONE*
20   *gets up.)*
21   MA: I dunno. How long do I have to do this?
22   LONE: Could you do it for three years?
23   MA: Three years? Don't be —
24   LONE: You couldn't, could you? Could you be a duck for
25   that long?
26   MA: Look, I wasn't born to to be either of those.
27   LONE: Exactly. Well, I wasn't born to work on a railroad
28   either. "Best of both worlds." How can you be such an
29   insect?! *(Pause)*
30   MA: Lone . . .
31   LONE: Stay down there! Don't move! I've never told anyone
32   my story — the story of my parents' kidnapping me from
33   school. All the time we were crossing the ocean, the last
34   two years here — I've kept my mouth shut. To you, I
35   finally tell it. And all you can say is, "Best of both worlds."

39

1   You're a bug to me, a locust. You think you understand
2   the dedication one must have to be in the opera? You
3   think it's the same as working on a railroad.
4 MA: Lone, all I was saying is that you'll go back too and —
5 LONE: You're no longer a student of mine.
6 MA: What?
7 LONE: You have no dedication.
8 MA: Lone, I'm sorry.
9 LONE: Get up.
10 MA: I'm honored that you told me that.
11 LONE: Get up.
12 MA: No.
13 LONE: No?
14 MA: I don't want to. I want to talk.
15 LONE: Well, I've learned from the past. You're stubborn. You
16   don't go. All right. Stay there. If you want to prove to me
17   that you're dedicated, be a locust till morning. I'll go.
18 MA: Lone, I'm really honored that you told me.
19 LONE: I'll return in the morning. *(Exits.)*
20 MA: *(Alone)* Lone, that's ridiculous. You think I'm gonna stay
21   like this? If you do, you're crazy. Lone? Come back here.
22
23
24
25
26
27
28
29
30
31
32
33
34
35

A PEEP INTO THE TWENTIETH CENTURY
by Christopher Davis

Scene for two white males in their forties.

This drama was first developed as a workshop production at the Seattle Repertory Theatre in 1986, and in 1989 it received its professional premiere at the Philadelphia Festival Theatre for New Plays. This scene takes place in 1890 when a public outcry against the horror of hanging led the New York State Legislature to see a gentler way to kill a man within the law. Electricity, a new symbol of progress, was their choice, and so the electric chair was born. In the following scene, McDade and Kernahan are prison guards on death row, and Rupert Weber (on-stage but stubbornly silent) is the condemned man. Kernahan may be fiddling with some electrical instrument as the scene begins, while McDade is thumbing through Weber's mail.

KERNAHAN: What did the warden say to your request for a transfer, McDade? *(Pause)* Turned you down? Maybe he smelled the gin. I can smell it from here. *(Pause)* No peace for me. Double shift. I go straight from this to assist Mr. George Taggart. I'm an electrician now, assistant executioner.

MCDADE: Rupert isn't deaf, Kernahan. And that newspaper of yours is contraband. Take it with you when you leave.

KERNAHAN: The corridor gate out there was unlocked when I come on. That's your dereliction, ain't it?

MCDADE: *(To Weber)* Good morning, Rupert. *(No response)*

KERNAHAN: Not a squeak all night. The parson was down. Weber spit in the bucket and turned from him. The code says his lawyer's come upstate to plead him crazy since the appeal is denied and he's so silent. He has a case. Not a syllable in ten days. He don't use his walk-around time, stays in his cell. *(To Weber, loudly)* You understand a lot of

41

1   the drainpipe telegraph now, don't you, Weber? It says
2   the new electrician's in the prison and your expensive
3   lawyer's come up to see you.
4 MCDADE: You're off duty, Kernahan. Rupert, I've brought
5   your kites. *(MCDADE takes the letters and looks them over.*
6   *Reads:)* "Dear Weber, if the heart was a letter to read, I
7   think you would be persuaded of my sincerity. Put
8   yourself into the hands of the good Reverend Snow. He
9   knows what's what." Underlined. "Word of your long
10   silence comes to us above you on B-Wing. All here implore
11   you to believe upon G." Odd. He don't spell it out. "If the
12   high court denied your writ, so be it, Mr. Weber. Now act
13   the man and let religion fill your heart and guide your
14   faltering steps." ... Here's one. "Dear Good-Looking —"
15   *(Snorts, crumples note, goes through the others.)* Here, Rupert.
16   "Rest assured in the hearty thoughts of each on C-Wing,
17   level one. Now your stay is lifted we are with you all the
18   way. Be of good courage. Signed Thomas Catwright for
19   all." I don't know the con. It's an honest message. Here's
20   this from your brother in Philadelphia ... "Dear Brother,
21   we have word your petition on the cruel and unusual is
22   denied and hope you bear it like a man. Act in good faith
23   and repent your terrible crime. The papers say you are
24   baptized by God's grace. It will surprise you to learn that
25   three years ago I too was baptized in secret. I blame our
26   family's neglect of this rite for much that came
27   afterwards of ill to us all. You are famous here as the
28   first in history to be done by electricity. Myself, I praise
29   the power if it will deliver your soul to our Father instant
30   and painless as advertised. I thank the fellow who reads
31   this to you. Sincerely yours ..." He isn't aware you've
32   learned to read some in prison, thanks to Mrs. Snow.
33   *(Offers letter, no response.)* You've got the doctor coming.
34   Get ready.
35 KERNAHAN: You're a fool then.

1   MCDADE: *(Drinking from a flask)* **I'd hoped I was only a drunk.**
2   *(Takes reading glasses and puts them on, opens a pamphlet.)*
3   **Here. Let's get done with your devil's catechism. What's**
4   **the little ammeter thing then?**
5   KERNAHAN: *(An effort)* **The ammeter measures electrical**
6   **current by means of heat in the wire.**
7   MCDADE: **All right. And your — what's this? "Rheostat"?**
8   KERNAHAN: **Rheostat. A resistor. Regulates current.**
9   MCDADE: **Regulates the devil. What's amperes?**
10 KERNAHAN: **One of them's equal to one volt in a conductor**
11 **with a resistance of one ohm.**
12 MCDADE: **And there's your ohm again. That's a terrible cruel**
13 **joke. Let's get done. The alternating?**
14 KERNAHAN: **That's the current we're using here on Weber.**
15 **Westinghouse's. It switches direction inside the wire by**
16 **intervals, builds up a hell of a lot of power. It's why we**
17 **use it. The direct goes only one way, continuous, and**
18 **don't build in frequency. That's what Edison sells, calls**
19 **it safe power, but Mr. Taggart says it won't do the work.**
20 MCDADE: *(Tosses booklet at him.)* **You do your work at least.**
21 **Tell Taggart I give you an alpha-plus, and tell him it's all**
22 **the devil when it isn't what the bull drops in the pasture.**
23 *(Drinks.)* **Jesus, it's good to get off shift in this dungeon.**
24 KERNAHAN: **Why stay?**
25 MCDADE: **My wife won't let me drink at home and the**
26 **saloons are full of reporters.**
27 KERNAHAN: **Don't I know it! They keep asking me about**
28 **his silence. I don't know what to say. What do you tell**
29 **them?**
30 MCDADE: **He's minding his business.**
31 KERNAHAN: **I said how it was the last thing he spoke. "It**
32 **don't do." They give you a beer and half a dollar and**
33 **expect the secrets of the universe. Take it down in short-**
34 **hand, "It don't do." What the hell is that, they said, got**
35 **mad at me.**

43

1　MCDADE:　I wish I had shorthand. A man should have skills
2　　　　to give him a choice. *(Drinks.)* Here's a proposition,
3　　　　Kernahan. Wouldn't the two of us be better off, better
4　　　　men I'm suggesting, out on construction somewhere with
5　　　　a shovel and pick, or working a farm? Isn't that better,
6　　　　I ask, than going in to help them kill this young fellow
7　　　　while Edison and the other one quarrel over who's to
8　　　　profit and reporters write their stories? A young fellow
9　　　　in health, not much different to you and me. I'm only
10　　　inquiring to see what you'll say.
11　KERNAHAN:　Look what he done.
12　MCDADE:　Took a life. I know what he did. We're policemen.
13　　　　We're supposed to safeguard life. Just consider it.
14　KERNAHAN:　It's the law. The majesty of the law.
15　MCDADE:　Made by men. Like us.
16　KERNAHAN:　I don't mind my work.
17　MCDADE:　I mind mine. And they can put that down in
18　　　　shorthand. I'm not religious, but I can read the Bible,
19　　　　and read correct the Bible is a cunning book. Weber is a
20　　　　man, not a dog. Begin there. So you don't put him down.
21　　　　Take Cain in the Bible. He was cast out. If he went to
22　　　　farm, the earth was sour. He was cursed, but he wasn't
23　　　　put down like a dog because God knew when to stop,
24　　　　which we don't.
25　KERNAHAN:　It's always the atheist quotes the Bible. Weber
26　　　　forfeit his life when he took the woman's, and that's the
27　　　　end of it. You don't want shorthand. Learn electricity
28　　　　like me. There's a skill for the future.
29　MCDADE:　You shouldn't be messing with their devil's
30　　　　electricity for a few extra dollars in your pay envelope,
31　　　　man.
32　KERNAHAN:　Your kids are grown, McDade. Mine ain't. I
33　　　　notice you take home your death-watch bonus.
34　MCDADE:　I do. I shouldn't. *(Drinks. Quiet)* I tell you I dislike
35　　　　my job and I'll quit it.

1   **KERNAHAN: No, you won't.**
2   **MCDADE: Well, bugger you. You're not so stupid as you look,**
3   **Mr. Kernahan. I say I will every time and never do.** *(Pause)*
4   **The majesty of the law, is it? Maybe this time I'll do it. I**
5   **mean to be shut of it.**
6
7
8
9
10
11
12
13
14
15
16
17
18
19
20
21
22
23
24
25
26
27
28
29
30
31
32
33
34
35

1 # INCOMMUNICADO
2 ## by Tom Dulack
3
4 *Scene for one black male, thirties, and one white male, forties.*
5
6 This drama was developed in 1988 under a grant from the Fund for New
7 American Plays. It received its premiere at Philadelphia's Wilma
8 Theatre, and in 1989 was presented at the Kennedy Center in
9 Washington, D.C. The play deals with the imprisonment of the famous
10 American poet Ezra Pound by Allied Forces, following the victory in
11 Italy in 1945. Pound had delivered a series of radio broadcasts for the
12 Italian Fascist government during the war. According to the author,
13 Pound embodies "the great moral failure of Western Man in the 20th
14 century." In this scene, Pound is in solitary confinement, writing in a
15 notebook, immediately after the execution of a fellow prisoner with whom
16 Pound had become friendly.
17
18 MP: Heard you had yourself a nervous breakdown.
19 POUND: You heard wrong.
20 MP: Nervous breakdown. Thrashing around like a fish on a
21   hook. Just 'cause they went and shot some low-bottom
22   nigger shoulda been shot years ago.
23 POUND: Killing off the public for my poetry's the way I look at
24   it. Only public I got in here.
25 MP: Till! Who's Till? Makes me ashamed to be colored. I'd of shot
26   him myself they give me the chance.
27 POUND: Picture of Christian charity and compassion, Bo.
28 MP: Trash like Till hurts all of us.
29 POUND: Oh yeah? How's he hurt you, Booker T.?
30 MP: We finally get a chance to do our part, earn the white man's
31   respect, show him we belong, that it's our country too. Then
32   along comes some trash like Till give all the colored troops
33   a bad name.
34 POUND: Well, not being a colored troop myself, I'm not ashamed
35   to say I found him a credit to the human race, and I miss him.

1   MP: Anyway, you're living in the lap of luxury now.
2   POUND: Yeah, but I already miss the Spartan rigors of the
3   other joint. What does Confucius say? "A handful of rice
4   to eat, a jar of water to drink, life in a mean street —"
5   MP: Confucius come out of Chicago by any chance? Sounds
6   like the way I grew up. Life in the mean streets. Shit, we
7   didn't have it so good. Least you don't have no rats in
8   your bedroom. Least you get three squares a day.
9   POUND: What's that you've got there? Looks like a book.
10   MP: It is a book. It's a dictionary. An English dictionary.
11   POUND: You decided to learn a second language?
12   MP: Some law against my buying a dictionary?
13   POUND: You *bought* a dictionary?
14   MP: Yeah, you wanna make something of it?
15   POUND: But this could be serious. Have you ever bought a
16   book before?
17   MP: Naturally I've bought books before.
18   POUND: What kind of books have you bought? I don't mean
19   collections of pornographic pictures, I don't mean comic
20   books, Lil' Abner, the Katzenjammer Kids. I'm talking
21   about *books!* What the hell books have you ever bought?
22   MP: You want the titles? I don't remember the titles.
23   POUND: *Paradise Lost,* perhaps? *Madame Bovary?*
24   MP: Yeah, among others.
25   POUND: How much did you pay for this dictionary?
26   MP: None of your business.
27   POUND: But it's entirely my business. Books are my
28   business exclusively. Where did you buy it?
29   MP: In Florence.
30   POUND: In Florence?! You went to Florence?! What earthly
31   reason could you have for going to Florence?
32   MP: To look around.
33   POUND: To look around at *what?*
34   MP: Pictures, churches, statues.
35   POUND: *(After a moment of critical scrutiny)* I knew it. Minute

1   I laid eyes on you, I said to myself, "This one's *ripe* for
2   culture!" Brother, are you ripe! You don't give a damn
3   the old girl's all clapped up, you're just going to jump
4   right in. Careful, Sergeant, I'm warning you. You think
5   you're a long way from the center of that frozen lake,
6   you imagine there's a whole African continent's worth of
7   fiery real estate between you and the bottom of the pit.
8   But once you take that first leap, look out! — the rest of
9   the way is such an exhilarating slide. You think you're
10   flying.
11 MP: What are you talking about?
12 POUND: Hell! There some other topic? I worry about you,
13   Amos.
14 MP: You don't worry about nobody 'ceptin' yourself.
15 POUND: Don't say " 'ceptin'," Jesus Christ! "Except!" You
16   want to be a Bloomsbury aesthete and get invited to tea
17   *chez* Virginia Woolf, you can't go around talking the
18   mother tongue like some coon on a chain gang.
19 MP: *(Dropping the dictionary)* Here. It's for you.
20 POUND: *(Startled out of a reverie)* What's this?
21 MP: I bought it for you. *(POUND doesn't know what to say.)* I
22   thought you might . . . need it. In your work. *(POUND is*
23   *embarrassed. At length he picks up the book and turns it over*
24   *caressingly in his hands. He stands, takes a length of broom*
25   *handle that's been lying on the ground, and strolls up and down,*
26   *looking into the sky, gesturing with the broom handle which he*
27   *employs as a walking stick, elegant and jaunty, as a rapier, as*
28   *a pool cue, as a baseball bat.)*
29 POUND: Betelgeuse. Star called Betelgeuse. Over there is
30   Ursa Major. *(Pointing. The MP doesn't look.)* What's going
31   on outside?
32 MP: Outside where?
33 POUND: I hear the English threw Churchill out of office. Is
34   that true?
35 MP: There ain't been no change in your status. I'm not

1   supposed to give you information about the outside.
2   POUND: Yeah, of course, I can understand that. You gotta
3   obey orders. Wouldn't want it any other way. You're
4   probably already stretching a point bringing me that
5   dictionary.
6   MP: Don't tell nobody where you got it, that's all.
7   POUND: That was thoughtful, soldier. My manner is a little
8   . . . a little "crusty" from time to time. In general, one's
9   social graces don't improve living in a dog kennel. You
10   could have spent the money on a piece of ass. A
11   dictionary's a wonderful thing, even when you know all
12   the words. Just to be able to hold it, something to hold
13   onto, one of the few things in this world.
14   MP: Just keep your mouth shut about it, that's all.
15   POUND: What's Florence look like? How'd you pass your
16   time? Where'd you go? What did you see?
17   MP: That's classified. Classified information far as you're
18   concerned.
19   POUND: There's a place called Fiesole up in the hills above
20   the city. Ain't a thing on earth can match the view from
21   there at sunset with the mists rising from the river, or
22   at midnight, in the full moon, when the town looks
23   translucent, as though it were spun out of silk shot
24   through with silver . . .
25   MP: I liked it. It's nice, a nice friendly little place.
26   POUND: Old whore bitch of a city! Can't beat it for treachery.
27   They *invented* treachery in Florence. There's a statue
28   says it all about Florence, bird named Donatello, carved
29   out of wood. Mary Magdalene, old snaggle-toothed hag
30   after a lifetime in the desert, trying to bake the sin out
31   of her bones . . . *(For a moment, he is transported on a wave*
32   *of painful nostalgia.)* But there persists after everything,
33   the sensuality still smoldering inside — deep down —
34   like a fire in a peat bog . . . Because, after all that suffering
35   the old gal's got still more suffering to do, more expiating,

1   before she's purified. *(There is a silence.)* **Don't suppose you**
2   **caught the Mary Magdalene?**
3 **MP:** No. Didn't see nothing like that.
4 **POUND:** They're fucking with my *brain*, Kingfish!
5 **MP:** Who is? Who's fucking with your brain?
6 **POUND:** The psychiatrists. It's revenge for what they think
7   I did to the Jews. They're trying to kill me with Freudian
8   analysis.
9 **MP:** They're doctors. You had a nervous breakdown. They're
10   trying to fix you up.
11 **POUND:** What do you know about these ... these so-called
12   death camps the Germans were running?
13 **MP:** Not much. What I see in *Stars and Stripes*.
14 **POUND:** You believe it? You believe millions of Jews died in
15   those camps?
16 **MP:** I dunno.
17 **POUND:** You know anybody saw one of these camps with his
18   own eyes?
19 **MP:** No. But I saw some newsreel footage.
20 **POUND:** Yeah? Did it look authentic?
21 **MP:** I don't know. I guess so. Don't know how they can fake
22   something like that.
23 **POUND:** You know how much I got paid for those broadcasts?
24   Three hundred and fifty *lire* for each one. That's about
25   seventeen goddam bucks a week. You think a man's
26   gonna sell his country down the river for seventeen bucks
27   a week?
28 **MP:** What the hell exactly did you say in them broadcasts?
29   Nobody I know ever heard one.
30 **POUND:** Never mind. It's all ... too abstract for you ...
31 **MP:** Talk comin' out of the infirmary is that you got yourself
32   some kinda problem with the Jews.
33 **POUND:** Talk's inaccurate.
34 **MP:** How the hell you people can turn against your own kind
35   like that. You're all white, ain't you?

1   POUND: What's been your experience with Jews, Amos? They
2   own the ghetto, they suck your people dry.
3   MP: Me? I don't have no trouble with Jews. Never did, and
4   I never will. The Jew's the only white man would ever
5   do business with us.
6   POUND: The business is called usury.
7   MP: The business is called "survival" where I come from.
8   Shit, lotta niggers in my neighborhood be dead by now
9   'ceptin' for Hymie Goldberg the pawnbroker, 'ceptin' for
10   Hymie Goldberg the loan shark. Them Goldbergs kept us
11   all alive many a time, kept shoes on our feet, kept food
12   in our mouths. Without the Jews we all be dead. Nobody
13   else do business in our part of town. You must of had a
14   different experience. What happened? They pull
15   somethin' on you personally? You have a bad experience
16   with a pawnbroker?
17   POUND: *(Evasively)* You're out of your depth, Booker T. You're
18   in over your head.
19   MP: Oh no I ain't! You're the one in over his head. Way over
20   his head! You think I don't know anything, you think I
21   can't learn? You such a genius, what the hell you doing
22   locked up in here? Maybe you belong here after all. Maybe
23   you *belong* here with the likes of Till.
24   POUND: Hey, Rochester, I didn't mean ...
25   MP: And my name ain't Rochester. It ain't Rochester, it ain't
26   Bo, it ain't Buck, it ain't Booker T.!
27   POUND: Sorry, Sergeant. Sorry. What *is* your name?
28   MP: Never mind! I don't know why I waste my time on you!
29
30
31
32
33
34
35

FRANKENSTEIN: THE REAL STORY
by Gail Erwin

Scene for two men, indeterminate ages.

In this version of the classic tale, the young scientist, Victor Frankenstein, has brought to life a Creature who kills Victor's dearest relatives as a plea for love and understanding. Victor fails at first to recognize the Creature's plight, and in this scene he has just attempted — unsuccessfully — to strangle the Creature. Victor holds a burning branch (or other weapon) throughout the scene to keep the Creature at bay.

VICTOR: Vile creature! You are Satan incarnate!

CREATURE: No. You are the one who would be God.

VICTOR: You have killed my baby brother and his nurse! I will grind you to dust!

CREATURE: Ashes to ashes, dust to dust. I did not ask to come into this world. You fathered me and orphaned me in the same moment.

VICTOR: You can't blame me for your evil deeds.

CREATURE: You left me to wander the world with no speech, no protection, no knowledge! But I have learned goodness from another as I learned evil from you.

VICTOR: What are you talking about?

CREATURE: My friend. He taught me philosophy and history. He taught me to read and to write and to speak. He gave me all of the good that is in me.

VICTOR: What goodness? If you have any conscience, you will beg my forgiveness. You have killed my brother!

CREATURE: I owe you nothing. It is time you do your duty to me.

VICTOR: My only duty is to kill you!

CREATURE: Impossible! You sewed together this muscle and sinew. You know how strong I am.

1   VICTOR: I was the greatest of fools.

2   CREATURE: You never thought of the consequences. Was it
3   glory you sought? To do a trick no one had done before?
4   But I didn't turn out right. I wasn't a beautiful, well-
5   behaved toy. So you left me to wander like an animal.
6   Eating berries, sleeping in the dirt, hiding from the
7   hunter. Why did you give me feelings? Why could I not
8   be a machine?

9   VICTOR: I see that you have suffered.

10   CREATURE: Alone. I have no William. No Henry. No
11   Elizabeth. I will never laugh with a friend, or comfort a
12   lover.

13   VICTOR: I did not know the result of my experiment before
14   I finished. How could I?

15   CREATURE: You must have done other experiments. Surely
16   I am not the only one. Perhaps there is someone else.
17   Someone even uglier. Take me to him. I will understand
18   him. I will be his friend.

19   VICTOR: There is no one like yourself.

20   CREATURE: Why can't I die of this sadness? The pain goes
21   on and on. You must give me someone. You must create
22   a mate for me!

23   VICTOR: No! Never!

24   CREATURE: Have a care! I have it in my power to destroy
25   you. You will curse the day you were born!

26   VICTOR: I already have.

27   CREATURE: Do this one thing. We will go far away. To the
28   jungle. We will live on nuts and berries. We will make
29   our bed on dried leaves and leave mankind in peace.

30   VICTOR: How can you? You crave man's company. You have
31   even learned how to talk to him.

32   CREATURE: My mate will give me the companionship I crave.
33   You know how to re-create life now. Your next experiment
34   will be perfect. You can learn from your mistakes.

35   VICTOR: If only I could right the terrible wrong I have done.

1 CREATURE: After she is created, your responsibility is
2   ended. I will teach her to speak, to read. I will have
3   someone to belong to. I beg you! My life began in misery.
4   I am as frozen and alone as the mountain peaks above
5   us! You have it in your power to give me happiness. Let
6   me die without cursing my maker.
7 VICTOR: You swear to be harmless?
8 CREATURE: I swear.
9 VICTOR: You swear to leave the places where men dwell
10   and go into the jungle forever?
11 CREATURE: I swear by the sun above and the ground
12   beneath, I will go. I swear by the ice-blue cold of my
13   loneliness, once my mate is with me you will never see
14   me again.
15 VICTOR: God help me. I can't look at you without pity. Even
16   after what you've done. Perhaps this is the way to atone
17   for my sin. Very well. I'll do it, I'll create a mate for you.
18 CREATURE: Soon. If you do not keep your promise, I will
19   kill everyone you love. It is surprisingly easy. You have
20   made me so strong. I will not be far away. I shall be
21   watching you.
22 VICTOR: I will not be moved by your threats.
23 CREATURE: Sweet hate will be my companion, and I will
24   ride the wheels of Revenge!
25 VICTOR: Murderer!
26 CREATURE: Remember, I will be with you on your wedding
27   night!
28
29
30
31
32
33
34
35

1 # DIESEL MOON
2 ## by Robert Auletta
3
4 *Scene for two men, thirties.*
5
6 This play was first produced by Chicago's Victory Gardens Theatre
7 in 1990. It explores the surrealistic world of Cap, a Vietnam veteran
8 and renegade trucker, and his wife Martha, who have taken refuge
9 in the Rocky Mountains from their crumbling dreams of America.
10 Cap is searching for some faith in life that can dispel his
11 disillusionment. In this scene he confronts his friend Tunnel, a tough
12 and cynical Vietnam veteran, who urges Cap to join the truckers'
13 protest against working conditions. The locale is a tavern. The off-
14 stage jukebox music is important and can be cued in from a portable
15 cassette.
16
17 **TUNNEL: How you doing, Cap? Long time ... no**
18 **communicado.**
19 **CAP: How are you, Tunnel?**
20 **TUNNEL: I'm doing fine, Cap. But the real story is all the**
21 **activity starting to pop around here. Truckers ain't**
22 **gonna take it anymore, Cap. Government regulations**
23 **have become too vicious and strangulating.**
24 **CAP: Yeah, I know.**
25 **TUNNEL: You've heard all about this, haven't you, Cap?**
26 **CAP: Yeah, I have.**
27 **TUNNEL: Of course. You're a trucker, and you live around**
28 **here. But we missed you at our first meeting.**
29 **CAP: I was busy.**
30 **TUNNEL: That's too bad, because it was a real interesting**
31 **meeting. But no need to get heartbroken about it, because**
32 **we're gonna have another one tomorrow night at Little**
33 **Joe's. You be there or you be square, right?**
34 **CAP: Right, right, Tunnel.**
35 **TUNNEL: Because truckers ain't gonna take this shit no more.**

1   CAP: But we're independents, Tunnel. Independents don't
2   get together and strike.
3   TUNNEL: You're from around here and you're one of us —
4   sometimes you are, anyway. Right, Cap? *(He laughs.)* Once
5   in awhile when you get it together you're one of us. So
6   we're gonna see you tomorrow night, right, Cap? It's
7   definite now, isn't it? Little Joe's.
8   CAP: I'll tell you someting, Tunnel. One man gambles, one
9   man saves. One man loves, another man raves.
10   TUNNEL: What the fuck's that supposed to mean?
11   CAP: I really have no idea. *(They both laugh.)*
12   TUNNEL: Let me buy you a drink, Cap. *(They grab beers. The*
13   *music blares. Suddenly they both seem quite drunk.)*
14   CAP: Let me ask you, let me ask you, Tunnel: is there a
15   tollbooth? Do they charge you for a toll?
16   TUNNEL: What are you talking about? What kind of toll you
17   mean?
18   CAP: To hell, to get into hell. Do they charge you a toll to get
19   into hell, Tunnel?
20   TUNNEL: *(Laughing)* No, Cap, no! They let you in for nothing!
21   They don't charge you a damn thing! But if you wanta
22   get out, if you're interested in getting out, they take
23   everything you fucking got and then some.
24   CAP: But you got back, didn't you, Tunnel? You're here.
25   TUNNEL: Part of me anyway, Cap.
26   CAP: So you paid your price and you're back, you're here.
27   TUNNEL: The last I noticed.
28   CAP: You think some people have to pay a higher price than
29   others? You think some people have to leave more than
30   others? I'm thinking of one person in particular. I'm . . .
31   thinking of my father.
32   TUNNEL: Who really gives a shit?! I certainly don't.
33   CAP: Maybe you're right, Tunnel. Maybe you're right. *(They*
34   *drink, the music blares.)* But there's another thing I really
35   want to ask you, something that really bothers me . . .

1   TUNNEL: Yeah, what's up, Cap?

2   CAP: Did you ever wish somehow, thought maybe, that
3   maybe it would have been better if it ended over there,
4   finished up, instead of coming back here and having to
5   face it every day, every living day? Did you ever find
6   yourself feeling that way ... Wyatt?

7   TUNNEL: What'd you call me? No, wait. I heard what you
8   called me. I heard it very clear and distinct. You called
9   me Wyatt.

10   CAP: I didn't mean any harm.

11   TUNNEL: Of course you meant harm. Now let me put it all
12   together, let me get the package straight so you can really
13   see it, Cap. See it there at my feet? It says Wyatt Anderson
14   on it. That's who it's addressed to. My birth name. And
15   maybe it's got a million dollars in it. But I got a problem,
16   you see, I've got a big problem with it: I can't accept it,
17   I can't even goddamn look at it! *(He kicks and begins*
18   *trampling the invisible package.)* I can't even stand the
19   thought of it, that name you just called me, Cap. That
20   name I haven't heard for years. Because it's empty, it's
21   false, it's phony. It's a man's job, to find his real name, to
22   get a hold on his real name, then brand it to him, right
23   to his living flesh, so everybody can know, so everybody
24   can see what the real truth is; because otherwise that
25   phoniness starts running infectious, and before you
26   know it you've become everybody's dog running to
27   everybody's whistle. *(Staring at CAP)* Only you, Cap, only
28   you could ... *(He trails off.)*

29   CAP: What, Tunnel?

30   TUNNEL: Talk to me, the way you just did, using that name
31   you mentioned. *(He suddenly laughs.)* You have your work
32   cut out for you, Cap?

33   CAP: What's that, Tunnel?

34   TUNNEL: Surviving. Surviving with your life in this world.
35   *(He laughs.)* Yeah, you're gonna have to keep working on

1   it. *(Staring at CAP)* **You asked me if I ever thought it would**
2   **be better staying over there full time, forever.** *(A slight*
3   *smile)* **Well, let me tell you: sure, why not? Lots of times**
4   **I wished to hell I never made it back. You wake up those**
5   **nights thinking of those thousands and thousands of days**
6   **ahead and feeling, what's the use, man? How can I work**
7   **this out? How can I negotiate these details? But you know**
8   **what stops me from drastically changing my situation?**
9   CAP: No, Tunnel.
10 TUNNEL: My utter contempt for death! Death is a bullshit
11 operation. It's MGM, it's Hollywood, it's just not real.
12 Sure, in the beginning anyway it's got the power to grab
13 you around your scrawny throat and shake you until
14 your shit turns to freeze, but somehow after you survive
15 that a few times, the chill is over, the fear is gone. *(Softly,*
16 *but menacing now)* **Does that make me some kind of freak**
17 **in your estimation?**
18 CAP: I don't know, Tunnel. I couldn't say, because I don't
19 know what death is to me either.
20 TUNNEL: Well, then there's something wrong with your
21 goddamned ears, because I just said I know what death
22 is to me: it's nothing. *(Pause)* **And I've seen guys die, so**
23 many really, and it's never added up, never really
24 amounted to much for me — they were just gone, not to
25 be known anymore. It was no big deal. C'est la vie, as
26 they say. C'est la shit, as they say. *(Pause)* **You see, I like**
27 it here, where I am, on this earth. I guess you might say
28 that I'm in my natural element.
29 CAP: Not me, somehow. I don't feel that there's anything
30 natural about it at all.
31 TUNNEL: That's too bad, Cap, because every man needs to
32 find his proper element in order to flourish.
33 CAP: *(Starting to leave)* **See you, later, Tunnel.**
34 TUNNEL: Tomorrow night, Little Joe's, about 8:30. You be
35 there.

1   CAP: But we're independents, Tunnel. We're cowboys.
2   Striking is not something we do.
3   TUNNEL: The time has come.
4   CAP: We're independents. We've always made our own way.
5   When and how and where we work.
6   TUNNEL: I fought for America, so it could make a living, a
7   respectable living, so that it could hold up its head in the
8   world; and now I'm going to fight it, if I have to, if it tries
9   to stop me from making my living, from holding my head
10   up in the world. *(CAP starts to leave.)* **Cap.** *(He stops.)*
11   Cowboys and Indians are gone. You understand. Even
12   the cattle are different. They're engineered different.
13   They're fatter. They don't respond to the world the way
14   they used to.
15   CAP: Then what's left? What the hell are we then?
16   TUNNEL: *(Thinking for a moment)* Maybe just ... survivors,
17   just goddamned lonely robot survivors, standing our
18   ground. Maybe that's not good enough for you, but I'll
19   accept it, I'll drink to it. *(Calling out)* Jody, give me a
20   whiskey. There's something I've got to drink to.
21
22
23
24
25
26
27
28
29
30
31
32
33
34
35

<table>
<tr><td>1</td><td></td></tr>
</table>

1	# WELCOME HOME
2	## by Kathryn Schultz-Miller
3	
4	*Scene for two men, late teens.*
5	
6	This imaginative and socially critical play was first produced in 1990
7	by the ArtReach Touring Theatre of Cincinnati, where the author is
8	Artistic Director. It deals with a Vietnam veteran, his wife, and
9	teenage son, and the memories of war that haunt him. But as the
10	following scene reveals, the play also comments upon the human
11	history of that war, moving from idealism to disillusionment, as it
12	affected American life. The following scene takes place in a "hootch"
13	or barracks, where the central character arrives in Vietnam and
14	meets his buddy, Billy.
15	
16	BILLY: Hey, hey, hey. Look what we got here, Another
17	patriotic son, a brand new fearless warrior ...
18	RON: Hi, I'm Ron.
19	BILLY: Come to fight for our country and protect the
20	American way.
21	RON: Yeah, well, hi guys. *(He unpacks.)*
22	BILLY: So where you from, Rod?
23	RON: Ohio. It's, uh, Ron.
24	BILLY: Ohio? What part of Ohio, Bob?
25	RON: It's Ron.
26	BILLY: Like I say, Rick, you from Cleveland or that other
27	city? Whaddaya call it? Begins with a C.
28	RON: Cincinnati and it's *Ron.*
29	BILLY: Yeah, yeah, Columbus, Ohio. What a happening town.
30	How long you live there, Joe? *(RON grabs BILLY by the*
31	*collar.)*
32	RON: What's the matter with you? You got some gripe with
33	me? The name's *Ron. Use it. (Lets him go.)* I figure this
34	whole Vietnam routine is going to be tough enough on
35	its own. I came here to fight the Viet Cong. Not you. So

1   knock it off.
2   BILLY: OK, OK. Geez. A guy makes one little mistake.
3   *(Thinking)* **Ohio.**
4   RON: Ohio, what?
5   BILLY: I'll just call you Ohio if that's all right with you. I'm
6   having a little trouble remembering that other name. So
7   what do you say, Ohio?
8   RON: *(Tired of it)* Fine, fine. And I'll call you Mississippi.
9   BILLY: I'm Big Bad Bill. *(Shows his hat.)* See, it says so right
10   here.
11   RON: Well, Big Bad Bill, I hope your mouth doesn't always
12   run on automatic like this. I'm the strong and silent type,
13   you know what I mean?
14   BILLY: Oh, you'll get over that soon enough. You need every
15   buddy you can get in Vietnam, man. Plus, you got a lot
16   to learn.
17   RON: About what?
18   BILLY: Peanut butter, for one.
19   RON: Peanut butter?
20   BILLY: It's one of Charlie's favorite magic tricks. Charlie's
21   our pet name for the Viet Cong. He puts insect repellent
22   in a small can of peanut butter — booby trap. Now you
23   see the GI, now you don't.
24   RON: I guess you guys don't eat too much peanut butter.
25   BILLY: Clean lost my appetite for peanut butter. I wanna
26   grow old, if you know what I mean. Hey, want to see
27   something? *(He takes a picture from inside his hat.)* Is that
28   the most beautiful girl in the world, or what?
29   RON: She's a looker.
30   BILLY: One gorgeous babe. Linda, Linda, Linda. *(He kisses
31   the picture.)* I know, I know what you're thinking. How did
32   somebody with a mug like mine rate a chick that is one
33   hundred percent prime time gorgeous like her.
34   RON: *(Laughing)* I was wondering.
35   BILLY: She loves me for my mind.

1   RON: Oh, man, get outta here.

2   BILLY: Hey, it just happens that I got a very high I.Q.

3   RON: Yeah, right.

4   BILLY: Hey, I was a brain surgeon before I got drafted.

5   RON: A brain surgeon?

6   BILLY: But I was getting pretty bored with it. Yeah, I think

7   when I get out I'll go into a new line of work. Criminal

8   law, maybe. Hey, lookit here. *(He hands RON another*

9   *picture.)*

10   RON: Wow. You got a kid?

11   BILLY: He's got my profile. See?

12   RON: Wow. Hold old is he?

13   BILLY: Six months.

14   RON: Boy, I bet you hate being over here with your kid still

15   a baby and all.

16   BILLY: That's why I gotta stay healthy. I'm a daddy now.

17   April 15, 1968 — my DEROS.

18   RON: What's that?

19   BILLY: Date Expected to Return from Overseas — the day I

20   fly this coop. You got a girl?

21   RON: Yeah. Her name's Beverly. *(He hands BILLY a picture.)*

22   We got engaged before I came over here.

23   BILLY: Hey, you must have a high I.Q., too.

24   RON: I don't think you have noticed how extremely good

25   looking I am.

26   BILLY: Oh, I forgot to tell you, I'm blind in one eye.

27   RON: Get outta here.

28   BILLY: *(Hops to bunk and gets comfortable.)* **So, did you come to**

29   **win the war, hero?**

30   RON: Sure did.

31   BILLY: How long do you think it'll take?

32   RON: Well, the way I figure it, we got all the best equipment

33   plus tanks and choppers. They don't even have horses,

34   man. These VC can't hold out more than a few months.

35   BILLY: Eight or nine, maybe ten months.

1   RON: Right.
2   BILLY: Then we'll all go sailin' home sweet home.
3   RON: Right.
4   BILLY: Right. *(Silence)*
5   RON: What?
6   BILLY: Nothing.
7   RON: You seen any action?
8   BILLY: *(Laughs.)* That's funny. Whew, there you go. That's a
9   joke for you.
10   RON: What?
11   BILLY: Action. Ain't no action in Nam, Ohio.
12   RON: What do you mean?
13   BILLY: Charlie's invisible, man. He's out there, he's
14   everywhere. He's in the trees, he's in a tunnel in the
15   ground, he's hiding in the elephant grass. But you never
16   see him. Man, Charlie could be right in front of your face
17   and you wouldn't even know he was there. And what's
18   he doing? I wouldn't call it "action."
19   RON: What's he doing?
20   BILLY: You'll know soon enough, Ohio. Soon enough.
21
22
23
24
25
26
27
28
29
30
31
32
33
34
35

Scenes for Two Women

1   # ROOTS IN WATER
2   ## by Richard Nelson
3
4   *Scene for two females, indeterminate ages.*
5
6   This scene takes place in June's office in a very pricey marketing
7   research firm. April has come to June's firm for help in boosting
8   memberships in April's conservation organization.
9
10   **JUNE:** *(Looking through a file)* **I see your organization is non-**
11   **profit. That helps. That certainly does help.**
12   **APRIL: Why does that help, Ms. Hayes?**
13   **JUNE: Because of the discount. I'll be able to offer a**
14   **discount, April. Well, it's not exactly a "discount," but**
15   **that's what it boils down to ... for you.** *(Looking through*
16   *the file)* **I see, twenty-one thousand members ...**
17   **APRIL: What sort of discount are we talking about?**
18   **JUNE: Shall we say ten percent? Our normal commission is**
19   **sixty, so let's say we'll knock off ten from that, make it**
20   **an even fifty percent. April, you've picked the right time**
21   **of the year to be nonprofit.**
22   **APRIL: Right time? We've always been nonprofit.**
23   **JUNE: The right time for *us*, dear. But I'm sure I don't have to**
24   **tell you about that.**
25   **APRIL: Why don't you tell me about it?**
26   **JUNE: It's December, April. It's the end of the year. It's**
27   **closing-the-books time. Taxes, April. Taxes. And I don't**
28   **think it's boasting to say this year has been quite good**
29   **to Stone's Phone Solicitations. Very good. You've come**
30   **at the right time, just when a deduction wouldn't hurt.**
31   **APRIL: A deduction?**
32   **JUNE: So it's settled, we'll take a fifty-percent commission,**
33   **with of course the understanding that we are in fact**
34   **taking our normal sixty, only giving ten percent back, as**
35   **our way of contributing to the serious and deeply**

67

1	important work your organization has been doing. I'll
2	need your nonprofit tax number, if you don't mind. *(Beat)*
3	APRIL: Fifty percent?
4	JUNE: Of course we'll expect to be listed among your patrons
5	or whatever you call your large donors ...
6	APRIL: Excuse me, Ms. Hayes — fifty percent of what?
7	JUNE: Of what? Of all the contributions our service solicits
8	for you, of course. Perhaps you could even give us a page
9	in your program, that often goes with a donation of this
10	size, doesn't it? Something with our letterhead,
11	congratulating you on your year — you write the copy,
12	just send it over for approval when you get the chance ...
13	APRIL: What program, Ms. Hayes?
14	JUNE: The program you hand out to your audience, April.
15	What program do you think I'm talking about?
16	APRIL: We don't have a program. We don't have an audience.
17	JUNE: No audience? I'm sure you're exaggerating, but still
18	you're in worse shape than I thought. Think of it, an
19	opera society without an audience.
20	APRIL: What opera society? We're not an opera society.
21	JUNE: Yes you are, April.
22	APRIL: No.
23	JUNE: No?
24	APRIL: We're an environmentalist group.
25	JUNE: An environmentalist group? Where did I get the idea
26	you were an opera society?
27	APRIL: I have no idea.
28	JUNE: You are sure you —
29	APRIL: No opera, Ms. Hayes. Clean air, clean water,
30	endangered species, but no opera.
31	JUNE: Huh. *(Beat)* It must have been your logo that confused
32	me, this big cloud blowing air. *(Beat)*
33	APRIL: I hope your operators will be informed about our
34	organization before they begin their calls.
35	JUNE: Informed? In this case, April, I shall even do the

1   informing myself. Which is not always the way; all of our
2   clients are not so fortunate. An environmentalist group?
3   APRIL: That is correct. *(Beat)*
4   JUNE: I'll have to be very clear about that with our
5   operators.
6   APRIL: I'd hope you —
7   JUNE: *(Snaps her fingers.)* April, what do you think when I
8   say — "women"? Quick!
9   APRIL: I don't —
10   JUNE: You think — mothers. You think — motherhood. You
11   think — mother nature. And what's closer to the
12   environment than mother nature? You following me?
13   APRIL: No, I —
14   JUNE: We use only women operators for this campaign. I
15   mean if you'd just been a rinky-dink opera society men
16   would have been fine, but for the environment, it's
17   obvious it's got to be just women, don't you agree?
18   APRIL: I don't know.
19   JUNE: The female voice. Don't ever underestimate the sex
20   appeal of the female voice.
21   APRIL: I won't. But getting back for a second to the fifty
22   percent. That sounds a little steep to me.
23   JUNE: You've never used a professional telephone
24   solicitation company before, have you?
25   APRIL: We've always tried to call ourselves. We've had
26   volunteers.
27   JUNE: Volunteers are nice. They're sweet. In fact you have
28   to ask yourself where would this country be without
29   volunteers? I'll tell you where — it'd be bored. *(She laughs.*
30   *Suddenly serious)* April, there is a time and place for the
31   professional. Let me show you. How much did you solicit
32   last year? I have it right here: $11,912. I can guarantee,
33   April, that after one day of our phoning, that figure will
34   be tripled. And tripled comes to . . . $33,760. Take away our
35   fifty percent, and you have $17,880. Now you see what I mean.

1   APRIL: You can triple our pledges?

2   JUNE: Mr. Stone only allows us to guarantee a tripling, but

3   generally the jump is a great deal more.

4   APRIL: Still, fifty percent. I don't know what our

5   membership would think if they knew that one-half of

6   their pledges weren't going to us. We're a very grassroots

7   organization, our members are very committed to what

8   we do.

9   JUNE: Commitment is always a good place to begin, but in

10   this day and age, we'll have to set our sights a bit higher

11   than just commitment. *(Beat)* If there is anything we have

12   learned in the last fifteen years it is that. Let me show

13   you what we can do. *(Takes out a large computer printout*

14   *book from her desk.)* Do you know what this is? The names

15   and phone numbers of everyone within a three-state

16   radius who has an American Express card.

17   APRIL: I doubt if too many of our members have American

18   Express cards.

19   JUNE: That is what we're about to change, don't worry.

20   APRIL: But . . .

21   JUNE: Let me finish. I want you to know just how much we

22   can do for you. First we'll pick a Sunday night to call.

23   Why a Sunday, you ask? *(Beat)* Because that's when

24   *Masterpiece Theatre* is on, so the chances are the right

25   people will be home. Let's say, the third Sunday of the

26   month, that's before the callees have received their bills

27   from American Express, so they'll feel a little more free

28   with their expressions of support. And that goes double

29   if you let them charge their pledges to their American

30   Express cards — so you lose a few percent, but believe

31   me, you more than make it up in the long run. Of course,

32   if we're getting heavy into plastic, I advise we look into

33   the Diner's Club as well — you'd be very surprised how

34   many people don't have both. I never could figure that

35   one out, one could write a dissertation on just that

1   conundrum, April. I'd avoid Mastercharge, I mean
2   Mastercard — why the hell did they change the name, as
3   if life weren't complicated enough already; in any case,
4   I'd avoid it — too many women, and they're always saying
5   they have to talk to their husbands who by and large
6   already have either Diner's or American Express, so what's
7   the point really, you're just duplicating. You follow me?
8   APRIL: I . . .
9   JUNE: What we need is men. *Our* women talking to *those*
10   men. That's the real selling point, you see. Young women
11   callers with sweet *natural* voices. Girls these men can
12   picture wearing khaki hiking shorts and knee socks.
13   That's the image we have to work to get across. *(Beat)*
14   Now, have we discussed the red book?
15   APRIL: What red —
16   JUNE: We keep that in the safe, otherwise I'd show you.
17   APRIL: What's to —
18   JUNE: It lists those who are paying off their credit card
19   charges in installments. And those people, believe it or
20   not, are the ones most likely to give. It's true. *(Beat)* They
21   live life on the edge, month to month, paycheck to
22   paycheck; they're loose, they're free, and besides, in this
23   case, it's a good bet that in the last six or seven months
24   they've had to *use* the environment as they usually are
25   without enough cash in their pockets to even go out to
26   a movie. And you don't need cash to take a walk in the
27   woods, just the right clothes — and that's what they've
28   got their American Express cards for. Of course, these
29   kinds of people usually like to *get* something for their
30   money, that's why I'm suggesting you seriously think
31   about a magazine. *(Beat)* There are plenty of nature
32   pictures floating around you could pick up for a song —
33   even for no song, especially if the magazine is getting
34   into the right homes because these photographers know
35   with the right exposure they just might pick up a little

1	work with an ad agency or two. *(Beat)* **While we're on the**
2	**subject of gifts, you'll need something for your large**
3	**donors, the fifty-dollar people; say a bird book, a bird**
4	**feeder, maybe a tote bag with a bird on it; I wouldn't use**
5	**your logo on it, it would look too much like an opera tote**
6	**bag.** *(Beat)* **Maybe a record of wind and waves for the**
7	**twenty-five dollar givers; wind and waves are royalty**
8	**free, so it won't cost you much.** *(Beat)* **But what we really**
9	**need to bang our heads about is what to give the really**
10	**big guns, the thousand-dollar-and-up people. I would**
11	**have suggested a safari, but these money people don't**
12	**have the time for that sort of thing, you have to get into**
13	**their heads and figure out what they really want.** *(Beat)*
14	**What do they want?** *(Beat)* **I'll tell you. They want to meet**
15	**people, people like themselves with money and position;**
16	**they want to make contacts, you give them that and**
17	**they'll bite, April.** *(Beat)* **What about a big dinner and a**
18	**show, a couple of orchestra tickets to a Broadway hit,**
19	**like CATS, that's it: CATS — cats are animals, that's**
20	**nature, and afterwards a party so they can mingle — I'll**
21	**bet a group like yours has got a lot of pull with some of**
22	**those old folk singers from the sixties; we can call it a**
23	**sixties nostalgia party — what we have to keep**
24	**reminding ourselves, April, is that a lot of these big**
25	**executives were kids themselves in the sixties, it's *their***
26	**music — hard to fathom, isn't it, but it's true and we just**
27	**have to face it.** *(Beat)* **Now to get the ball rolling, we can**
28	**get a few stars, that's never as hard as it sounds, get them**
29	**to give a little of their money — it's tax time for them**
30	**too — or give a little of their time, or just their name, or**
31	**even just an old necktie to auction off, whatever, just**
32	**depends how aggressive we want to be. On second**
33	**thought, forget the necktie, what the hell does a necktie**
34	**have to do with nature? Walking shoes, walking sticks,**
35	**walking anything would be more like it, but who the hell**

1   walks in Hollywood, I don't know.
2   APRIL: *(Standing up)* Excuse me, I have to —
3   JUNE: One second, I want to write down Perrier for the
4   party — that's clean water.
5   APRIL: I'll talk all this over with my committee.
6   JUNE: Picture this: we kick the whole thing off with a
7   protest. Talk about nostalgic!
8   APRIL: Ms. Hayes —
9   JUNE: We ask people to strike a match and burn a bill say,
10   an electric, or their oil bill, any damn bill — I'll tell you,
11   I wouldn't mind burning my phone bill, but that's my
12   own fault for going with a guy who's bi-coastal. But I'm
13   not alone. There are a lot of people just like me.
14   APRIL: I'm sure. Thank you.
15   JUNE: If they want to they can burn the stub they don't have
16   to send back, what the hell, you have to start somewhere.
17   *(Calls.)* April!
18   APRIL: What?
19   JUNE: It'll be just like old times.
20   APRIL: Like?
21   JUNE: It'll feel so good to be back in a movement again.

GLEANING/REBUSCA
by Caridad Svich

Scene for two women in their twenties.

This play was developed at New York's INTAR Hispanic Playwrights Laboratory, and was first performed in New York and Los Angeles in 1989 and 1990. The two characters are young Cuban-American women who have been roommates and close friends for some time. Barbara is sorting make-up from a box, and Sonia is clipping items from a shopping catalog. The setting is their apartment in Florida.

SONIA: So, it's official?

BARBARA: We're engaged. *(Slight pause)* That's it.

SONIA: That's something.

BARBARA: *(After a pause)* Until we have a ring ...

SONIA: Gotta have a ring.

BARBARA: Or else what's the point? *(Slight pause)* I think it'll be good. Don't you?

SONIA: At least you'll have something.

BARBARA: It'll be good.

SONIA: *(After a pause)* He loves you.

BARBARA: I can't wait to marry him.

SONIA: Then what?

BARBARA: Then we'll be together.

SONIA: *(After a pause)* You could live with him.

BARBARA: No. I want a wedding. I want it to be permanent. It's the only way.

SONIA: I'll be lucky if I see you.

BARBARA: Huh?

SONIA: Nothing. *(Slight pause)* You've thought about the dress?

BARBARA: I don't have a ring yet.

SONIA: The tailors around here are super busy. You go waiting around taking your time and —

1   BARBARA: I'll make an appointment.

2   SONIA: You better make it soon.

3   BARBARA: I'll make an appointment.

4   SONIA: If you don't make it soon —

5   BARBARA: Sonia!

6   SONIA: *(After a pause)* I haven't said a word.

7   BARBARA: I told you I'd do it.

8   SONIA: If you mess up, you mess up.

9   BARBARA: *(To herself)* And you keep on and on.

10   SONIA: If it's a disaster, it's a disaster. It's not my business.

11   *(Slight pause)* You're gonna do pink or white? Don't tell

12   me one of those strange colors like peach or blue que va

13   a look like los carnavales.

14   BARBARA: White. I'll do white.

15   SONIA: *(After a pause)* Babi, Orlando's a treasure. Thinking

16   about Rudy won't help.

17   BARBARA: I'm not.

18   SONIA: Your eyes are doing something.

19   BARBARA: I'm thinking.

20   SONIA: About Rudy.

21   BARBARA: Just thinking. What are you, wound up today?

22   SONIA: *(After a pause)* Every time I say something . . .

23   BARBARA: It's too much! The engagement, the wedding,

24   this, that. I don't have time to pee and now I have to

25   think about these things? It's too much.

26   SONIA: *(After a pause)* Ay!

27   BARBARA: What?

28   SONIA: A fly.

29   BARBARA: Where is it?

30   SONIA: Flew away. Una picazón.

31   BARBARA: Don't scratch.

32   SONIA: It itches.

33   BARBARA: That's what they want. Damn flies want you to

34   scratch, scratch, scratch 'til it swells up like a bowling

35   ball. I'll get the Caladryl.

1   SONIA: I'm all right.

2   BARBARA: It's the best thing.

3   SONIA: I won't scratch.

4   BARBARA: Well, remind me to put some on you later. 'Cause

5   if not . . .

6   SONIA: I know.

7   BARBARA: *(After a pause)* I wonder who'll come visit. Didn't

8   your mami used to tell you that? When a fly comes in,

9   that means someone will come visit?

10   SONIA: No.

11   BARBARA: Mine did. Whenever a fly would come in, I'd

12   spend the next day or two waiting. Somebody always

13   showed up.

14   SONIA: Really?

15   BARBARA: Without fail.

16   SONIA: *(After a pause)* Sometimes I think no one's going to

17   come along.

18   BARBARA: You got Polo.

19   SONIA: Yeah, he's intense, but I'm talking about someone.

20   I'll see him, he'll see me, and I know he'll be someone.

21   With Polo, I still feel like I'm waiting.

22   BARBARA: You don't see each other enough.

23   SONIA: We see each other plenty. But when we're in bed

24   together, it's like it's just me, me and what I'm thinking.

25   *(Slight pause)* We could be so good we could be great.

26   BARBARA: There are other guys.

27   SONIA: I want to work it out with him. You worked it out

28   with Orlando.

29   BARBARA: We're engaged.

30   SONIA: Exactly. You're going somewhere.

31   BARBARA: *(After a pause)* Doesn't hurt to look.

32   SONIA: If I look, I'll start touching.

33   BARBARA: So?

34   SONIA: So what would Polo think?

35   BARBARA: *(Selects lipstick from box.)* He'll think you're hot.

1   **SONIA:** Yeah?
2   **BARBARA: Candela.** *(BARBARA puts on lipstick. SONIA*
3   *watches her.)*
4
5
6
7
8
9
10
11
12
13
14
15
16
17
18
19
20
21
22
23
24
25
26
27
28
29
30
31
32
33
34
35

1 # THIS ONE THING I DO
2 ### by Claire Braz-Valentine
3 ### in collaboration with Michael Griggs
4
5 *Scene for two women in their thirties.*
6
7 The original text of this play was first produced by Bear Republic
8 Theater in Santa Cruz, California in 1982, and was published by
9 Samuel French in 1989. The two characters in the scene are the
10 famous women's rights activists Elizabeth Cady Stanton and Susan
11 B. Anthony. The setting is Elizabeth's bedroom, late 1800s.
12
13 **SUSAN: So, I rush back to you and here you are, fat and**
14 **complacent like a fine cow in your chambers. The least**
15 **you could do is look a little pale.**
16 **ELIZABETH:** *(Holds out her arms.)* **Oh, darling Susan. Come**
17 **here and let me hug you. Let you hug me.**
18 **SUSAN:** *(Goes to ELIZABETH's bed, sits and they hold each other.)*
19 *SUSAN pats her back and rocks her gently.)* **How is it with**
20 **you, little Elizabeth?**
21 **ELIZABETH: I'm too old for this, Susan. No more children.**
22 **I have only so much energy. I want my last years to be**
23 **spent alongside you on the platform. I want so terribly**
24 **to change something in my life.**
25 **SUSAN: Oh? And wasn't it you who just appeared before**
26 **Congress? Wasn't it you who spoke in Utah three months**
27 **ago? And isn't it you who is managing and writing** *The*
28 *Revolution?* **Isn't it you who has led campaigns in over**
29 **twenty states in the last fifteen years?**
30 **ELIZABETH: It never seems enough. There's just so much to**
31 **do.**
32 **SUSAN: That is the question, I suppose. If there is enough**
33 **to give, can we give it?**
34 **ELIZABETH: We try.**
35 **SUSAN: I only do one thing, Elizabeth. This one thing and**

1 now I feel with the suffrage movement split and women
2 running off in all directions that even I am ineffective.
3 ELIZABETH: *(Pause)* Henry's gone again.
4 SUSAN: For how long?
5 ELIZABETH: Four months . . . maybe three.
6 SUSAN: *(Touches ELIZABETH's stomach.)* And this birth. He
7 will miss this one also?
8 ELIZABETH: I suppose he will . . . You know, Susan, in a
9 way, I think birth frightens men. It is such an . . . an awful
10 thing . . . you know, not awful . . . awesome. Our
11 strength . . . this thing our bodies do . . . open up, and put
12 forth another being . . . a totally different being . . .
13 *(Pause)* Did you see the children? They've been making
14 me mad asking when you'd return.
15 SUSAN: Yes, I saw them, the little monsters. They have
16 already gone through my valise and snatched away their
17 presents, weasled six pennies from me, and made me
18 promise them a story at bedtime.
19 ELIZABETH: They do love you, Susan.
20 SUSAN: And I them. But it's their mother I'm concerned
21 about. So what are you doing in bed? You've been the
22 one preaching about modern birth. Why, your last child,
23 you weren't in bed more than fifteen minutes. Barely long
24 enough to get the poor thing born.
25 ELIZABETH: I think I will amend my campaign so that it's
26 directed toward active pregnancies for younger women
27 only.
28 SUSAN: Pshaw! Younger indeed. *(Pause)* Well, I guess this
29 means you won't be hearty enough to make the journey
30 with me to Wyoming. When are you full term?
31 ELIZABETH: Six more weeks. When do you make the trip?
32 SUSAN: Four weeks.
33 ELIZABETH: Oh, and I did so want to join you. This is such
34 an exciting time there. Pretty soon Wyoming will be
35 admitted into the Union, God and the Democrats willing.

1   The first state. Can you believe it, Susan, the first state

2   with women's suffrage? Well, get my papers and pens. I

3   feel guilty enough about not being able to attend. At least

4   I can write you a humdinger of a speech. Why do I always

5   feel guilty? I think it has something to do with

6   motherhood. The minute you become a mother you begin

7   to feel guilty.

8   SUSAN: *You* begin to feel guilty.

9   ELIZABETH: *I* begin to feel guilty. *(Pause)* I felt guilty about

10   the bloomers. The minute you appeared in public you

11   were almost tarred and feathered.

12   SUSAN: Ah yes, the great bloomer caper. Well, Mrs. Stanton,

13   you deserve a little guilt on that one.

14   ELIZABETH: Don't you miss them, though?

15   SUSAN: Indeed I do. But as you said, the bloomers called

16   too much attention to the clothes and not the people

17   inside.

18   ELIZABETH: Do you feel we're before our time, Susan?

19   SUSAN: Well, my girl, we're certainly not behind it.

20   ELIZABETH: I'm going to write you a speech so wonderful

21   they'll never forget you in Wyoming.

22   SUSAN: I don't care if they forget me. Let them forget me.

23   People, individual people aren't the issue here.

24   ELIZABETH: *(Pause)* They are, though, actually, aren't they?

25   SUSAN: Yes. *(Turns to leave the room.)*

26   ELIZABETH: I hope it's a girl, Susan. I'll call her Susan

27   Stanton.

28   SUSAN: Fine, call her that. But what I hope is . . . *(Pause)* I

29   hope it's the last.

30

31

32

33

34

35

1 # TABLES AND CHAIRS
2 ## by Stanley Rutherford
3
4 *Scene for two women, indeterminate ages.*
5
6 In this wacko comedy, Naomi, Spencer, and Howard are staying as
7 guests in the home of Alice, a fantastically wealthy spinster. Spencer
8 is Off-stage during the scene, and Howard is not seen by the audience,
9 even though the women refer constantly to him. Howard should
10 probably be "placed" downstage in an empty chair.
11
12 **ALICE:** Howard says that —
13 **NAOMI:** I don't care what Howard says . . . if Howard wants
14 to say something, Howard can say it for himself . . . isn't
15 that right, Howie? *(She glares at HOWARD.)*
16 **ALICE:** Howard is very shy.
17 **NAOMI:** *(Screams.)* **Speak, Howard! Speak!**
18 **ALICE:** *(Pause, as she stares at Howard lovingly)* **Isn't Howard**
19 **wonderful?**
20 **NAOMI:** Howard is a Neanderthal.
21 **ALICE:** Howard is the man I love.
22 **NAOMI:** Alice, Howard has been married about seventeen
23 times, maybe more . . .
24 **ALICE:** Howard is the man of my dreams.
25 **NAOMI:** The longest marriage lasted about seven weeks, the
26 shortest exactly eighteen hours . . . remember her,
27 Howard? Gloria Garton? The ventriloquist? And then
28 there was Mary Louise Menderman and Mieu-Mieu-
29 Rohrbach and Allison Kildaire . . .
30 **ALICE:** *(Pause)* **Naomi . . . Howard has asked me to be his**
31 **bride.**
32 **NAOMI:** *(With a deep sigh)* **Oh, Alice . . .**
33 **ALICE:** Howard has asked me to join him in eternal wedlock.
34 **NAOMI:** Alice, you need professional help.
35 **ALICE:** Howard wants to sanctify our love.

1   NAOMI: Alice, Howard will get what he wants from you and
2   then he'll dismiss you.
3   ALICE: He wants to *marry* me.
4   NAOMI: He wants to marry everyone ... it's his plan for
5   world peace. A world with one husband and five billion
6   wives. Five billion wedding ceremonies with five billion
7   wedding presents. Howard plans to return all of the
8   wedding presents and use the cash to eliminate all
9   international debt.
10 ALICE: *(Gasps.)* Isn't that wonderful!
11 NAOMI: It's sick.
12 ALICE: Howard will win the Nobel Prize.
13 NAOMI: Howard will be indicted for polygamy. Howard will
14   spend the rest of his life behind bars: handcuffed,
15   tethered, and gagged. *(Pause, then gently to ALICE)* Alice,
16   Howard is a psychopath.
17 ALICE: I love Howard.
18 NAOMI: Howard is a sociopath. He's a barbarian who preys
19   on unsuspecting women, especially those with a healthy
20   bank account.
21 ALICE: I have bags of money.
22 NAOMI: That's what Howard wants.
23 ALICE: Howard can have it all.
24 NAOMI: He wants it all.
25 ALICE: Isn't Howard wonderful?
26 NAOMI: Alice, Howard is a Casanova who has ruined the
27   lives of countless women ... Mieu-Mieu Rohrbach, Mary
28   Louise Menderman ...
29 ALICE: I love Howard.
30 NAOMI: Claudia Grierson, Melonie Camberwell, Dottie
31   Leachman, Mimi Nash ...
32 ALICE: Naomi ... Howard and I are going to be married this
33   evening. And I would like you to be my maid of honor.
34 NAOMI: *(Thinking quickly)* I'm going to be having major
35   surgery.

1   **ALICE:** *(Imploring)* **Naomi ...**

2   **NAOMI:** Major *exploratory* surgery.

3   **ALICE:** It would mean so much to us both.

4   **NAOMI:** I am going to be in the depths of anesthesia.

5   **ALICE:** We want it to be special ... just Howard and I and
6   our very special friends, Naomi and Spencer ... just the
7   four of us ... our family.

8   **NAOMI:** *(Dryly)* I wish I'd known sooner.

9   **ALICE:** We wanted it to be a surprise ... Howard wants me to
10   wear his mother's wedding dress ...

11   **NAOMI:** Alice ...

12   **ALICE:** The very dress that she wore when she married
13   Howard's father.

14   **NAOMI:** Alice, Howard wants *everybody* to wear his mother's
15   wedding dress. I'm surprised he's not going to wear it
16   himself. Everyone else has: Mieu-Mieu Rohrbach,
17   Melonie Camberwell, Gloria Garton. Have you ever seen
18   Howard's mother's wedding dress?

19   **ALICE:** Howard wants it to be a surprise.

20   **NAOMI:** Alice, Howard's mother was a saint, God knows ...
21   but she had a hump, a very large hump back here ... *(She*
22   *indicates.)* ... and so does the dress ... you'll have to pad
23   yourself to fill it out. *(ALICE is starting to have doubts.)* **Alice,**
24   we have known Howard since infancy ... and he was the
25   same then as he is now. He's still an infant ... Alice,
26   Howard's greatest claim to fame was his role as a donkey
27   in our Sunday school Christmas pageant, when he pulled
28   down his pants and did a b.m. in the middle of the manger
29   scene. Alice, Howard needs help, he's not self-
30   sufficient ... he can't get up in the morning, and Spencer
31   and I have graciously taken responsibility for his care
32   and protection ...

33   **ALICE:** Howard says that *he* takes care of *you*.

34   **NAOMI:** *We* take care of *him*. It's a long story, Alice, awfully
35   long and awfully tragic. Howard needed someone to take

1   **care of him after his mother died. He couldn't take care**
2   **of himself, and so Spencer and I adopted him. Howard**
3   **is our son. We'll be your in-laws if you marry him.**
4 **ALICE:** *(Very confused and upset. To HOWARD)* **Howard?**
5 **NAOMI:** **Honey, Howard's having one of his quiet days.**
6 **ALICE:** **Howard, talk to me . . . I need some answers, Howard**
7   **. . . simple answers to some simple questions.**
8 **NAOMI:** **Honey, all of Howard's answers are simple. Howard**
9   **has a learning disability. He's retarded, Alice. His mind**
10   **is mush.**
11 **ALICE:** *(Utterly distraught, screaming)* **Howard . . . Howard . . .**
12   **Howard, talk to me!** *(Long pause as ALICE recovers her*
13   *composure and moves to NAOMI for comfort.)* **I don't know**
14   **why I love him.**
15 **NAOMI:** **Honey, he's not worth it.**
16 **ALICE:** **Don't you love Spencer?**
17 **NAOMI:** **No.**
18 **ALICE:** **Doesn't Spencer love you?**
19 **NAOMI:** **No.**
20 **ALICE:** **Don't you want to have Spencer's child?**
21 **NAOMI:** **No.** *(Pause)*
22 **ALICE:** **I thought you loved Spencer. I thought he loved you.**
23 **NAOMI:** **Alice, this is life . . . this is *real* life. This isn't like**
24   **anything your mother ever told you about.**
25 **ALICE:** **My mother never told me anything . . . that's the**
26   **problem.**
27 **NAOMI:** **Honey, love is a heartache. You're better off without**
28   **it. It's overrated. It's an enzyme. You can get the same**
29   **feeling from eating chocolate.**
30 **ALICE:** *(Pause. Stunned)* **I didn't know.**
31 **NAOMI:** **I didn't either. I had to learn.**
32 **ALICE:** **And I've watched and I've listened trying to learn**
33   **the movements, the attitudes, the right things to say and**
34   **do, when to say it, when to keep it to myself . . .**
35 **NAOMI:** *(Comforting)* **Honey, you're doing just fine.**

1	ALICE:	I'm not a real person. I'm a pretend person.
2	NAOMI:	You're a very nice person, Alice. Too nice.
3	ALICE:	*(Hysterical)* *I am not a person!*
4	NAOMI:	Honey, you've got to relax.
5	ALICE:	*I have no personality!*
6	NAOMI:	Alice, honey, you don't *need* a personality to be a
7		person.
8	ALICE:	I want a personality.
9	NAOMI:	Personality is a completely overrated commodity.
10	ALICE:	I want to be like you. You're fun.
11	NAOMI:	I am?
12	ALICE:	Everyone thinks you're fun.
13	NAOMI:	I didn't know that.
14	ALICE:	I want to be fun too.
15	NAOMI:	You are fun.
16	ALICE:	No I'm not . . . I'm neurotic.
17	NAOMI:	Alice . . .
18	ALICE:	*I'm neurotic!*
19	NAOMI:	Alice, I don't like that word.
20	ALICE:	*(Loudly)* *I am neurotic!*
21	NAOMI:	*(Louder)* *I don't like that word!*
22	ALICE:	*(Screams into NAOMI's face.)* *Neurotic!*
23	NAOMI:	Alice, there are certain words that I simply cannot
24		tolerate being used in my presence, and that word is one
25		of them. It is a bad word, Alice.
26	ALICE:	I'm manic-depressive.
27	NAOMI:	Alice . . .
28	ALICE:	I'm schizophrenic.
29	NAOMI:	*(Loudly)* Bad words! Bad words! Bad, bad, "psychology"
30		words.
31	ALICE:	*(Shocked)* I love psychology!
32	NAOMI:	Psychology is dead. *(ALICE is pretty stunned by this*
33		*news.)* There is no more psychology . . . it's all
34		over . . . they've told us to forget the whole thing.
35	ALICE:	I love psychology.

1   NAOMI: They killed it off quite some time ago, Alice. You
2   can't even major in it anymore. It's dead. Very, very dead.
3   ALICE: *(Pause. Very stunned and confused)* **What am I supposed**
4   **to do?**
5   NAOMI: Forget about it.
6   ALICE: I disappear when other people leave the room. I
7   vanish. I am a planet. I have no light source of my own.
8   I need other people, light-giving people off of whom I can
9   reflect.
10   NAOMI: You need to eat more chocolate.
11   ALICE: I need Howard.
12   NAOMI: *(Annoyed)* **Alice** . . .
13   ALICE: I need you. *(She opens her arms to NAOMI.)*
14   NAOMI: *(Embracing ALICE)* **Alice** . . .
15   ALICE: I'd like you to be my sister.
16   NAOMI: Alice, I don't like that word.
17   ALICE: I've never had a sister.
18   NAOMI: It's not you I don't like, it's the institution.
19   ALICE: We'd be so close.
20   NAOMI: We *are* close.
21   ALICE: Even closer.
22   NAOMI: Let's just be friends.
23   ALICE: *(Gasps. Thrilled. Moved)* **I've never had a friend. I want**
24   both of you to be in my wedding so very much.
25   NAOMI: Honey, I'm having major surgery.
26   ALICE: Couldn't you have it tomorrow?
27   NAOMI: It's urgent . . . it has to be done as soon as possible.
28   ALICE: Maybe we could fit it in before the wedding . . .
29   NAOMI: We are *not* going to fit it in before the wedding.
30   ALICE: . . . cut you open, move things around, sew you up . . .
31   So why don't we have major surgery and then a little
32   supper — a nice postoperative, prenuptial supper . . .
33   NAOMI: I don't think I'm going to be up for it.
34   ALICE: And then we'll have the wedding!
35   NAOMI: And then we'll have the consummation, the

1   disenchantment, the lamentations, and then we'll have
2   the divorce.
3 ALICE: *(Oblivious)* I'm so happy.
4 NAOMI: Alice ...
5 ALICE: I want to have babies.
6 NAOMI: Alice ...
7 ALICE: And I want them to look like Howard.
8 NAOMI: Alice ...
9 ALICE: Howard's eyes and Howard's nose ...
10 NAOMI: Alice ...
11 ALICE: I want them to sound like Howard and smell like
12   Howard ...
13 NAOMI: You need professional help.
14 ALICE: I had never experienced *real life,* I mean, *real, real,*
15   *life,* until that wonderful moment when I opened my door
16   and saw this beautiful man standing on my doorstep and
17   then he smiled and I was terrified, my heart was
18   pounding, I was confused ... and he asked me if I wanted
19   to buy a vacuum cleaner ...
20 NAOMI: He'd stolen it.
21 ALICE: ... but I didn't need a vacuum cleaner ...
22 NAOMI: No one does.
23 ALICE: I already had a vacuum cleaner, and then he said his
24   name was Howard and I said my name was Alice, and I
25   was paralyzed with fear and joy, and then he asked if he
26   could come in and then he said he wanted to marry me
27   and make a million babies, and then he told me about
28   his friends. He said that you had fallen on hard times
29   and had no place to live and needed a place to stay for
30   a few days and maybe, he said, that I might have a place
31   for you to stay and maybe I might be able to spare some
32   food. *(Pause)* I was thrilled. I'd always wanted someone
33   to live with me, someone who needed me, because my
34   life had been nothing but pain and loneliness and every
35   day was solitude and terror in the face of an enormous

1   and terrifying world ... I had nothing to hold on to, no
2   one to tell me that things were going to be all right until
3   I met Howard and got to know his wonderful friends.
4   NAOMI: Alice, Howard and Spencer and I are not nice
5   people. We are not the kind of people you want to have
6   lying around your home. We don't have a real home. We're
7   on the run, we're fugitives. We're wanted in all fifty
8   states ... shoplifting, petty theft, extortion ... it's been
9   hell. There are posters out with pictures of us. It was the
10   Howard-the-Evangelist episode that pushed us over the
11   edge ... an awful period, Alice. We'd set up a nine
12   hundred number and Howard was passing himself off as
13   a television evangelist ... call Howard and find salvation.
14   And he wasn't washing his hair and he'd let his fingernails
15   grow to record-breaking lengths, even for Howard ...
16   and you'd dial the nine hundred number and get a
17   prerecorded message from Howard. An "inspirational"
18   message ... it was quite lucrative ... They're after us for
19   fraud. Alice, we've had to resort to a life of crime.
20   ALICE: *(Momentarily confused and troubled, but then resolved*
21   *and enthusiastic)* I want you to know that you can stay
22   here forever. I will hide you and feed you and we'll create
23   our own beautiful world safe from the outside.
24   NAOMI: Alice, you'd be aiding and abetting.
25   ALICE: I *want* to aid and abet!
26
27
28
29
30
31
32
33
34
35

1   **FOR HER**

2   **by Annie Evans**

3

4   *Monolog or scene for two women, one sixteen and the other thirty-six*

5   *to forty.*

6

7   The older female is the mother, and this role can either be played

8   from Off-stage, or done in shadow/silhouette. The locale is the family

9   home.

10

11   *(HER enters. She carries with her a clear glass that contains*

12   *urine. She holds under her arm a first response pregnancy test.*

13   *She also holds an overly large alarm clock. She sits on the floor.*

14   *She places the glass and clock down carefully. She tentatively*

15   *reads the directions on the box. She opens the box, takes out the*

16   *contents and begins to read the directions. She opens the wrapper*

17   *around the plastic indicator. She does all this as if it were fine*

18   *glass, or if she makes any noise the alarm will sound. MOM*

19   *enters.)*

20   **MOM:**   **Sweetheart, are you home?** *(HER reacts with quiet fear.*

21   *She starts to proceed with the directions on the pregnancy test*

22   *with a bit more urgency.)* **Sweetheart? Honey?**

23   **HER:**   **I'm home.**

24   **MOM:**   **Good. Did you have a nice day?**

25   **HER:**   **A-huh.**

26   **MOM:**   **Good.**

27   *(MOM hesitates, then crosses Off-stage. HER breathes a sigh of*

28   *relief. She sets up the test. She looks at the clock to mark out the*

29   *time. MOM re-enters. She carries a laundry basket full of men's*

30   *shirts. She begins to fold them. HER for the next five minutes*

31   *constantly looks back and forth from the clock to the test.)*

32   **MOM:**   **I hope you aren't too hungry 'cause your father's going**

33   **to be late and he's picking up dinner at Steak & Stein. I**

34   **told him we'd rather have that take-out Chinese you like**

35   **so much but you know your father. I was going to cook**

1	some chicken parmigiana but the house I've been trying
2	to sell, you know, the Taylors who moved to Miami? I had
3	a last-minute showing, people from Chicago, getting out
4	of the city before it gets them, they said. Hey, honey, did
5	you want to drive into Bloomington with me Saturday?
6	Do some shopping? You never said yes or no. Honey?

7 HER: No.

8 MOM: Are you sure? I've never heard you say no to shopping.
9 Didn't you say you need a blouse to go with your plaid
10 skirt since the beige one ripped under the arm?

11 HER: I'm sure.

12 MOM: Why don't you come out and help me fold these? I
13 hardly see you lately.

14 HER: I'll be out in five minutes.

15 MOM: OK. It's nice you're so busy. I know Mrs. Reynolds
16 says she never sees Nancy either. She had a field hockey
17 game all the way in Indianapolis, can you imagine? I'm
18 glad you just like working for this newspaper. I'm told
19 that it looks good to college admissions people, working
20 on the newspaper. Is Nancy still seeing Dr. Koenig's son?

21 HER: Yes.

22 MOM: I'm surprised you two aren't a couple. You played
23 together since you were five. You used to chase each other
24 around the yard for hours. Remember?

25 HER: He likes Nancy, Mom.

26 MOM: I'm just saying he likes you too. You'd run around and
27 then come in and ask for Bosco and peanut butter on
28 toast. Never peanut butter and jelly. I had all those jams
29 your brother liked so much and you two always turned
30 up your noses. Remember?

31 HER: That was a long time ago.

32 MOM: I know, I'm just saying you'd make a cute couple, that's
33 all. *(MOM crosses off and brings on more men's shirts.)* I'd
34 appreciate some help out here? Sweetheart?

35 HER: I said five minutes.

90

1 MOM: Whatever happened to that nice boy who took you to
2   the Halloween dance? Bill, Bob — what was his name?
3   He seemed like a nice boy. I hope he was, wasn't he?
4   Honey? Well, he seemed nice to me. You father, well, you
5   know your father, no one is good enough for his baby.
6   He was nice, wasn't he? Your father thought he was a bit
7   full of himself. What was he, middle man on the soccer
8   team, something like that? Well, you know what to say if
9   he isn't nice. You say take me home. What are you doing
10   in there that's taking so long? Sweetheart? What are you
11   doing? Huh? What are you doing?
12 HER: *Don't come in here!*
13 MOM: Why not?
14 HER: 'Cause — I'm not dressed.
15 MOM: Oh. Sorry. *(HER relaxes. Looks again at clock and test.)* I
16   hope you aren't still mad because we won't give you the
17   car Friday night. It's not that we don't trust you, but a
18   rule is a rule. Your brother couldn't drive after dark until
19   he was seventeen either. Are you still mad? Well, I'd
20   rather be safe than sorry, if you get my meaning. We'll
21   just pick you up once you've put the paper in the bed,
22   however late. *(HER laughs to herself at MOM's mistake.)* We
23   do trust you. And we don't have to tell you we're very
24   proud of you. Being an editor. I certainly wouldn't begin
25   to know how to make a newspaper work. You know that,
26   don't you? We're very proud. *(In frustration HER leaps to
27   her feet.)* Before you know it, you'll be driving to college,
28   day or night. OK?
29 HER: I can't wait.
30 MOM: Is that what it is? You're still mad? Well, to be perfectly
31   honest, I think we could lighten up on that rule for you.
32   You certainly haven't been the worry your brother was
33   when he was your age. But you know your father.
34 HER: I don't care about the car.
35 MOM: You sure?

1   HER: I'll get someone to drive me.
2   MOM: How about that Bill or Bob? He could drive you.
3   HER: It's Brian — no he won't drive me.
4   MOM: Then we will.
5   HER: I said I don't care.
6   MOM: Obviously you do.
7   HER: I don't.
8   MOM: Then why are you raising your voice?
9   HER: Christ! Can we drop this, please?!
10   MOM: Watch your language.
11   HER: I'm sorry.
12   MOM: Well, you do what you want, but we'll pick you up if
13   it's necessary.
14   HER: Thank you.
15   MOM: You know if you're upset you should just tell me. You
16   need any help?
17   HER: I can get dressed by myself.
18   MOM: Of course you can. *(They each are possibly about to say*
19   *something. The alarm clock suddenly goes off. HER runs to turn*
20   *it off.)* What's that?
21   HER: Something's wrong with the alarm. Don't come in. *(She*
22   *tries to turn off the alarm. It's won't. In her frustration she kicks*
23   *over the pregnancy test. HER frantically tries to get the cup before*
24   *it all spills.)* Shit!
25   MOM: What's going on in there?
26   HER: It's nothing. I spilled some water.
27   MOM: You need paper towels?
28   HER: I got it. *(HER stuffs the plastic indicator into the glass and*
29   *puts it out of the way of the spill, not bothering to notice the*
30   *possible results of the test. HER looks frantically for something*
31   *to wipe up the spilled test. She finds nothing and starts to use*
32   *the end of her shirt.)*
33   MOM: You sure?
34   HER: Yes, yes.
35   MOM: Let me at least get the alarm. Oh shoot — your father's

1   **home.** *(MOM quickly puts the laundry in the basket.)* **Come**
2   **out and set the table. You should have done it earlier.**
3   **Put out the salad and the bowls, and that low cholesterol**
4   **dressing for your dad. Pull out any lettuce that may be**
5   **brown. Maybe you should add in some tomatoes, what**
6   **do you think? Can you try to turn that off, honey, please?**
7   *(She exits with the laundry. HER is frantically wiping up the*
8   *spill. The alarm blares. Blackout.)*
9
10
11
12
13
14
15
16
17
18
19
20
21
22
23
24
25
26
27
28
29
30
31
32
33
34
35

Scenes for a Man and a Woman

1		# SIGNS OF LIFE
2		## by Debbie Baley

3

4 *Scene for one male and one female, indeterminate ages.*

5

6 This play was first produced at the Perseverance Theatre in Douglas,
7 Alaska, in April of 1990, where Debbie Baley is a company member.
8 In this opening scene of the play we meet Sal and Abe, two ordinary
9 people who journey back and forth across America in search of their
10 dreams. The action is self-explanatory, but the author reminds us
11 that "the style of the play draws heavily from vaudeville.
12 Consequently, the actors should bear in mind that there is usually
13 a 'straight man' in each scene."

14

15 *(A rest stop along a highway in the Great Salt Lake Desert. Early*
16 *morning. Lights up on a Chevy Vega. In the front of the car, on*
17 *the ground lies a large mound covered with a blanket. The mound*
18 *moves. A man's arm and a woman's leg pop out. The mound*
19 *shifts again and lies still for a moment, before the blanket is*
20 *tossed aside and a woman sits up suddenly.)*
21 **SAL:** **Abe! Where are we?**
22 **ABE:** **Hmmmm?**
23 **SAL:** **Where are we? Tell me where we are!**
24 **ABE:** **On the road, Sal.**
25 **SAL:** **But where?**
26 **ABE:** *(Yawns.)* **Salt Lake.**
27 **SAL:** **Salt Lake?**
28 **ABE:** **Utah.**
29 **SAL:** *(Pause)* **We never shoulda come!**
30 **ABE:** **Sal . . .**
31 **SAL:** **We never shoulda left!**
32 **ABE:** **Will you knock it off!**
33 **SAL:** **This whole thing was a bad idea!**
34 **ABE:** **Quit worryin' and go back to sleep!**
35 **SAL:** **Leavin' everything at the drop of a hat, comin' out here**

1   on a whim —

2   ABE: *(Sits up.)* It wasn't a *whim!*

3   SAL: It was too a whim!

4   ABE: It was a *sign!* A very important sign!

5   SAL: When you jump in the car and drive to Utah because

6   the stars have come out in New Jersey, that's a whim!

7   ABE: Sal. We're not goin' to Utah. We're goin' someplace else.

8   SAL: Where? Where we goin'?

9   ABE: I dunno!

10   SAL: If you're gonna abandon everything and charge off

11   'cross the country, you better know where you're goin'!

12   ABE: How many times I gotta tell ya! All I know is we're

13   followin' the stars!

14   SAL: But Abe! We've been followin' 'em for three days! I think

15   it's time you figured out where we're followin' 'em to!

16   ABE: I can't do that, Sal!

17   SAL: Why not!

18   ABE: Because! I dunno! Look! All I know is I saw the stars!

19   I was sittin' in the car during the power outage, listenin' to

20   the radio and watchin' the smoke float by from the landfill.

21   And the smoke lifted...and I looked up...and

22   ...the sky *turned on!* As I was watchin' it! The stars *popped*

23   *on,* like somebody had plugged 'em in. And as I was sittin'

24   there, a voice comes on the radio and says "Follow the stars!"

25   so I jiggle the dial to a different channel and the voice comes

26   back on again! And says "Follow the stars" — a second time!

27   And when I heard that, I knew what it was! It was the stars

28   talkin' to me through the radio! Well, next thing I know, you

29   come outta the trailer with a flashlight and tell me you went

30   to Diamond Eddie's and got a tattoo...a tattoo of a *star*, on

31   your breast! And when you shine the flashlight on the

32   tattoo...BAM! The power comes back on! Well, when that

33   happened, I knew we had to come. There was no

34   mistakin'...it was a *sign.* We had to follow it. And that's

35   what we're doin'! We're followin' it!

1	SAL:	I know! But Abe, we've been followin' the stars for three
2		days! And you haven't found this place yet! Doesn't that
3		tell ya something?
4	ABE:	What?
5	SAL:	That maybe it doesn't exit? That maybe you imagined
6		this whole thing?
7	ABE:	Imagined? You think I imagined *that?*
8	SAL:	*(Pause)* Yes.
9	ABE:	Sal! I didn't imagine nothin'! It happened! And you saw
10		it too! You said it gave you a good feelin'! That's when
11		we decided to come!
12	SAL:	It didn't give me a good feelin'. It gave me the creeps.
13	ABE:	Sal . . . you said funny things had been happenin' to you
14		all day and that it gave you a good feelin'.
15	SAL:	Nothin' funny happened that day!
16	ABE:	Since when do you go to Diamond Eddie's and get a
17		tattoo? *(SAL doesn't answer.)* You never done nothin' like
18		that before! And why did you get a star of all things? *(SAL*
19		*doesn't answer.)* No, Sal! When the power came back on
20		and I told ya everything I had heard and seen, you stood
21		there and said that you had a feelin' *this* would be the
22		answer to . . . your little problem . . . you know, the
23		*female* problem you been havin'!
24	SAL:	I didn't say that!
25	ABE:	That's a *quote*, Sal!
26	SAL:	Well . . . maybe I did.
27	ABE:	There's no maybe about it! I mean, Sal! When you said
28		*that*, I started the car! 'Cause we tried everything. I
29		bought ya all those books! I bought ya bottled water! And
30		when *you* said that *this* would do the trick, that settled
31		it! So don't sit there and tell me it gave you the creeps.
32		It gave ya a good feelin', an' ya know it! *(Long pause)* You
33		know, Sal, when ya flip-flop like this all over the place,
34		it makes me feel like ya don't believe in me, like ya don't
35		trust what I'm tryin' to do.

1   SAL: I trust ya. I wouldn't of drove 'cross the country with ya
2   if I didn't trust ya.
3   ABE: 'Cause we're in this together. And I take good care of
4   ya. I ain't never let ya down.
5   SAL: No, ya haven't.
6   ABE: Well, quit carryin' on then! You ain't stopped since we
7   left.
8   SAL: I know ...
9   ABE: What's eatin' at you anyway?
10 SAL: I'm just nervous.
11 ABE: About what?
12 SAL: *(Pause)* The TV. I left it on.
13 ABE: What?
14 SAL: Just as we were leavin', I ran back into the trailer and
15   turned it on.
16 ABE: You went back into the trailer and turned on the TV?
17   Deliberately?
18 SAL: Uh-huh.
19 ABE: Oh my God!
20 SAL: I think we should go back and turn it off.
21 ABE: But Sal! We been drivin' for three days!
22 SAL: I can't stand the thought of sittin' here in Utah while
23   our TV is on in New Jersey.
24 ABE: Well, you shoulda thought of that before you went back
25   into the trailer!
26 SAL: I'd feel much better if we just went back and turned it off.
27 ABE: But — but — now, wait a minute! Sal. Sal! We *left* the
28   TV! We *left* the trailer! We *left* New Jersey! *For good!* We
29   ain't never goin' back! It doesn't matter if the TV is still
30   on or not! We left everything behind! Remember?
31 SAL: Yeah.
32 ABE: What we gotta do is look ahead! We gotta think about
33   the future! We gotta follow the stars!
34 SAL: Right. *(Long pause)*
35 ABE: Did you leave anything else on?

1   SAL: I'm tryin' to remember if I unplugged the coffee pot.
2   ABE: The coffee pot!
3   SAL: I'm sure I did.
4   ABE: Well, I hope so!
5   SAL: No. I did. I definitely did. *(Pause)* Well, don't look at me
6   like that! I unplugged it!
7   ABE: You could burn the whole place down!
8   SAL: Well, what d'ya expect? You start carryin' on about
9   signs and stars and the next thing I know I'm in the car
10   headin' west! I'm sure I unplugged it. I didn't have time
11   to pack my toothbrush, but I did remember to unplug
12   the coffee pot.
13 ABE: Did you unplug it before or after you turned on the TV?
14 SAL: We decided to go and the first thing I did was pull the
15   plug. I remember now! That's right! I pulled the plug.
16 ABE: Well, good. That's settled. *(Pause)*
17 SAL: I'm sure I pulled it.
18 ABE: Sal!
19 SAL: Maybe I just think I pulled it.
20 ABE: This is a helluva thing!
21 SAL: Maybe I'm imagining the whole thing.
22 ABE: Will you knock it off?
23 SAL: I can't.
24 ABE: Just forget about the coffee pot. Just forget about the
25   television.
26 SAL: I can't. They're burned in my mind!
27 ABE: Well, burn 'em out!
28 SAL: They're burned in your mind too!
29 ABE: No they're not!
30 SAL: Yes they are! You'll just keep drivin' around the country
31   with nothin' but the coffee pot and TV on your mind. Just
32   wait.
33 ABE: *(Long pause)* All right. All right. But I'm tellin' ya, we're
34   comin' *right back.* As soon as we get everything
35   unplugged, we're turnin' around and comin' back! You

101

1   **understand?**
2   **SAL: Uh-huh.**
3
4
5
6
7
8
9
10
11
12
13
14
15
16
17
18
19
20
21
22
23
24
25
26
27
28
29
30
31
32
33
34
35

STUMPS
by Mark Medoff

Scene for a man in his thirties, a woman in her twenties.

Emily, a "porn princess" star with the stage name "Fawn," is reading for a part in a serious film with a young writer, Jerry. Jerry is in a wheelchair. Emily's manager, Cal, dominates and abuses her, and has just left to go fishing for a couple of hours. The scene is outside Jerry's trailer on the bank of a river.

JERRY: What's in your purse that he doesn't want you to put down your throat, up your nose, or into your veins?

EMILY: Nothin'. I mean, I got, see, these allergies and he doesn't like me to take my antihistamines cuz they make me real kinda like loggy. He doesn't like me to be loggy.

JERRY: I buy that. Because I'm new to earth. Emily, I been around virtually nothin' but addicts of one sort or another the last decade. You wanna play "Guess My Addiction"? What was the medication you both took awhile ago?

EMILY: Vitamins.

JERRY: What he gave you looked like some kinda antibiotic. What's in your purse? I'd guess from your behavior, it's maybe a little cocaine.

EMILY: I think we should just like work the scene now. Help me do our first scene, about the painting, OK?

JERRY: No, not that one, uh-uh. The one that starts on page twenty-seven. We'll just read through it once. Can you see without your glasses?

EMILY: Oh, I don't need 'em at all. I just wear 'em so I won't look like, you know, what everyone thinks I am. *(She takes the glasses off, puts them aside. She finds the scene.)* Oh. Gee. Don't ya think this scene's kinda ... ya think we should do maybe a different one?

1   **JERRY:**   **Uh-uh. This one.** *(Pause)*

2   **EMILY:**   **OK.** *(She invents a "door," opens it, and enters, beginning*

3   *the scene with some clichéd "porn queen" sexuality. JERRY does*

4   *the scene from memory.)*

5   **"CATHERINE":**   **"A lotta guys are real slobs. This is nice,**

6   **you keep your atarpment — you keep your tapart — your**

7   **apart**ment . . .**"** **Oh, wait, I'm starting over, OK?**

8   **JERRY:**   **Relax. You don't have to work at being sexy. Be**

9   **yourself. Be you. Be Emily. Not Fawn.**

10   **EMILY:**   **Oh — OK. Emily. Emily.** *(She shakes herself out, tries*

11   *to get loose, starts over, doing it essentially the same way.)*

12   **"CATHERINE":**   **"A lotta guys are real slobs. This is nice, you**

13   **keep your apart**ment **very nice. Can I take my** *jacket* **off?"**

14   **"JOSH":**   **"Sure, please."**

15   **"CATHERINE":**   **" 'Please'? I don't want you to get the wrong**

16   **idea. Guys often think if you take your** *jacket* **off, it's an**

17   **imitation — an in***t***imation — an** *invitation* **to —"** *(EMILY*

18   *breaks out, dumps the script, starts away.)* **Oh, gee, God, I'm**

19   **so terrible!**

20   **JERRY:**   **No, you're not.**

21   **EMILY:**   **I'm so crappy and awful and . . .** *crappy!*

22   **JERRY:**   **I said you're —**

23   **EMILY:**   **Ya can't give a stupid person a smart person to play.**

24   **JERRY:**   **Emily —**

25   **EMILY:**   **I'm such a hammerhead, I can't even read!**

26   **JERRY:**   **Hey, hey! Miss! Come back here! Come on!** *(She*

27   *returns.)* **Now, are you just nervous because you're afraid**

28   **Cal's got the trees bugged or do you have some kind of**

29   **reading problem?**

30   **EMILY:**   **I have some kind of** *moron* **problem!**

31   **JERRY:**   **Look at me, Emily. Read my eyes.** *(She does.)* **You're**

32   **not terrible and you're not a moron.**

33   **EMILY:**   **I am too!**

34   **JERRY:**   **No, you're not.**

35   **EMILY:**   **Am!**

1   **JERRY:**   Not!

2   **EMILY:**   Am!

3   **JERRY:**   **Not!** *(This is repeated several more times . . . until they*

4   *laugh at the childishness of the exchange.)* **It's not you. It's**

5   **the script. My fault. She shouldn't say anything**

6   **suggestive. Bad writing. We'll rewrite, we'll fix it. Let's**

7   **just relax a minute, whudduya say? Do a little yoga, have**

8   **a little chat. For instance, no big deal, but ya know I can't**

9   **help wondering just how you met his divinity, the Rev.**

10   **Calvin Rhodes.** *(She isn't forthcoming with a response.)*

11   **Church social?** *(She shakes her head.)* **Confessional booth?**

12   **EMILY:**   **His religion, they don't have confession.**

13   **JERRY:**   **Bar Mitzvah?**

14   **EMILY:**   **What's that?**

15   **JERRY:**   **A Jewish praying and eating event.**

16   **EMILY:**   **I'm not Jewish.**

17   **JERRY:**   **I never woulda guessed.**

18   **EMILY:**   **Calvin was only kidding.**

19   **JERRY:**   **Calvin wasn't kidding. Calvin was goading, but I**

20   **didn't bite because I was being cool; perhaps you noticed.**

21   **So where'd ya meet? Simple question. Hell, as far as I'm**

22   **concerned you can lie if you want to. I just want you to**

23   **relax.**

24   **EMILY:**   **I'm relaxed, we can try the scene again.**

25   **JERRY:**   **But now I'm tense. Why, today, Emily, parts of me**

26   **incapable of tenseness are tense.**

27   **EMILY:**   **You have a nice sense of humor. I bet a lotta guys in**

28   **like, you know, guys that are in wheelchairs aren't real**

29   **funny.**

30   **JERRY:**   **Tell ya the truth — some of them are downright**

31   **austere. But I'm a ramblin', fun kinda guy, so you don't**

32   **wanna talk, fine. Let's do the scene.**

33   **EMILY:**   **I was selling men's shirts and ties outside the Port**

34   **Authority bus station in New York City and Cal, ya know,**

35   **he comes up and wants like a striped shirt to go with a**

1	chalk stripe suit, he says. But the thing is, he didn't really
2	care about the shirt, though, see, it was a trick; he was
3	really tryin' to get me away from these two whackos I
4	was workin' for that were like, you know, kinda holdin'
5	me prisoner in their apartment.
6	JERRY: So he rescued you from the street and promoted you
7	to porn princess.
8	EMILY: Well, you know, there are some parts like in between.
9	JERRY: No, I don't know. Why don't you tell me? *(When she*
10	*doesn't)* Do a lotta the runaways he takes off the street
11	end up in pornographic movies?
12	EMILY: No. He helps a lotta kids, Jerry.
13	JERRY: How?
14	EMILY: He just does — lotsa ways. He talks to 'em and gets
15	'em jobs or lotsa times he makes 'em go home to their
16	moms . . .
17	JERRY: Who's Carlos?
18	EMILY: A man that, you know . . . a kinda businessman that
19	Calvin sorta works for.
20	JERRY: He putting up Cal's share of the movie money?
21	EMILY: I guess kinda.
22	JERRY: So, this project is important to Cal, isn't it? He sees
23	my script as *his* way out too, doesn't he?
24	EMILY: Can I make a suggestion?
25	JERRY: Is this called "Changing the Subject"?
26	EMILY: I think you should, ya know, like definitely keep
27	the title. Of the movie. "Catherine Liberty."
28	JERRY: Why?
29	EMILY: You can't tell Calvin. Do you promise?
30	JERRY: Sure, I promise.
31	EMILY: I went to the library one day, ya know, by myself,
32	and I looked up the painting and this writer said he was
33	like, the painter, that Delacroix, ya know, he didn't know
34	whether he . . . about his like sexual preference, ya know,
35	so I thought like Liberty's breasts are exposed maybe

1   because she scares him — women do, I mean — and so,
2   whachamacallit, *unconsciously* he could humiliate her by
3   putting her in front of all those guys half naked, not
4   carrying a thing ... a *weapon*, not carrying a weapon like
5   the guys, but only that — ya know, the guys' flag like.
6   JERRY: Their banner.
7   EMILY: Yeah. And so after I thought about all that, then I
8   understood a lot about what you felt maybe about
9   Catherine and Josh and that it was ... well, you know,
10   that it was a really, really, good title and the discussion
11   they have about the painting's pretty important. *(Pause)*
12   Is what I just said like really dumb?
13   JERRY: No. What you just said reconfirmed for me what I've
14   written is right. I was sitting in there wondering if I
15   should lose all that Delacroix stuff. Thank you very much.
16   EMILY: Really?
17   JERRY: Yes.
18   EMILY: You swear?
19   JERRY: I swear.
20   EMILY: Gosh, that's so nice. I mean usually it's like as soon
21   as guys know who I am and what I've, ya know, *done* and
22   that I got a tenth grade education, they don't take me
23   too serious.
24   JERRY: Not many women take me seriously.
25   EMILY: People really like to pigeonhole people, ya ever
26   notice that?
27   JERRY: Nope, never did.
28   EMILY: Ya haven't?
29   JERRY: I'm kidding.
30   EMILY: That's nice too. Nobody kids me neither unless it's
31   like, you know, really mean. *(Pause. Eyes locked together.*
32   *EMILY breaks away.)* God, I wish I had me a trailer on a
33   river. Grill a T-bone outside on a dealy like that. One a
34   those food chopper things that you can shoestring up
35   some taters for a guy ya really like. Go in the

1   supermarket and know the produce guy like by name.
2   "Hey, Armando, how's the Boston Bibb Lettuce today —
3   you recommend it?" Except I'll probably never have a
4   place like this cause Calvin, he wants to be president of
5   Paramount Pictures, and we'll probably end up living
6   some place like Beverly Hills ... You respect women,
7   don't ya?
8   **JERRY:** I got no respect for men, so I'm tryin' women.
9   **EMILY:** Did you have to like, ya know, kill anyone in
10   Vietnam?
11   **JERRY:** Yeah, I was, like, required to do that.
12   **EMILY:** Who'd you have to kill?
13   **JERRY:** Oh, ya know, a nice assortment of slant-eyed
14   individuals of like various ages and sexes.
15   **EMILY:** You're making fun of how I say "like" and "ya know."
16   I'll try not to say them. *(Pause)* Did you want to move to
17   Israel like Josh and be in the Israeli army? Before
18   you're ... before you ...
19   **JERRY:** Before I became a paraplegic? Yeah, that's what I
20   wanted to do. Wear short pants, year round tan, kick a
21   lotta Arab and Palestinian ass. *(He sings the first bars of*
22   *"Hatikvah" quietly and stares into her eyes.)*
23   **EMILY:** Calvin doesn't like Israel.
24   **JERRY:** Another shocker. *(He continues to sing "Hatikvah"*
25   *until ...)*
26   **EMILY:** Don't look at me like that.
27   **JERRY:** Like how?
28   **EMILY:** Like that. It's not good. OK?
29   **JERRY:** I have an idea.
30   **EMILY:** What?
31   **JERRY:** Let's go inside and work on the scene.
32   **EMILY:** We're too tense.
33   **JERRY:** It's a tense scene. I should have realized from the
34   beginning that precisely what it needs is a lotta tension
35   between the two participants. Help me up the ramp. *(He*

1   *resumes singing "Hatikvah" as she helps him up the ramp and*
2   *into the trailer.)* **All right, ready to resurrect the**
3   **emotionally dead?**
4   **EMILY: OK. But one thing, OK? This is real, real awful**
5   **important to Calvin *and* to me.**
6   **JERRY: Oh, it's real, real awful important to me too, Emily,**
7   **have no doubt about that.**
8   **EMILY: OK. So you gotta make me better.**
9
10
11
12
13
14
15
16
17
18
19
20
21
22
23
24
25
26
27
28
29
30
31
32
33
34
35

1   # THE CINDERELLA WALTZ
2   ### by Don Nigro
3
4   *Scene for one male and one female, twenties.*
5
6   This comedy was first performed by the Indiana State University
7   Summer Repertory Theatre in 1978. Several new characters have
8   been added to this modern version of the classic tale, in particular
9   Zed, the village "idiot." In the following scene, Zed meets Rosey
10   (Cinderella) just after she returns from the Prince's ball. The wicked
11   stepsisters are named Goneril and Regan, and the fairy godmother
12   is Mother Magee.
13
14   **ZED: Hark. Silence.**
15   **ROSEY: Oh, hello.**
16   **ZED: How was the prom? Nice music?**
17   **ROSEY: Zed, it was wonderful. I danced so many times with**
18   **the Prince. He danced with me more times than with**
19   **anybody else. And he danced with Regan, too, and he**
20   **asked Goneril several times but she just gnawed on her**
21   **lip and stared at his codpiece and then she went off into**
22   **the corner and drank seventeen margaritas.**
23   **ZED: Nice girl.**
24   **ROSEY: Regan danced a whole lot with Mr. Troll, who's very**
25   **sweet and makes bird call imitations when he's had too**
26   **much to drink, and September drank a whole punch bowl**
27   **and rolled under the table with the Queen's dog. They**
28   **didn't even recognize me. And the King showed us how**
29   **he could talk and burp at the same time.**
30   **ZED: Very chic.**
31   **ROSEY: Everybody was looking at me. They were all so rich.**
32   **They had purple clothes and fat red jewels and all the**
33   **women wore dead animals around their shoulders with**
34   **eyes that looked back at you and made you feel odd for**
35   **being so rich when they were so dead, only I wasn't rich,**

1 but I WAS, I think the Prince liked me a lot. It was
2 wonderful.
3 ZED: Sounds like it.
4 ROSEY: What's the matter?
5 ZED: Nothing.
6 ROSEY: And just before midnight I realized I had to get home
7 or I'd turn into a bowl of fruit or something, so I ran out
8 and nearly killed myself on the lawn sprinkler and
9 everybody ran after me but I was gone. Oh, Zed, I want
10 so bad to be rich, you can't believe how wonderful it is,
11 it's like a different world, so cultured and refined and
12 sophisticated, and everybody's got diamonds and
13 emeralds and rubies and they speak French and laugh
14 at jokes I don't understand and sniff things up their noses
15 and the Prince looked like he stepped out of a painting
16 or something, he knew what to do and he knew how to
17 dance and he made me laugh and put me at ease and
18 talked to me so gently and whirled me around, it was
19 just like my dream, it was JUST like my dream, oh, I want
20 to go back, I want to go back so bad — what's wrong?
21 ZED: I have to go.
22 ROSEY: You don't have to go.
23 ZED: Yes I do.
24 ROSEY: Where does the village idiot have to go? Stay here
25 and talk to me.
26 ZED: You don't want to talk to me. I'm incoherent.
27 ROSEY: No you're not. As a matter of fact, you're talking
28 better than I am this morning.
29 ZED: That's because you're talking bullshit.
30 ROSEY: Pardon?
31 ZED: I, on the other hand, am speaking in tongues and
32 various Romance and non-Romance languages. Amo,
33 amas, amat. Veni, vidi, vici. Ho person il passaporto. Ou
34 est la bibliotheque? Mein freund Herbert und ich sind
35 Studenten aus Amerika. La Vida Es Sueno. Futari no

111

1   heyaga hoshii desu. Kufungua kata hapa. Toy boat, toy

2   boat, toy boat. Rubber baby buggy bumpers. She sells sea

3   shells by the sea shore. The Leith police dismisseth us.

4   ROSEY: What happened to you? You're talking perfectly fine.

5   You're talking so well, I don't know what the hell you're

6   saying.

7   ZED: I'm drunk. I'm thoroughly plotzed. I'm incoherent

8   when sober, but I enunciate exquisitely when snookered.

9   Give up, don't care, talk fine. Thanks to Mother Magee,

10   and her wonder gin. I danced many dances with Mother

11   Magee. It was wonderful.

12   ROSEY: *(Big discovery)* Zed, you're not an idiot.

13   ZED: Of course I'm an idiot. I act like an idiot, hole in the

14   woods, that's VERY idiot. Act like an idiot. *(He puts his*

15   *fingers to his mouth and burbles his lips.)* BLABLABLABLA-

16   BLABLABLA. I belong to the village idiots union, I go to

17   the convention every year, I'd show you my membership

18   card but I think I ate it. I eat like an idiot, berries, leaves,

19   grass. No chickens, though. Don't like that. Eyes look up

20   at you, little beady ones, say "Don't wring my neck, I've

21   eggs to lay, poems to write, roads to cross, SQUAWK!" So

22   I just dress them up in little sweaters and let them go. I

23   look like an idiot, think like an idiot, walk like an idiot,

24   I think I must be an idiot, all the evidence seems to point

25   in that direction.

26   ROSEY: I don't understand. How did you get to BE like

27   this — I mean, how you are when you're not drunk —

28   when you —

29   ZED: Oh, I worked hard. Practice, practice, practice. You

30   can, too, if you want. Go to balls, hang around with the

31   upper classes.

32   ROSEY: Why would anyone want to practice to be an idiot?

33   ZED: Because, because, because, because, BECAUSE. Saw

34   out the corners of things. Patterns, ghost stuff, just on the

35   edge, little ghostly mechanisms, couldn't touch, nobody

1   else could see, reach out, they run off. Different. Is bad.
2   Maker of things. Not useful. Go now, go to the palace,
3   devour small animals, make them into party hats. You'll
4   be a big star.
5   ROSEY: You're not being very nice to me this morning. I
6   thought you were nice.
7   ZED: You thought I was an idiot. Safe.
8   ROSEY: Well, what's wrong with being rich and living in a
9   palace? Do you mind if I dream about it a little, when I'm
10   not shoveling out the barn? I mean, is that a problem for
11   you? My mother used to tell me such beautiful stories
12   about —
13   ZED: Oh, God bless Mother. Bless her little heart. Pass the
14   petunias.
15   ROSEY: She was a good mother.
16   ZED: Sure, for a three year old.
17   ROSEY: What does THAT mean?
18   ZED: Sorry. Drunk. It's my brain, you see. My brain gets to
19   running in high gear and I can't stop it. And this affects
20   my mouth, which begins to move, and prose comes out.
21   Your mother was a saint. The Prince is a prince. Rich
22   people are God's gift to the poor. Wallowing at their feet
23   is a great privilege.
24   ROSEY: You're the one that made me go in the first place. I
25   was scared to go and you taught me to dance.
26   ZED: That's what you wanted, wasn't it?
27   ROSEY: Yes. So what's your problem?
28   ZED: Oh, I haven't got any problems. What, me? The village
29   idiot? Have any problems? No, far be it from me to try
30   and explode your infantile delusions.
31   ROSEY: They're not like us, they're REAL. And they SMELL
32   good. And I've got a right to dream, I'm an oppressed
33   person here, it's not easy being good all the time, you
34   know, when your stepmother is a geek and your
35   stepsisters are a freak show and your father can't find his

1   pants —

2   ZED: You can handle them.

3   ROSEY: Who can?

4   ZED: You can run rings around those people every which way.

5   ROSEY: Then how come they push me around so much? Huh?

6   ZED: You let them.

7   ROSEY: No I don't.

8   ZED: Yes you do. Safe. *(He looks at her.)* **Idiot. Jealous. Sorry.**

9   **No brain. Sorry.** *(He puts a finger to his head and pulls the*

10   *trigger with his thumb.)* **Bang. Sorry. Stupid. Nice ball, nice**

11   **girl, very sorry, I gotta go now.**

12   ROSEY: **Wait a minute. Just wait a minute. You can't talk to**

13   **me like that and then just walk away.**

14   ZED: **Yes I can. I'm an idiot. I can do anything I want. That's**

15   **the beauty of it.**

16   ROSEY: **What are you trying to do? Make me feel as**

17   **miserable as possible? Because if you're not, then please**

18   **explain to me right now just what the hell you think**

19   **you're talking about?**

20   ZED: *(After a big sigh)* **To dream of romance is natural. To hide**

21   **conveniently behind one's dream is neurotic. To worship**

22   **the rich is cretinous. You don't remember your mother.**

23   **You just remember remembering your mother. You hide**

24   **behind the memory of this remembering in order to avoid**

25   **the danger of having to experience any further growth,**

26   **thus misunderstanding and subverting the whole**

27   **purpose of the archetypal folk motif in the first place. Do**

28   **you wish to have money? Why do you wish to have money?**

29   **So you can give it away to other poor people? Then you**

30   **will have no more money. Do you wish to marry a prince?**

31   **Why do you wish to marry a prince? So you can act like**

32   **a princess? How does a princess act? How, for example,**

33   **does she urinate?**

34   ROSEY: **I think you're being terribly unfair. Many of those**

35   **rich people are very nice. They can't help it if they're rich.**

1   They're just people, just like you and me.

2 ZED: Then why do you want to be rich?

3 ROSEY: Because it's better than this.

4 ZED: Why is it better than this?

5 ROSEY: Because this stinks.

6 ZED: Why does this stink?

7 ROSEY: Because everybody treats me like dirt.

8 ZED: I don't treat you like dirt.

9 ROSEY: You're treating me like dirt right now.

10 ZED: I'm treating you like an adult.

11 ROSEY: Well, stop it, I don't like it, this is a fairy tale.

12 ZED: The question is, what fairy tale is it?

13 ROSEY: It's MY fairy tale, so why do you keep butting into

14   it?

15 ZED: I've been trying to get the hell out of here all morning,

16   but you keep calling me back to explain myself, then

17   when you don't like what I say, you want me to go away

18   again. Make up your mind, why don't you?

19 ROSEY: Zed, that palace is like a dream to me. I'm just

20   striving here to throw off the shackles of my

21   oppressors —

22 ZED: So you can turn into one.

23

24

25

26

27

28

29

30

31

32

33

34

35

1   # FIVE SCENES FROM LIFE
2   **by Alan Brody**
3

4   *Scene for a black male, thirty-four years old, and a white female,*
5   *thirty-six years old.*
6

7   The setting is an empty classroom in the educational block of a
8   maximum security prison somewhere in the northeast. Nina, a
9   university professor, teaches an extension course for special inmates.
10 Political science class has just ended and Nina is shuffling student
11 papers. Bobby, a student, is still hanging around.
12

13 **NINA:** You're going to be late for lock-up.
14 **BOBBY:** I got permission.
15 **NINA:** Trusty?
16 **BOBBY:** Sort of. *(Pause)* My paper's not in there. Somebody
17   ripped off my books. I was going to do a thing on the Bill
18   of Rights, you know? But somebody ripped it off. The
19   book.
20 **NINA:** Not the bill.
21 **BOBBY:** You think I could have yours?
22 **NINA:** What about the library?
23 **BOBBY:** It's hard to get time.
24 **NINA:** You can find it.
25 **BOBBY:** I just wanted you to know why it's late. Is that OK?
26   *(NINA gestures as if to say there's nothing she can do about it.)*
27   You're a good teacher.
28 **NINA:** Thanks.
29 **BOBBY:** You don't take no shit. Like when Abingdon was
30   doing his number on civil rights and you told him ...
31   what did you say?
32 **NINA:** I just stopped him.
33 **BOBBY:** You said this course wasn't Black Rage 101 and if he
34   had a point to make he should make it. That was tough.
35 **NINA:** I wouldn't have stopped him if I believed him.

1   BOBBY: That's what I mean. He does that number in every
2   class. You're the first one to ever stop him. You know
3   what he's in for?
4   NINA: I don't want to know what anyone's in for.
5   BOBBY: You don't bullshit us, either. Some of the other
6   dudes come in here, you know. We can tell they're not
7   giving us the same shit they're giving the kids at the
8   college. Scaling down, y'understand me? Like intellectual
9   welfare. Mr. Garifole. You know him? *(NINA nods. BOBBY*
10   *waits for more.)*
11   NINA: He's a little tense.
12   BOBBY: He would have given me his book.
13   NINA: Testing me?
14   BOBBY: Just pointing out the distinction. *(Pause)* Is this
15   what happens after your class? You wait in here till they
16   take you out?
17   NINA: Or in the hall.
18   BOBBY: That's rough, huh? Everybody checking you out.
19   NINA: Get your paper in next week. OK?
20   BOBBY: See, that's what I mean. No shit lady. Could I ask
21   you a personal question?
22   NINA: No.
23   BOBBY: How come you do this? I mean, it's easy to figure out
24   a lot of the other dudes. Who's doing it for the extra bread,
25   or out of, you know, guilt or politics. Bunch of guys locked
26   up here for murder and rape and doing drugs and shit
27   like that, and you come in once a week to give us a college
28   education.
29   NINA: I wanted to know what it was like. Whether there was
30   really any difference.
31   BOBBY: Difference?
32   NINA: You spend your life teaching the system to kids
33   who've been protected by it, it's a good idea to check out
34   how it works for the ones who weren't.
35   BOBBY: Wanted to find out what it's like to be black, too, huh?

117

1   NINA: What it's like to be white.

2   BOBBY: That's cool. That's exceptionally cool.

3   NINA: Why?

4   BOBBY: No do-good crap.

5   NINA: That's not my style.

6   BOBBY: Right on. Is there?

7   NINA: What?

8   BOBBY: A difference.

9   NINA: Not a lot. Same late papers. Different excuses. You

10   can't go to your grandmother's funeral all the time.

11   BOBBY: You don't believe me about the books.

12   NINA: It doesn't matter. The paper's late.

13   BOBBY: Hey. That's very existential. Am I making you

14   nervous?

15   NINA: Why?

16   BOBBY: Staying in here alone with you.

17   NINA: Mike is out there.

18   BOBBY: You are one cool lady.

19   NINA: Get your paper in next week. OK?

20   BOBBY: Any pointers?

21   NINA: Keep it simple.

22   BOBBY: Yeah.

23   NINA: And honest.

24   BOBBY: Mr. Chatsworth. You know him? That's all he

25   wanted in freshman English. Simple and honest. He had

26   a lot of rescue fantasies.

27   NINA: How did you do?

28   BOBBY: OK.

29   NINA: What's OK?

30   BOBBY: OK is OK.

31   NINA: I think you better get back now.

32   BOBBY: Yeah. One other thing. Next weekend. We got this

33   thing. Family Day. Anybody tell you about that?

34   NINA: No.

35   BOBBY: The busses come up from the city. Wives and kids

1 and mothers and aunts and ladies, if they're still
2 interested. And they get here with all these shopping
3 bags, see, and they're filled with barbecued chickens and
4 cole slaw and brownies. And presents like electric razors
5 and 8 x 10 portraits of the kids in full color and bunches
6 of cloth flowers that somebody's made who couldn't make
7 it up to, you know, brighten up the block. And when they
8 get here they have to lay it all out before they come in
9 so they can be sure nobody stuffed a barbecued chicken
10 with any shit or made the flowers out of cigarette paper.
11 So it takes a couple of hours for them all to get in 'cause
12 everybody has to wait in line until they take out the cole
13 slaw and the brownies and the electric razors and the
14 pictures and then put it all back in — except for the
15 electric razors which they put back after they go through
16 the metal detectors which also takes a long time because
17 the nails in somebody's shoes always sets the damned
18 thing off and then they have to do a body search. Then
19 everybody goes into the gym where they set up a
20 bandstand and a bunch of the cats play and some of the
21 cats' ladies sing, except they're already tired from the
22 bus ride and the taking out and putting back and taking
23 out again, and now they don't have as much time as they
24 thought they would so everybody's trying to be happy
25 fast and they get right down to the bump . . .
26 NINA: What?
27 BOBBY: . . . Bump. It's a dance. A little old-fashioned, but it
28 does what we need it to, so we hang onto it here. Anyway,
29 there's all these little kids dressed up to see their daddies
30 in jackets and ties and short pants or little starched
31 dresses and ribbons and their hair all pulled tight in
32 braids and cornrows and they end up running all over
33 the gym because Mommy and Daddy or whoever are busy
34 doing the bump. Except some of the other little kids do
35 it, too, like imitating. Then somebody makes a speech for

1   the local NAACP and somebody else for the Muslims and
2   they welcome all the visitors and tell them they hope
3   they had a good time and to please contribute or join the
4   NAACP or the Muslims. And by that time the little kids
5   are all stained with chicken drippings and cole slaw and
6   chocolate cake and they're tired from the bus ride and
7   the waiting and doing the bump and they're bored with
8   the speeches, so they're crying and getting slapped. Then
9   they send them all back to the busses. So everybody says
10   good-bye and hugs each other fast 'cause the busses are
11   waiting and the bells are going to ring for lock-up and
12   they got to do a body search on all of us to make sure
13   nothing got by when they checked outside and everybody
14   says how they can't wait for the next month. And that's
15   Family Day.
16 NINA: Sounds like the faculty picnic.
17 BOBBY: Except for the body search.
18 NINA: And the bump.
19 BOBBY: So you want to come?
20 NINA: What?
21 BOBBY: Next weekend.
22 NINA: I don't think I'd ...
23 BOBBY: Hey, I'm asking if you want to be my family.
24 NINA: That's very sweet.
25 BOBBY: Don't bullshit me.
26 NINA: Hey.
27 BOBBY: "Very sweet" is bullshit.
28 NINA: All right. No.
29 BOBBY: Why not?
30 NINA: You just asked me for what I think was a date, and I
31   said no. I don't have to explain.
32 BOBBY: I asked you to be my family.
33 NINA: Wife, mother, aunt, or lady?
34 BOBBY: *(Suddenly vulnerable)* **Just ... a friend.**
35 NINA: I'm sorry. *(She means it.)*

1   BOBBY: It's OK.
2   NINA: You don't have any family?
3   BOBBY: A lot of guys like that. Used to be they wouldn't
4   even let us into the gym if we didn't have visitors. Now
5   they do. So we hang around some friend's family — not
6   too long, though, 'cause they want to get some time alone
7   with each other, so all the guys with no visitors end up
8   horsing around on one side of the gym like those girls
9   who used to dance with each other at the high school
10   hops. You know what I mean?
11   NINA: Very well.
12   BOBBY: So I just thought I'd ask.
13   NINA: It wouldn't be too smart a move.
14   BOBBY: Why not? *(Quickly)* OK if I ask this time?
15   NINA: *(Smiles.)* It would be unprofessional.
16   BOBBY: You could figure it's part of my rehabilitation.
17   NINA: I'm not here to rehabilitate you. All I do is teach
18   Government 103.
19   BOBBY: That's not all you do.
20   NINA: There would be other students there. What do you
21   think they'd make of it if I showed up as your . . . friend?
22   And what would that do to the next time I walked in here?
23   BOBBY: You got somebody on the outside?
24   NINA: *(Quickly)* No.
25   BOBBY: Hey, I don't believe you.
26   NINA: Hey, I think this conversation is over.
27   BOBBY: You're not stringy.
28   NINA: What?
29   BOBBY: You know how some women have these skinny
30   necks with all the bones showing like they're always one
31   step ahead of a scream? That's stringy. It comes from
32   being alone. You're not like that. So I don't believe you.
33   I tell you what. Bring him along. Then you don't have to
34   worry about the class. He can hang around with the other
35   cons while we do the bump.

1   NINA: I'm going to wait in the hall.

2   BOBBY: I'll wait with you.

3   NINA: Don't come on to me, Bobby.

4   BOBBY: See? That's what I said. No shit lady.

5   NINA: I don't think I sent out any signals, but if I did, you

6   misread them.

7   BOBBY: Shit. I fucked up again.

8   NINA: And I tell you what. Just to make sure we're clear,

9   watch your language around me.

10   BOBBY: I didn't mean to make you mad.

11   NINA: I also know about put-ons.

12   BOBBY: *(Quickly)* I meant it. I wanted to invite you . . .

13   NINA: Not then. Now. You're too arrogant to be contrite.

14   BOBBY: I blew it.

15   NINA: I'm calling Mike.

16   BOBBY: So did you. *(She hesitates. He moves in quickly.)* **You**

17   **lost your cool. You knew what to expect when you started**

18   **teaching up here. You probably had training sessions on**

19   **what to wear and how to handle the love poems and the**

20   **sexy letters and the guys checkin' to see whether you got**

21   **a bra on and the looks in our eyes that tell you what's**

22   **going on behind them, and they taught you how not to**

23   **take it personal, because after all, the cons don't get to**

24   **see a lot of women so you have to understand it could be**

25   **anybody. But it's nothing a smart, mature lady with a**

26   **Ph.D. can't handle. Right? But you did take it personal,**

27   **so you blew it, too.**

28   NINA: You're right. I'm sorry.

29   BOBBY: Wrong. It was personal.

30   NINA: Oh, for Christ's sake . . .

31   BOBBY: No. Listen. I mean I *like* you. That's all I'm trying

32   to say. I'm not talking dirty pictures. I'm not talking about

33   goons like Mendes who got their hands in their pockets

34   all the time. I'm talking *like*.

35   NINA: Look, Bobby . . .

1   BOBBY: Just let me tell you. We've had lady teachers before.
2   And I've sat there with all the other goons watching
3   movies in my head while she talked about the English
4   Romantics or supply and demand and thought she was
5   doing just fine in the field. I came in here all ready to use
6   you like that, too. But you arrive dressed, you know, just
7   right, with that blouse buttoned so your neck was open
8   and the collar fell so that was all. Not scared, not pushy.
9   Just right. And you got down to business. We could tell
10   you knew what we were thinking, and you just let us.
11   And, yeah, I was thinking it, too, but it kept turning into
12   something else. Every time you smiled when some other
13   lady teacher would have laughed too hard, or when you
14   listened to one of us and came back — bam — dead on
15   the target so it showed you really were listening, I could
16   feel it turn into something else. I thought, hey, I like this
17   lady. I'd like to fucking *talk* to her. Sorry.
18   NINA: OK.
19   BOBBY: So I just wanted you to know. You make me feel
20   warm without burning, y'understand me? That's all I
21   meant. And I wanted to tell you. *(Long pause)*
22   NINA: How does it work? Family Day?
23   BOBBY: You sign this request. See? Inmate: Bobby Jones,
24   number 69-D-0591. Then you put down your name here.
25   Visitor: Dr. Nina Shenton. I give it to the Family Day
26   committee. You're already cleared for up here, so that's
27   all. You just arrive about 10:00 a.m. with your regular
28   pass.
29   NINA: Give it to me. *(She sits down with her roll book.)*
30   BOBBY: What are you doing?
31   NINA: Adding some names. I'll come as a guest of the class.
32   Can you let them know that?
33   BOBBY: One smart lady.
34   NINA: Read them out to me.
35   BOBBY: Abingdon, Edward, number 76-D-4723; Mendes,

1	**Rafael, number 43-B-0211; Napoli, Tony, number 34-C-**
2	**9652; Washington, James, number 62-C-0479.**
3	
4	
5	
6	
7	
8	
9	
10	
11	
12	
13	
14	
15	
16	
17	
18	
19	
20	
21	
22	
23	
24	
25	
26	
27	
28	
29	
30	
31	
32	
33	
34	
35	

1 # THE SCARLET LETTER
2 ## by Nathaniel Hawthorne
3 ## adapted by Frank Bessell
4
5 *Scene for a man in his thirties, and a woman in her twenties.*
6
7 This play was first presented in 1991 at the Berkshire Public Theatre
8 in Pittsfield, Massachusetts. The setting is a forest where Hester has
9 suddenly encountered Dimmesdale. In this scene from Frank Bessell's
10 adaptation of Hawthorne's famous story, Arthur Dimmesdale and
11 Hester Prynne achieve a reconciliation seven years after the birth of
12 their illegitimate daughter, Pearl, who is playing nearby.
13
14 **HESTER:** *(Faintly at first; then louder, but hoarsely)* **Arthur**
15 **Dimmesdale! Arthur Dimmesdale!**
16 **ARTHUR:** **Who speaks?** *(He steps closer and sees the scarlet letter.)*
17 **Hester! Hester Prynne! Is it thou? Art thou in life?**
18 **HESTER:** **Even so! In such life as has been mine these seven**
19 **years past! And thou, Arthur Dimmesdale, dost thou yet**
20 **live?**
21 *(With fear, and tremulously, ARTHUR puts forth his hand and*
22 *touches HESTER's hand. A distant roll of thunder. Without a*
23 *word, they glide back into the shadow of the woods and sit down*
24 *on a heap of moss. They don't speak right off.)*
25 **HESTER:** **There are clouds.**
26 **ARTHUR:** **Yes. Perchance a storm follows.**
27 **HESTER:** **Are you well?**
28 **ARTHUR:** **Reasonably so. And thou?**
29 **HESTER:** **Well enough.**
30 **ARTHUR:** **Good.** *(Pause)* **Hester, hast thou found peace?**
31 **HESTER:** *(Smiling and looking down upon her bosom)* **Hast thou?**
32 **ARTHUR:** **None! Nothing but despair. What else could I look**
33 **for, being what I am, and leading such a life as mine?**
34 **Were I an atheist — a man devoid of conscience, a wretch**
35 **with coarse and brutal instincts — I might have found**

125

1   peace long ere now. Nay, I never should have lost it! But,

2   as matters stand with my soul, whatever of good capacity

3   there originally was in me, all of God's gifts that were

4   choicest have become the ministers of spiritual torment.

5   Hester, I am most miserable!

6   HESTER: The people reverence thee. And surely thou

7   workest good among them. Doth this bring thee no

8   comfort?

9   ARTHUR: *(With a bitter smile)* More misery, Hester — only

10   more misery! As concerns the good which I may appear

11   to do, I have no faith in it. It must needs be a delusion.

12   What can a ruined soul, like mine, effect towards the

13   redemption of other souls? Or a polluted soul, towards

14   their purification? And as for the people's reverence,

15   would that it were turned to scorn and hatred! Canst

16   thou deem it, Hester, a consolation, that I must stand up

17   in my pulpit, and meet so many eyes turned upward to

18   my face, as if the light of heaven were beaming from it!

19   And then look inward and discern the black reality of

20   what they idolize! I have laughed, in bitterness and agony

21   of heart, at the contrast between what I seem and what

22   I am! And Satan laughs at it!

23   HESTER: *(Gently)* You wrong yourself in this. You have

24   deeply and sorely repented. Your sin is left behind you,

25   in the days long past. Your present life is not less holy,

26   in very truth, than it seems in people's eyes. Is there no

27   reality in the penitence thus sealed and witnessed by

28   good works? And wherefore should it not bring you

29   peace?

30   ARTHUR: No, Hester, no! There is no substance in it! It is

31   cold and dead, and can do nothing for me! Of penance I

32   have had enough! Of penitence there has been none! Else,

33   I should long ago have thrown off these garments of mock

34   holiness, and have shown myself to mankind as they will

35   see me at the judgment seat. Happy are you, Hester, that

1   **wear the scarlet letter openly upon your bosom! Mine**
2   **burns in secret! Thou little knowest what a relief it is,**
3   **after the torment of a seven years' cheat, to look into an**
4   **eye that recognizes me for what I am! Had I one friend —**
5   **or were it my worst enemy — to whom I could daily**
6   **betake myself, and be known as the vilest of all sinners,**
7   **methinks my soul might keep itself alive thereby. Even**
8   **thus much of truth would save me. But now it is all**
9   **falsehood. All emptiness! All death!**
10 **HESTER:**   **Such a friend as thou hast even now wished for,**
11   **with whom to weep over thy sin, thou hast in me, the**
12   **partner of it! Thou has long had such an enemy, and**
13   **dwellest with him under the same roof.**
14 **ARTHUR:**   *(Starts to his feet, gasping for breath and clutching*
15   *at his heart.)* **Ha! What sayest thou? An enemy! And under**
16   **mine own roof! What mean you?**
17 **HESTER:**   **Oh, Arthur, forgive me! In all things else, I have**
18   **striven to be true. Truth was the one virtue which I might**
19   **have held fast through all extremity; save when thy**
20   **good — thy life, thy fame — were put in question! Then**
21   **I consented to a deception. But a lie is never good, even**
22   **though death threaten on the other side! Dost thou not**
23   **see what I would say? That old man — the physician — he**
24   **whom they call Roger Chillingworth! He was my husband!**
25 **ARTHUR:**   *(Looks passionately at her, then sinks down on the*
26   *ground and buries his face in his hands.)* **I might have known**
27   **it! I did know it! Was not the secret told me in the natural**
28   **recoil of my heart, at the first sight of him, and as often**
29   **as I have seen him since? Why did I not understand? O**
30   **Hester Prynne, thou little, little knowest all the horror**
31   **of this thing! And the shame! The indelicacy! The horrible**
32   **ugliness of this exposure of a sick and guilty heart to the**
33   **very eye that would gloat over it! Woman, woman, thou**
34   **art accountable for this! I cannot forgive thee!**
35 **HESTER:**   *(Flinging herself on the fallen leaves beside him)* **Thou**

1   **shalt forgive me! Let God punish! Thou shalt forgive!**

2   *(With sudden and desperate tenderness, she throws her arms*

3   *around him and presses his head against her bosom. He tries in*

4   *vain to release himself. HESTER holds him fast.)*

5   **HESTER:** **Wilt thou yet forgive me? Wilt thou forgive? Wilt**

6   **thou forgive? Wilt thou not frown? Wilt thou forgive?**

7   **ARTHUR:** *(At length)* **I do forgive you, Hester. I freely forgive**

8   **you now. May God forgive us both! We are not, Hester,**

9   **the worst sinners in the world. There is one worse than**

10   **even the polluted priest! That old man's revenge has been**

11   **blacker than my sin. He has violated, in cold blood, the**

12   **sanctity of a human heart. Thou and I, Hester, never did**

13   **so!**

14   **HESTER:** *(Whispering)* **Never, never! What we did had a**

15   **consecration of its own. We felt it so! We said so to each**

16   **other! Hast thou forgotten it?**

17   **ARTHUR:** *(Rising from the ground)* **Hush, Hester! No, I have not**

18   **forgotten!**

19   *(They sit side by side, and hand clasped in hand, on the mossy*

20   *trunk of a fallen tree. They sit silently together. Then he starts*

21   *at a thought that suddenly occurs to him.)*

22   **ARTHUR:** **Hester, here is a new horror! Roger Chillingworth**

23   **knows your purpose to reveal his true character. Will he**

24   **continue, then, to keep our secret? What will now be the**

25   **course of his revenge?**

26   **HESTER:** **There is a strange secrecy in his nature, and it has**

27   **grown upon him by the hidden practices of his revenge.**

28   **I deem it not likely that he will betray the secret. He will**

29   **doubtless seek other means of satiating his dark passion.**

30   **ARTHUR:** **And I — how am I to live longer breathing the**

31   **same air with this deadly enemy? Think for me, Hester!**

32   **Thou art strong. Resolve for me!**

33   **HESTER:** **Thou must dwell no longer with this man. Thy**

34   **heart must be no longer under his evil eye!**

35   **ARTHUR:** **It were far worse than death! But how to avoid it?**

1   Be thou strong for me! Advise me what to do.

2 HESTER: Is the world so narrow then? Doth the universe lie
3   within the compass of yonder town, which only a little
4   time ago was a leaf-strewn desert, as lonely as this around
5   us? Whither leads yonder forest-track? Backward to the
6   settlement, thou sayest! Yes, but onward, too! Deeper it
7   goes, and deeper, into the wilderness, less plainly to be
8   seen at every step; until, some few miles hence, the yellow
9   leaves will show no vestige of the white man's tread.
10   There thou art free! So brief a journey would bring thee
11   from a world where thou hast been most wretched, to
12   one where thou mayest still be happy! Is there not shade
13   enough in all this boundless forest to hide thy heart from
14   the gaze of Roger Chillingworth?

15 ARTHUR: *(With a sad smile)* Yes, Hester, but only under the
16   fallen leaves.

17 HESTER: Then there is the broad pathway of the sea! It
18   brought thee hither. If thou so choose, it will bear thee
19   back again. In our native land, whether in some remote
20   rural village or in vast London — or, surely, in Germany,
21   in France, in pleasant Italy — thou wouldst be beyond
22   his power and knowledge! And what hast thou to do with
23   all these iron men? And their opinions? They have kept
24   thy better part in bondage too long already.

25 ARTHUR: It cannot be! I am powerless to go. Lost as my own
26   soul is, I would still do that I may for other human souls!
27   I dare not quit my post.

28 HESTER: Thou art crushed under this seven years' weight
29   of misery. But thou shalt leave it all behind thee! It shall
30   not cumber thy steps. Leave this wreck and ruin here
31   where it hath happened! Meddle no more with it! Begin
32   all anew! The future is yet full of trial and success. There
33   is happiness to be enjoyed! There is good to be done!
34   Preach! Write! Act! Do anything, save to lie down and
35   die! Give up the name of Arthur Dimmesdale and make

1   thyself another, and a high one such as thou canst wear
2   without fear or shame. Why shouldst thou tarry so much
3   as one other day in the torments that have so gnawed
4   into thy life! Up, and away!
5 ARTHUR: Oh, Hester! Thou tellest of running a race to a man
6   whose knees are tottering beneath him! I must die here.
7   There is not the strength or courage left me to venture
8   into the wide, strange, difficult world alone! Alone,
9   Hester!
10 HESTER: *(In a deep whisper)* **Thou shalt not go alone!** *(He gazes*
11   *into her face with a look in which hope and joy shine out, but*
12   *with fear and a kind of horror.)*
13 ARTHUR: If, in all these seven years, I could recall one
14   instant of peace or hope, I would yet endure, for the sake
15   of that earnest of Heaven's mercy. But now, since I am
16   irrevocably doomed, wherefore should I not snatch the
17   solace allowed to the doomed culprit before his
18   execution? Or, if this be the path to a better life, as Hester
19   would persuade me, I surely give up no fairer prospect
20   by pursuing it! Neither can I live any longer without her
21   companionship, so powerful is she to sustain, so tender
22   to soothe! Oh thou to whom I dare not lift mine eyes, wilt
23   thou yet pardon me!
24 HESTER: *(Calmly)* **Thou wilt go!**
25   *(ARTHUR turns slowly to her. He reaches for her. They embrace*
26   *in a passionate kiss of seven year's longing.)*
27 ARTHUR: Do I feel joy again? Methought the germ of it was
28   dead in me! Oh Hester, thou art my better angel! I seem
29   to have flung myself — sick, sin-stained, and sorrow-
30   blackened — down upon these forest leaves, and to have
31   risen up all made anew, and with new powers to glorify
32   him that hath been merciful! This is already the better
33   life! Why did we not find it sooner?
34 HESTER: Let us not look back. The past is gone! Wherefore
35   should we linger upon it now? See! With this symbol, I

1   **undo it all, and make it as it had never been!**

2   *(So speaking, she undoes the clasp that fastens the scarlet letter,*

3   *takes it from her bosom, and throws it to a distance among the*

4   *withered leaves. She heaves a long, deep sigh.)*

5   **HESTER:**   **Oh, exquisite relief!**

6

7

8

9

10

11

12

13

14

15

16

17

18

19

20

21

22

23

24

25

26

27

28

29

30

31

32

33

34

35

1   # JELLY BELLY

2   **by Charles Smith**

3

4   *Scene for one black male and one black female, in their twenties or*

5   *thirties.*

6

7   Charles Smith is one of this country's fastest-rising new playwrights.

8   A Chicago-based writer, he has penned scripts for stage and screen,

9   and has won a number of Obies, fellowships, and playwriting awards

10   for his work. This drama was first presented by Chicago's Victory

11   Gardens Theater in 1986, and has since been performed on many

12   regional theatre stages coast to coast. The action takes place on the

13   porch of an old house in an inner city neighborhood.

14

15   **BARBARA:**   *(Calling at a boy Off-stage)* **Hey, boy! You! Yeah, I'm**

16   **talking to you. What you doing messing with that car?**

17   **I'll tell you one thing, you better leave it alone. What? I**

18   **know your momma. I'll beat your ass. I'll beat your ass,**

19   **take you home and then your momma'll beat your ass.**

20   **That's right, go on about your business. Go ahead.** *(Under*

21   *her breath)* **Hard-headed little son of a bitch, you.** *(MIKE*

22   *enters.)*

23   **MIKE:**   **Kenny ain't here yet?**

24   **BARBARA:**   **Nope.**

25   **MIKE:**   **I wonder what happened to him.**

26   **BARBARA:**   **He's probably mad at you.**

27   **MIKE:**   **Wanna another beer? Last two.**

28   **BARBARA:**   **Thanks. He asleep?**

29   **MIKE:**   **Out like a light.**

30   **BARBARA:**   **He ought to sleep good tonight. Had a full day.**

31   **MIKE:**   **He was telling me about it. Said he wants to go back**

32   **tomorrow.**

33   **BARBARA:**   **That's good.**

34   **MIKE:**   **Rough, hunh?**

35   **BARBARA:**   **For a while there, I didn't think we was going to**

1   make it. God, I didn't know a little boy could be so full
2   of questions. "Is the school really big, Mommie? Mommie,
3   will we have cookies and milk at school? Can I take my
4   dog to school, Mommie? Mommie, do they have
5   bathrooms there?" We got there, he stopped, looked
6   around, folded his arms, nodded his head, looked up at
7   me and said, "Thank you, Mother. I think I'm ready to go
8   now." I tried to explain to him, no, Mike, this is school,
9   remember? You have to stay. But he wasn't having none
10   of that.
11   MIKE: Did he cry?
12   BARBARA: At first.
13   MIKE: What you do?
14   BARBARA: I told him that if he wanted to be like his daddy,
15   he couldn't cry.
16   MIKE: And it worked?
17   BARBARA: Works every time.
18   MIKE: I wish you wouldn't tell him that. *(To a boy Off-stage)*
19   Hey boy! What you doing messing with that car?
20   BARBARA: That's that little Paterson boy.
21   MIKE: *(To boy)* You better get away from that car.
22   BARBARA: I done told him once.
23   MIKE: *(To BARBARA)* Somebody ought to talk to that boy's
24   momma.
25   BARBARA: She don't care what that boy does.
26   MIKE: *(To boy)* Go on home, boy! Watch TV or something. Go
27   ahead! *(MIKE and BARBARA watch the boy leave.)* Damn
28   shame.
29   BARBARA: Somebody don't set that boy straight, he's going
30   to end up in prison, you mark my words.
31   MIKE: I wish Kenny would get here. I'm ready to go to bed.
32   BARBARA: Will you stop worrying about Kenny? Kenny's
33   going to have to learn how to take care of himself.
34   MIKE: Maybe I ought to call to see if he's at home.
35   BARBARA: Mike? Sit down and cool out, OK? *(MIKE sits.)* I

1   called my father.

2   MIKE: For what?

3   BARBARA: Just to talk.

4   MIKE: Shit.

5   BARBARA: Mike . . .

6   MIKE: I wish you wouldn't have done that.

7   BARBARA: He's my father.

8   MIKE: Yeah.

9   BARBARA: I'm allowed to talk to my father, ain't I?

10   MIKE: It depends.

11   BARBARA: On what?

12   MIKE: On what you two talked about.

13   BARBARA: We didn't talk about nothing. We just talked.

14   MIKE: Yeah, OK, just talked.

15   BARBARA: Mike, if you don't want to go back, you don't

16   have to.

17   MIKE: Right.

18   BARBARA: You could find another job.

19   MIKE: Where?

20   BARBARA: Anywhere. There are places out there that

21   would hire you in a heartbeat.

22   MIKE: Everybody's cutting back.

23   BARBARA: But you've got experience.

24   MIKE: Everybody's got experience.

25   BARBARA: You don't have to take this shit from them, Mike.

26   With all of the construction going on in this town, you

27   could find a job paying twice what you're making now.

28   MIKE: I already looked. There was nothing in the paper. I

29   went down to the unemployment office, but there was a

30   line. I can't see myself standing in line all day.

31   BARBARA: Then I'll get a job.

32   MIKE: You?

33   BARBARA: Damn right. Me.

34   MIKE: Doing what? Working with your father?

35   BARBARA: I don't have to. I can do other things.

1   MIKE: Yeah. Type.

2   BARBARA: They call it administrative management, baby.

3   Director of Interoffice Communications.

4   MIKE: Typing.

5   BARBARA: Don't knock it, baby. Typists make lots of money.

6   MIKE: Yeah, like your last job.

7   BARBARA: That's not quite what I had in mind.

8   MIKE: Call them. I'm sure they'll be glad to have you back.

9   BARBARA: That bitch was crazy, Mike.

10   MIKE: Tell me about it.

11   BARBARA: Come rubbing up on me telling me how I can

12   increase my cash flow.

13   MIKE: You should've told her something.

14   BARBARA: I did. Told her she didn't have enough cash to be

15   getting into my flow.

16   MIKE: So call her. Yeah, that'll be nice. You call up the dyke

17   and I'll quit my job and stay home with the kids.

18   BARBARA: I'm serious, Mike. You don't have to go back. If

19   worse came to worse, I could always go to work for my

20   father.

21   MIKE: See? That's what I thought.

22   BARBARA: Come on, Mike . . .

23   MIKE: That's exactly what he wants. For you to go to work

24   for him. His little girl. No. Absolutely not.

25   BARBARA: So I can go someplace else.

26   MIKE: Why you so set on getting a job? You don't have to go to

27   work. Not unless you really want to. I mean, if that's what

28   you want to do, say so. It's fine, by all means, go right

29   ahead. But you told me you wanted to stay home with

30   Mikey. And I mean, hell, we're doing alright. We got a

31   little money in the bank, we don't owe nobody nothing,

32   no where, no how. We are three steps ahead of everybody

33   else who are two blocks behind. I mean, we're not doing

34   that bad, Barbara.

35   BARBARA: I just want to make sure you don't have to do

1 anything against your will.
2 MIKE: I am doing exactly what it is I want to do. I am going
3 back tomorrow and act like nothing ever happened. I'm
4 going to be all smiles, handshakes, and grins, 'cause right
5 now, that's exactly where I need to be. But the day is
6 going to come when I won't need them anymore. The day
7 is going to come when I'm going to be my own boss, have
8 my own company, and that's the day I'm going to walk
9 into that office and tell them to kiss my ass. But until
10 that happens, I cannot quit, I will not quit, it's going to
11 take a lot more than this to knock me down.
12 BARBARA: Does this mean I have to stay home now?
13 MIKE: Not if you don't want. You can go back to work for the
14 dyke if you want.
15 BARBARA: Well, you know . . . she and I did have a certain
16 rapport.
17 MIKE: So call her.
18 BARBARA: You don't mind?
19 MIKE: Course not.
20 BARBARA: You sure?
21 MIKE: Positive. You just have to find you someplace else to
22 live, 'cause you sure as hell ain't staying here.
23 BARBARA: Boy! *(BARBARA slaps MIKE about the head. MIKE*
24 *tries to duck.)*
25
26
27
28
29
30
31
32
33
34
35

1   # THE SPEED OF DARKNESS
2   **by Steve Tesich**
3
4   *Scene for one female and one male, fifteen-seventeen years old.*
5
6   This play was first presented by the Goodman Theatre in Chicago in
7   1989. In addition to writing a number of highly successful stage plays,
8   Steve Tesich is also known for his successful screenplays of "Breaking
9   Away," "The World According to Garp," "American Flyers," and more.
10 In this scene, Eddie and Mary have been friends since childhood.
11 Mary's parents have gone out for the night. She has phoned Eddie
12 to come over and keep her company because she's feeling nervous
13 and unsettled and can't explain why. The brief phone call Mary
14 receives at the end after Eddie's departure should not be omitted
15 since it throws important light upon Mary's fears and the vague
16 anxiety she has felt during the preceding scene. For technical
17 purposes, Lou's lines over the phone can be done by an unseen actor
18 Off-stage.
19
20   **Scene 5**
21
22   *(February. Night. EDDIE, dressed in his regular school clothes,*
23   *is sitting facing the audience, blindfolded. His jacket and long*
24   *scarf are lying on the floor next to him. MARY stands nearby.)*
25 **EDDIE:**   **How much longer?**
26 **MARY:**   **It's only been five minutes.**
27 **EDDIE:**   **Is that all? Feels like . . .** *(Gestures. Falls silent.)* **It's not**
28   **a practical joke of some kind, is it?**
29 **MARY:**   **No. It's an experiment.** *(EDDIE turns his head in her*
30   *direction. Waits for elaboration. None comes.)*
31 **EDDIE:**   **What kind of an experiment?**
32 **MARY:**   **Pretend you haven't been here in a long, long time.**
33 **EDDIE:**   **Where have I been?**
34 **MARY:**   **You've been away. Far away. You haven't been to my**
35   **home in a long, long time. When I give the word you will**

1   **take off your blindfold and tell me what you see. What it**

2   **feels like to be here, now.** *(EDDIE, nervous, looks around in*

3   *his blindfolded way.)*

4   **EDDIE: Is something wrong?** *(MARY thinks but remains silent.)*

5   **Mary?**

6   **MARY: Yes.**

7   **EDDIE: Just checking.** *(A beat)*

8   **MARY: Do your parents keep secrets from you?**

9   **EDDIE: I hope so. I mean, I certainly hope there's more to**

10   **them than what I get to see every day.**

11   **MARY: Did you know that I was conceived before my parents**

12   **were married? A love child. Conceived in sin. I wonder**

13   **if thoughts are conceived like babies. Something enters**

14   **your head. You don't know where it came from. You don't**

15   **even know it's there. Life goes on. Everything seems fine.**

16   **And then, suddenly a thought is born and you don't know**

17   **what to do with it.** *(A short beat)* **I keep having these**

18   **thoughts, Eddie. But I don't know where they come from.**

19   **EDDIE: What kind of thoughts?**

20   **MARY: Dark, violent thoughts.**

21   **EDDIE: Can I take this off now?**

22   **MARY: No. Not yet.** *(A beat)*

23   **EDDIE: What kind of dark violent thoughts?**

24   **MARY: Father kills family then turns shotgun on himself.**

25   **Christmas presents still unwrapped under the tree.**

26   **EDDIE: Oh, that. That poor farmer. Everyone knows he did**

27   **it because they took his farm away.**

28   **MARY: Others in the area had their farms taken away. They**

29   **didn't kill themselves and their families. He did. I keep**

30   **thinking about him. He's sitting in his living room. It's**

31   **late. The family's asleep. He's just sitting there, listening**

32   **to the radio, reading the newspaper, when suddenly this**

33   **thought is born in his head. This horrible thought. He**

34   **doesn't want any part of it. He doesn't even want to admit**

35   **that he's having it. But it won't go away. And because it's**

1   night. And because he's alone —
2 EDDIE: That's it. That does it. I'm taking this off.
3 MARY: All right. Go ahead. *(EDDIE takes off the blindfold. Looks*
4   *around. Shrugs as if asking the question: What am I supposed*
5   *to see?)*
6 MARY: So?
7 EDDIE: Yes? *(He looks around some more.)*
8 MARY: You don't notice any change in here?
9 EDDIE: No.
10 MARY: It feels the same to you?
11 EDDIE: Yes.
12 MARY: Maybe I'm just imagining it all.
13 EDDIE: All what?
14 MARY: I don't know. You see, whenever I felt bad, or hurt, I
15   knew if I could only get home everything would be fine.
16   There was always this . . . this music . . . not real music,
17   you know, but this music of my home and my mom and
18   dad which made everything bad go away. Nothing bad
19   could ever come in here. It felt safe and warm.
20 EDDIE: And now?
21 MARY: Now it doesn't.
22 EDDIE: It sure does to me. And I'm just visiting. I can't even
23   imagine how nice it must be to live here. I grew up
24   hearing these stories about how your dad was delirious
25   with joy and how he shot up the night with his pistol on
26   the night you were born.
27 MARY: I know. And he stopped in every bar in town and
28   treated everyone to drinks and every round was
29   preceded by a toast: "To my little miracle. To Mary." I
30   know the stories, Eddie. My dad used to tell me when I
31   was very small how unhappy he was before I was born.
32   And how I entered "like a ray of sunshine" into his life.
33 EDDIE: So what's your problem, Mary?
34 MARY: That's just it. I don't know. It comes and goes. It felt
35   so nice this evening. My dad wanted to go and speak

1   against the Mesa Project at those rezoning hearings and
2   my mom and I insisted that he wear a nice suit and tie.
3   It was real nice dressing him up, doing his tie. And then
4   when they left I stood right here, looking out. A storm
5   was coming which was great because I love storms. The
6   wind picked up. The prairie grass began to move this
7   way and that like somebody was running a huge comb
8   through it. But then the wind got stronger and stronger.
9   The tops of the tall grass bent all the way to the ground
10   and it suddenly felt like something huge and invisible
11   was walking toward me ... stomping across the prairie
12   through the storm ... That's when I called you to come
13   over.
14   **EDDIE:**   You are so spoiled, it's unbelievable.
15   **MARY:**   Spoiled. What's that got to do with it?
16   **EDDIE:**   You want everything, Mary. It's not enough for you
17   that your parents adore you. Not just love. Adore.
18   Everyone knows they adore you. But that's not enough
19   for you. You're worried you'll go to college and there'll
20   be kids there like me talking about bad times they've had
21   growing up and you'll have nothing to say on the subject.
22   So now you're busy inventing problems so you won't be
23   left out of the conversation.
24   **MARY:**   Are you saying I'm imagining it all?
25   **EDDIE:**   I'm saying other kids don't enter "like a ray of
26   sunshine" into their parents' lives. I'm saying it's a rare
27   thing to've ever felt about your home the way you did.
28   For a lot of kids home is exactly where the bad stuff
29   happens, not where they get to go and hide from it. So
30   I'm not too sympathetic to your problems. *(MARY is very*
31   *eager to accept his verdict.)*
32   **MARY:**   You're right. I am spoiled. I'm sure that's all it is. I'm
33   just a spoiled little bitch. One of those horrible girls who —
34   **EDDIE:**   There you go again. Off to the other extreme. Now
35   you want to have all the faults in the world. You're like

1   **something Greek. I don't know the word for it but it's**

2   **Greek.** *(He picks up his jacket and starts to go.)*

3   **MARY:**   **Don't go. I'll try to be normal.**

4   **EDDIE:**   **It's terrifying just to think how you would**

5   **manhandle normalcy.** *(Looks at watch.)* **I promised my mom**

6   **I'd be home by nine. They're having this special on TV**

7   **about the earthquake victims of Peru. Brings us closer**

8   **together that kind of stuff.** *(Starts to go again. Stops.)* **There**

9   **was something I remembered when I was blindfolded. I**

10   **was five or six and your dad was building this house. The**

11   **wooden frame was up. You and your mom and a bunch**

12   **of other kids were watching him hammering away. And**

13   **then your dad came over and started throwing you in**

14   **the air. "More." You kept screaming and laughing.**

15   **"More." And then all the other kids wanted to be tossed**

16   **in the air too. They lined up in a single file and you stood**

17   **there like an usher while they went past you to have**

18   **their turn. The way you stood there, Mary. This is my**

19   **dad, you seemed to be saying. He loves all kids but he**

20   **loves me most of all. I'll never forget that day. The house**

21   **going up. Those kids flying up and down. And you**

22   **screaming for more.**

23   *(He smiles. A little wave. And exits. MARY seems to get tense*

24   *when alone. Looks around. Sees EDDIE's long scarf on the floor.*

25   *Picks it up as if intending to run after EDDIE with it. Stops.*

26   *Changes mind. In a series of very dramatic gestures, she wraps*

27   *the scarf around her head, blindfolding herself. Sits there for a*

28   *bit, blindfolded. A beat of this and then the phone rings. MARY*

29   *picks up the phone.)*

30   **MARY:**   **Hello.** *(She removes blindfold.)*

31   **LOU:**   **Hello.**

32   **MARY:**   **Yes?**

33   **LOU:**   **Is Joe there?**

34   **MARY:**   **No, he's not. He won't be back for a while.**

35   **LOU:**   **Is this Anne?**

1   MARY: No, Mom went with him.
2   LOU: This ... wouldn't by any chance be Joe's little girl
3   Mary I'm talking to, would it?
4   MARY: Yes, it would. I mean, yes, it is. And who're you?
5   LOU: Me? It just so happens I'm your godfather, that's who.
6   MARY: I didn't know I had a godfather.
7   LOU: You certainly do. And it's me. The thing is, Mary,
8   having a godfather like me is not exactly like suddenly
9   discovering that you have a fairy godmother who makes
10   wishes true and all that. I want to be right up front with
11   you and all that. If I could, I would, but since I can't, I'd
12   hate to have you get your hopes up. You must be ... what
13   ... almost eighteen by now.
14   MARY: Yes, almost.
15   LOU: Amazing. The last time I saw you, you were no bigger
16   than a loaf of bread. I touched your cheek with my finger
17   and it was like touching a piece of pumpkin pie, it was
18   so soft. Anyway, give my regards to Joe.
19   MARY: What's your name?
20   LOU: Lou. Tell him Lou called, OK?
21   MARY: All right.
22   LOU: Good night, Mary.
23   MARY: Good night.
24   *(She hangs up. MARY stands still for a beat or two and then,*
25   *feeling that same tension taking over her body, she stuffs EDDIE's*
26   *scarf under her sweater and, walking like a very pregnant lady,*
27   *exits.)*
28
29
30
31
32
33
34
35

1   # MINNA AND THE SPACE PEOPLE

2   **by Wendy Hammond**

3

4   *Scene for one male and one female, indeterminate ages.*

5

6   This comic, one-act playlet is part of a large piece entitled "Family

7   Life," published by Broadway Play Publishing in 1990. It was first

8   performed in 1989 at the Home for Contemporary Theater and Art

9   in New York. The scene is the visiting room of a mental asylum.

10 Brett, a junior businessman in a rumpled suit, is trying to persuade

11 his sister, a committed patient, to have an abortion.

12

13 **MINNA:**   **You will not kill my baby!**

14 **BRETT:**   **It's not killing. It's taking it out of your body for**

15   **awhile.**

16 **MINNA:**   **You have no right killing my baby!**

17 **BRETT:**   **They'll take it away from you! They don't let babies**

18   **stay in the nuthouse!**

19 **MINNA:**   **You won't kill my baby! I won't let you kill my baby!**

20 **BRETT:**   **I'm not killing it, the *doctor* is killing it! I didn't mean**

21   **that. Minna, you are driving me *crazy*!**

22 **MINNA:**   *(Pointing to her stomach)* **This baby is more important**

23   **than Jesus Christ.**

24 **BRETT:**   **Minna, they don't let lunatics raise babies in the**

25   **loony bin.**

26 **MINNA:**   **This baby will save the world from nuclear**

27   **holocaust.**

28 **BRETT:**   **Is that what you want, Minna? You want them to**

29   **give your baby away?**

30 **MINNA:**   **Jesus Christ didn't save the world from nuclear**

31   **holocaust. Jesus Christ just said to turn the other cheek!**

32 **BRETT:**   **You want maniacs getting ahold of it? You want the**

33   **Steinbergs raising your child?**

34 **MINNA:**   **They *won't* be raising it, that's what I'm trying to**

35   **tell you. You could call a sanity hearing. You could say**

1   **Mom and Dad made a mistake, that I'm *not* crazy. You're**

2   **my brother, you could tell them I never once did anything**

3   **crazy the whole time we were growing up.**

4   **BRETT:** **Minna —**

5   **MINNA:** **I never did anything crazy, right?**

6   **BRETT:** **This isn't the —**

7   **MINNA:** **The whole time we were growing up. Never once!**

8   **BRETT:** **We're off the subject.**

9   **MINNA:** **This *is* the subject. I never did anything crazy, right?**

10 **BRETT:** **The subject is you've got to have an abortion.**

11 **MINNA:** **I'm not talking to you till you tell me I'm right. I**

12   **never did anything crazy.**

13 **BRETT:** **Minna!** *(MINNA sits on the floor, closes her eyes, and puts*

14   *her fingers in her ears.)* **All right. You're right.**

15 **MINNA:** **About what?**

16 **BRETT:** **You're right about not being crazy when we were**

17   **growing up.**

18 **MINNA:** *(Jumping up)* **That's right. So all you have to do is tell**

19   **them that at the hearing and then buy me a little**

20   **apartment and a little crib and some food —**

21 **BRETT:** **I can't buy you an apartment —**

22 **MINNA:** **Yes you *can!***

23 **BRETT:** **I don't have the money.**

24 **MINNA:** **Yes you *do!***

25 **BRETT:** **No I *don't!***

26 **MINNA:** ***You and Rita make lots of money!***

27 **BRETT:** ***We also have lots of bills!***

28 **MINNA:** ***Cut back!***

29 **BRETT:** ***We can't!***

30 **MINNA:** ***Yes you can!***

31 **BRETT:** ***No we can't!***

32 **MINNA:** ***Yes you can!***

33 **BRETT:** ***No we can't! No we can't! No we can't!***

34   *(MINNA stomps her foot, then plops down furiously into a chair*

35   *facing away from BRETT. Then BRETT stomps his foot and*

1   *plops down furiously into a chair facing away from MINNA.)*
2   **BRETT:** OK, who's the father? Maybe I could figure this out
3   better if you told me who the father is.
4   **MINNA:** There isn't a father.
5   **BRETT:** There has to be a —
6   **MINNA:** The space people put her inside me.
7   **BRETT:** *(Considering this)* The space people.
8   **MINNA:** They took me into their spaceship and put a machine
9   on my stomach and told me I would now bear a girl child
10   who would save the world from nuclear holocaust.
11 **BRETT:** How did you get into their ship?
12 **MINNA:** They came to me at night — they're really weird
13   looking, I was scared out of my mind — and they made
14   me stand this certain way. Then all of a sudden I was out
15   of the hospital and zooming straight up in the air.
16 **BRETT:** Minna, there has to be a father. I was sitting right
17   next to you when Mom explained the facts of life to us,
18   so I know you know there has to be a father.
19 **MINNA:** Jesus Christ didn't have any father.
20 **BRETT:** Then who did you have sex with? You had to have
21   sex with *some*body!
22 **MINNA:** The space people told me not to have sex.
23 **BRETT:** Stop talking about the space people! There's no such
24   thing as space people!
25 **MINNA:** Then how come I talk to them all the time? How
26   come they tell me how to be happy? How come they want
27   to talk to you and tell you how to be happy too?
28 **BRETT:** I am happy.
29 **MINNA:** You fight with Rita all the time.
30 **BRETT:** I do not.
31 **MINNA:** Rita drinks so much you have to call her work and
32   make excuses. Sometimes she hits you just like Mom did.
33 **BRETT:** *(Flaring)* She doesn't —!
34 **MINNA:** Sometimes she throws things at you.
35 **BRETT:** *(Collecting himself)* Rita drinks no more than anyone

1   else and she never hits me.

2   MINNA: Then how come you have a giant bruise on your
3   back?

4   BRETT: I don't have a bruise on my back.

5   MINNA: Yes.

6   BRETT: No!

7   MINNA: The space people told me. You were fighting. You
8   turned away. She threw the vacuum cleaner at your back.

9   BRETT: We're off the subject again! The subject is you
10   having an abortion!

11   MINNA: *(Jumping up) I will not have an abortion!*

12   BRETT: *(Jumping up) You don't have a choice!*

13   MINNA: *You have a choice! You can save my baby!*

14   BRETT: *I can't save your baby!*

15   MINNA: *All you have to do is get me out of here and give me a*
16   *little money!*

17   BRETT: *I don't have a little money!*

18   MINNA: *Then get me out of here and I'll find the money!*

19   BRETT: *I can't get you out of here! You're not ready to get out*
20   *of here!*

21   MINNA: *Yes I am!*

22   BRETT: *No you're not!*

23   MINNA: *Says who?*

24   BRETT: *Says your doctors!*

25   MINNA: *What do they know?*

26   BRETT: *They know that you're crazy!*

27   MINNA: *I am not crazy!*

28   BRETT: *You believe in space people! That's crazy!*

29   MINNA: You mean you're not going to help me?

30   BRETT: No.

31   MINNA: You won't help save the saviour of the world?

32   BRETT: No.

33   MINNA: What if Jesus had been aborted? Think of that.

34   BRETT: Jesus' mother didn't live in a nuthouse. *(MINNA*
35   *kicks a chair, then plops down into it, facing away from BRETT.)*

1   Minna, someday, if you do everything the doctors tell
2   you, maybe you'll get out of here. And then you'll find a
3   job and a husband and then you can start a family, a
4   normal family. Isn't that what you really want? Isn't that
5   the way you really want it? *(MINNA doesn't respond.)*
6   Minna, come on, talk to me, OK? *(MINNA doesn't respond.)*
7   I just think it'll be easier to have this abortion now than
8   to give the baby away later. *(MINNA doesn't respond.)* You
9   know I'm right. I know you know I'm right. *(MINNA doesn't*
10   *respond.)* Minna, we gotta talk about this. We're not going
11   to get anywhere if we don't start talking. *(Pause.)*
12   MINNA: What do you care?
13   BRETT: You don't think I care?
14   MINNA: The only reason you're here is because Nurse Doyle
15   called you and said you better make me get an abortion
16   quick.
17   BRETT: That isn't the only reason.
18   MINNA: You never visited me before.
19   BRETT: I call you all the time but you always hang up on me.
20   Why do you always hang up on me?
21   MINNA: Why didn't you stop Mom and Dad from putting me
22   in here?
23   BRETT: How? I wasn't around.
24   MINNA: No. You ran away and left me here.
25   BRETT: I had to run away. You know I had to.
26   MINNA: You could've taken me with you.
27   BRETT: You were too young.
28   MINNA: Yeah. Well, they were worse after you left. I got all
29   of it. And then Dwayne got me pregnant but Mom made
30   me have the baby. I had to drop out of school, I had to
31   give the baby away, and then I started having these
32   temper problems and I couldn't stop yelling at people
33   and once I threw eggs at the front door and the
34   windows — I broke some of the windows — so Mom
35   brought me here and told them I was crazy.

147

1   **BRETT:**   **Jesus, Minna, I didn't know all that.**

2   **MINNA:**   **You could have found out.**

3   **BRETT:**   **Didn't you tell the doctors what happened?**

4   **MINNA:**   **I couldn't stop crying long enough to talk. No**

5   **matter what drug they gave me, no matter how hard I**

6   **tried, I couldn't stop crying.**

7   **BRETT:**   **You're not crying now.**

8   **MINNA:**   **Not for years. Not since the space people taught me**

9   **how to be happy. They've even give me a baby again.**

10   *(MINNA reaches under her dress and pulls out a mascara wand*

11   *hidden in her underwear. She unscrews the wand, talks into one*

12   *end and listens to the other.)* **Yes. Now?** *(To BRETT)* **They**

13   **want to talk to you.**

14   **BRETT:**   **The space people?**

15   **MINNA:**   **Yeah.**

16   **BRETT:**   *(Upset)* **Minna —**

17   **MINNA:**   *(Talking into the wand)* **I don't think he's in the mood**

18   **. . . OK . . . Will he give it back? . . . If you say so . . .** *(To*

19   *BRETT)* **You can talk to them in private. Drop it off in**

20   **my room when you're done. Oh yeah. They say they've**

21   **figured out how you can earn a lot more money so you**

22   **can support me and the baby.** *(MINNA sets the mascara*

23   *wand on the table in front of BRETT and exits, humming a*

24   *Christmas carol.)*

25   **BRETT:**   *(Calling after her)* **Minna! If you think I'm going to talk**

26   **into this thing you're out of your mind!**

27   *(But she's gone. BRETT gathers up his belongings, starts to*

28   *leave, but then stops. He looks at the mascara wand. He picks it*

29   *up, looks it over, then raises it to his ear and listens. His eyes*

30   *widen.)*

31   **BRETT:**   *(Into the wand)* **Yeah? . . . Yeah? . . .**

32

33

34

35

1   # THE GEOGRAPHY OF LUCK
2   ## by Marlane Meyer
3

4   *Scene for a male and female in their thirties.*
5

6   This play has been professionally produced in 1990 by the Los Angeles
7   Theatre Company and Chicago's Steppenwolf Theatre. It was
8   published as part of TCG's "Plays in Process" series in 1990. Dixie,
9   an ex-convict and country-western musician, has looked up Teddy
10   who is supposedly the daughter of his ex-cellmate in prison. The scene
11   is Teddy's shack in the Nevada desert outside of Las Vegas, where
12   Teddy is sorting through boxes of photos.
13

14   **TEDDY: Dutchy is not my father, he's my stepfather. He**
15   **married my mother or didn't marry her. As I remember**
16   **now he used to hit her which he never hit me and he**
17   **wasn't an alcoholic which was OK except he did some**
18   **sort of drugs.**
19   **DIXIE: Morphine.**
20   **TEDDY: He wrote me, I just . . . I don't know, I hate to write.**
21   **DIXIE: I can't write.**
22   **TEDDY: I can't read either. I got dyslexia. It's a boy's disease,**
23   **but I got it.**
24   **DIXIE: Dutchy says I have some sort of aphasia.**
25   **TEDDY: That movie by Walt Disney which I hated 'cause it**
26   **bugged me when Mickey couldn't stop the broom from**
27   **filling the house with buckets of blood it makes you**
28   **scared to do housework.**
29   **DIXIE: So . . . Dutchy is not your father.**
30   **TEDDY: No, not really, my dad, my real dad . . . the only thing**
31   **I remember about him is his snoring. One day he just**
32   **walked into the garage where he kept his gun and boom.**
33   *(Luxuriating)* **He used to have this gold doubloon set on a**
34   **ring, a pinky ring? My mom told me that when he died**
35   **that coin would be my inheritance but then the mortuary**

1	guy said that his finger was too fat to get the ring off?
2	So I snuck in there at night with the bolt cutters and
3	snapped that digit clean. You can still see the bruise those
4	shears left on my hand, it must have been ten years ago.
5	I used to date a priest that said it was stigmata.
6	DIXIE: Dutchy is missing a finger.
7	TEDDY: You know I took that ring to a hockshop, guess how
8	much they wanted to give me . . . ?
9	DIXIE: Dutchy is missing the same finger.
10	TEDDY: Twenty-five dollars. Some inheritance. *(Rubs the*
11	*bruise on her hand.)* Next time I'm gonna use an ax and
12	take the hand, fingers shrink by themselves and rings
13	roll right off. You have small hands for a man, I bet you're
14	a Pisces.
15	DIXIE: *(He drops his hands beneath the table.)* I'm a Leo. What are
16	all those boxes?
17	TEDDY: Celebrity photos, rock stars. I sell them at the
18	swaps. You ever go to the swap meets?
19	DIXIE: How could I?
20	TEDDY: *(Stands.)* Who's your favorite?
21	DIXIE: Favorite what?
22	TEDDY: *(Moves to the boxes.)* Don't you like any singers?
23	DIXIE: I used to like Elvis.
24	TEDDY: How old are you?
25	DIXIE: I don't want to say. *(TEDDY pulls out a ring binder of*
26	*Elvis photos, flips through them.)*
27	TEDDY: I don't like to like the big stars, 'cause they take it
28	for granted.
29	DIXIE: Elvis had a gift.
30	TEDDY: You don't know the half of it. *(She hands him a photo.)*
31	I have heard these stories about his sex life. He was
32	studly.
33	DIXIE: This looks like Gladys.
34	TEDDY: That photo never moves, but if you want . . . you
35	could buy this one? *(She holds up a photo of Elvis in "Jailhouse*

1   *Rock.")*
2   **DIXIE: How much?**
3   **TEDDY: Two dollars.** *(They swap money for photo.)* **I think it's**
4   **OK to like him if you're old or have kids 'cause he's dead**
5   **anyway but I prefer my idols live.**
6   **DIXIE: I forgot he was dead.**
7   **TEDDY: Died of a drug overdose.**
8   **DIXIE:** *(Stares at the photo.)* **I forgot.** *(TEDDY rummages in box*
9   *and pulls out a white scarf.)*
10   **TEDDY: I got this at a concert he did at Caesar's. He took it**
11   **from around his neck and gave it to me, not to** *me,* **but**
12   **whoever was fast. Smell.**
13   **DIXIE:** *(He does.)* **Brut.**
14   **TEDDY: Sex appeal. As fat as he was? He reeked.**
15   **DIXIE: Sex, here on a rag, years later. God. You'd think the**
16   **world would have the decency to forget about the man.**
17   *(He hands back the picture and the scarf.)* **I don't want these.**
18   **TEDDY: No refunds.** *(He gives her a look.)* **Just kidding.** *(She*
19   *hands back his money.)* **You know, if you work the swap**
20   **with me I could introduce you to a lot of stars.**
21   **DIXIE: Like who?**
22   **TEDDY: Del Sherman.**
23   **DIXIE: Del is alive and Elvis is dead.**
24   **TEDDY: Yeah.**
25   **DIXIE: He only had one hit.**
26   **TEDDY: If it weren't for that one hit, Mister High and**
27   **Mighty, many of us would not have been born.**
28   **DIXIE: How much do you think I could make workin' the**
29   **swap?** *(TEDDY rummages and finds a guitar.)*
30   **TEDDY: Look. You are not gonna work the swap. That was**
31   **just my weird sense of humor, OK? Don't you think I**
32   **could recognize you? Where do you think I got that**
33   **poster? I was president of the Mojave Chapter of your**
34   **fan club.**
35   **DIXIE: I'm changed.**

151

1   TEDDY: I could still recognize you. *(She hands him the guitar.)*

2   Here's an old guitar of Duane Eddy's. It practically plays

3   itself. Let's hear what you got.

4   DIXIE: I got ... scars on my vocal chords.

5   TEDDY: Scars, scared, fear, it's a drive, like any of your basic

6   motivations, greed, lust, envy, they are there to keep your

7   blood pounding.

8   DIXIE: You can't be with me five minutes without trying to

9   make me sing.

10   TEDDY: What are you supposed to be if you ain't a singer?

11   DIXIE: Leslie Gore is selling real estate.

12   TEDDY: She did not strangle her wife. *(DIXIE is silent.)* What?

13   DIXIE: What you are saying is what?

14   TEDDY: My saying something is what's wrong ... ?

15   DIXIE: Yes.

16   TEDDY: You don't ever talk about it.

17   DIXIE: No.

18   TEDDY: You *never* talk about it? *(DIXIE is silent.)* You should

19   talk about it.

20   DIXIE: No.

21   TEDDY: OK then, we'll just be quiet with each other.

22   DIXIE: It was an accident.

23   TEDDY: Man, I don't know about accidents.

24   DIXIE: You ever been in love?

25   TEDDY: It's not about me.

26   DIXIE: It can reduce a man.

27   TEDDY: That love you're talking about there is the love of

28   stupes for their stupidity 'cause they do not feel worthy

29   of love ...

30   DIXIE: I bet you never been married ...

31   TEDDY: Sheila only married you 'cause you were famous ...

32   DIXIE: *(He stands to exit.)* I bet you never even been close ...

33   TEDDY: Tommy Roe wrote that song for her when she was

34   what, twelve years old, she was one of the most famous

35   groupies ever, and when you started to slide she started

1   to slip. Isn't that about the size of it? Where are you
2   going . . . ?
3   DIXIE: I didn't drive twenty-five million miles across the
4   burning desert to be insulted by a screwball like you.
5   TEDDY: I'm making dinner.
6   DIXIE: *(Exiting)* Good luck in the nuthouse.
7   TEDDY: OK, hey, wait. STOP. *(He stops.)* I'm sorry. I live alone.
8   I forgot I'm talking to real people.
9   DIXIE: Bet you're not a very happy person, are you?
10   TEDDY: Oh happy, right, let's all be happy.
11   DIXIE: I bet you never have any dates. *(TEDDY stands. She*
12   *stares at him. She puts her hands on her hips.)*
13   TEDDY: People who make up lies about the past that keeps
14   them from moving into the future never want to have a
15   date with me, so if you want to date somebody, go back
16   out into the desert and find yourelf somebody to lie to.
17   *(They watch each other.)*
18   DIXIE: You ever let up or you're just full on?
19   TEDDY: Full on pretty much of the time. Yeah it's like
20   genetic. *(Long pause. DIXIE sits.)*
21   DIXIE: I don't have anyplace to go.
22   TEDDY: *(Pause)* You want some Ripple with your fish sticks?
23   DIXIE: If that's the dish.
24
25
26
27
28
29
30
31
32
33
34
35

1 # TAINTED BLOOD
2 ### by Tom Jacobson
3
4 *Scene for a man and a woman in their twenties.*
5
6 This play was first produced at Houston's Main Street Theatre in
7 1990. In this version of the vampire story, three famous young men —
8 Oscar Wilde, Sir Arthur Conan Doyle, and Bram Stoker — all join
9 forces to search for the villain. The action takes place at Oscar Wilde's
10 country estate in Ireland, where the men are joined by Wilde's fiancée
11 and her aunt. In this scene Sir Arthur finds himself alone with Wilde's
12 precocious servingmaid, Miss Quimby, just after Wilde's fiancée has
13 left the room.
14
15 **ARTHUR:** *(To FLORENCE who has just exited)* **Good night.**
16 **QUIMBY:** **Cold-blooded as a worm, that one.**
17 **ARTHUR:** **That's a bit unfair, isn't it?**
18 **QUIMBY:** **Gives Mister Oscar nothing but chills, I bet. But**
19 **some gentlemen like icy ladies, don't they, Mister Doyle?**
20 **ARTHUR:** *(Embarrassed)* **If you don't mind —**
21 **QUIMBY:** **I never mind.** *(He can only stare.)* **What kind of**
22 **woman do you enjoy, sir? If I may inquire?**
23 **ARTHUR:** **Miss, I . . . uh . . .**
24 **QUIMBY:** **Oh, dear me! What a forward girl I am! Let's change**
25 **subjects, shall we? How old are you, lad?**
26 **ARTHUR:** **Almost twenty.**
27 **QUIMBY:** **Twenty's a pretty age. Man of science, are you?**
28 **ARTHUR:** **I . . . uh . . . attend medical college at Edinburgh.**
29 **QUIMBY:** *(Moving closer)* **Doctor Doyle, then, is it?**
30 **ARTHUR:** **Not yet.**
31 **QUIMBY:** **Have you had much experience with anatomy?**
32 **ARTHUR:** **Oh, yes, I've dissected several cadavers in various**
33 **states of decay —**
34 **QUIMBY:** **Oh, no, I'm talking about live anatomicals.**
35 **F'rinstance, I've a terrible swelling right here —** *(She*

1   *places his hand on her bosom.)* **Could you get me some relief**
2   **for it, Doctor?** *(He tries to take his hand away but she replaces*
3   *it.)* **I'd like a thorough examination, if you don't mind.**
4   **P'rhaps I should pay a visit to your office later this evening?**
5   **ARTHUR:**   *(Clears his throat.)* **I'm afraid I'm sharing quarters**
6   **with Mr. Stoker.**
7   **QUIMBY:**   **Of course, of course. Mustn't disturb that two-**
8   **faced bag of wind. I'm in with the cook, unfortunately,**
9   **but there's always the stable. It's warm, the hay smells**
10   **sweet, and if I drop a copper to Ty and the other stableboy**
11   **I'm quite sure they'd oblige us and disappear.**
12   **ARTHUR:**   **Miss, I quite confess you're very . . . I mean, I'm**
13   **rather . . . or actually *very* inclined, however . . .**
14   **QUIMBY:**   **What a sweetie! So shy! For you, it's only three**
15   **shillings.**
16   **ARTHUR:**   **Three shillings!**
17   **QUIMBY:**   **Usually it's a crown.** *(Takes a dainty brandy bottle*
18   *from her bodice.)* **Care for a tipple?**
19   **ARTHUR:**   *(Getting up, with great effort)* **Consider yourself lucky**
20   **I do not inform Mr. Wilde of your activities. I'm quite**
21   **certain he would not be pleased —**
22   **QUIMBY:**   **He knows. And says not a word. My regular wages**
23   **are next to bloody nothing —**
24   **ARTHUR:**   **Why, you're inebriated.**
25   **QUIMBY:**   **He says not a word and I say not a word. An even**
26   **exchange.**
27   **ARTHUR:**   **Surely you're not accusing your employer —**
28   **QUIMBY:**   **He's a nice boy. Very upright and decent. Awfully**
29   **religious of late, but not a man who ought to get married.**
30   **ARTHUR:**   *(Trying to leave)* **Good night, Miss Quimby.**
31   **QUIMBY:**   *(Producing a syringe)* **Dr. Doyle, look what I found**
32   **peeping out of your medical bag.**
33   **ARTHUR:**   *(Trying to take it)* **I'm a doctor! Of course I have —**
34   *(QUIMBY touches her finger to the needle then rubs it on her*
35   *gums.)*

1   QUIMBY: I ain't as ignorant as you might suppose. Every
2   man's got his weakness. *(He takes the syringe.)* P'rhaps you've
3   more than one. *(She leaps up and kisses him full on the mouth.*
4   *He doesn't actually respond, but she has taken his breath away.*
5   *After a moment she pulls back.)* Half an hour then?
6
7
8
9
10
11
12
13
14
15
16
17
18
19
20
21
22
23
24
25
26
27
28
29
30
31
32
33
34
35

1   **LITTLE VICTORIES**
2   **by Lavonne Mueller**
3
4   *Scene for one man and one woman, twenties.*
5
6   This play was first produced at the American Place Theatre in New
7   York in 1983. It portrays the early lives of two historical pioneers,
8   Susan B. Anthony and Joan of Arc, and the following scene is actually
9   two scenes condensed into one from the original script. Here Susan
10   meets Ben Caleb, a surveyor, as she travels through the American
11   West gathering signatures for her women's suffrage petition, and
12   Ben offers a strong temptation for her to give up her cause for the
13   sake of marriage. As the scene opens, Ben and Susan have just shared
14   a stagecoach ride together and he is sketching.
15
16   **BEN: A beautiful moonlight night.**
17   **SUSAN: I'm afraid I don't like moonlight nights. It's when the**
18   **Indians raid.**
19   **BEN: Is that why you can't sleep at night?**
20   **SUSAN: I'm not used to hearing tom-toms all night . . .**
21   **BEN: And the splashing of oars.**
22   **SUSAN: And the war songs of braves, Mr. Caleb.**
23   **BEN: After ten days on the Miles-Deadwood Overland . . .**
24   **intimately thrown together by every bump in the**
25   **road . . . I think we're entitled to call each other by our**
26   **first names. *(Pause)* Ben. Please.**
27   **SUSAN: Susan. *(Pause)* Ah, yes, the Miles-Deadwood stage.**
28   **Five miles an hour except when the horses are frightened**
29   **by Indians.**
30   **BEN: Then it's thirty miles an hour while the harness holds.**
31   **SUSAN: Thanks again for getting that soldier to change**
32   **seats with me. I hate to ride with my back to the horses.**
33   **BEN: I could see you were having a bad time of it.**
34   **SUSAN: I get sick riding backwards.**
35   **BEN: Especially with silly frills poking at you. That Southern**

1   belle sat next to you all the way from Eagle Rock to
2   Meeteetse.
3   SUSAN: When she finally got out ... I used a ruler to
4   measure the empty space she left. Five feet ten inches!
5   *(They laugh.)*
6   BEN: Why don't you take the Butterfield? It's roomier.
7   SUSAN: And the nickel-plated harness shines in the sun.
8   BEN: And it stops at hotels.
9   SUSAN: That's the long way.
10   BEN: Ah, a lady in a hurry.
11   SUSAN: I hurry when I can, but the West is deceptive.
12   Nothing here is located where it really is.
13   BEN: The West is a ... mystery. Trains are spreading
14   civilization into the wilderness ... everywhere, little
15   depots, eating houses ... and the old Conestoga wagon
16   rolls along the Boseman Trail and ends mid-journey at
17   a station for modern pullman cars. The nineteenth-
18   century and the Middle Ages meet each other daily on
19   the prairie.
20   SUSAN: *(Takes the sketch from BEN.)* Is that ... ?
21   BEN: You. *(Pause)* Susan, sit by the fire with me.
22   SUSAN: Shall we throw on some more logs?
23   BEN: The white man builds a big fire and stands way back.
24   The Indian builds a small fire and stands up close. *(They*
25   *sit on the ground and BEN continues sketching.)* I'll miss our
26   lively talks, Susan. Tomorrow morning, you take the
27   boat ... I catch a train. There's no guarantee I'll have any
28   good conversation.
29   SUSAN: Trains are packed with interesting people.
30   BEN: Pretty ones? *(He shows her the sketch.)*
31   SUSAN: *(Shyly)* You've drawn the hair much too full.
32   BEN: Did you know Choctaw widows mourn by never
33   combing their hair? For the full term of their grief.
34   SUSAN: What made you come to love the Indians?
35   BEN: Their fragileness. *(He continues drawing.)*

1   SUSAN: I don't think Indians are fragile.

2   BEN: Their race is.

3   SUSAN: Sioux steal cattle and molest homesteaders.

4   BEN: There are outlaw Indians just as there are outlaws

5   among us. *(Pause)* The early French explorers named

6   them "Sioux." It means "Little Snakes." *(Pause)* They call

7   themselves "Dakotas" now. *(Pause)* I've met over a

8   hundred different tribes and maybe twenty thousand

9   Indians, and I've never been threatened with any

10   violence.

11   SUSAN: I should think the Indian is doing well enough. We

12   have federal agencies set up for them. That's more than

13   women have.

14   BEN: Ahh ... but think ... who's the first lady of this land?

15   SUSAN: *(After a long pause)* The squaw?

16   BEN: Of course. *(SUSAN smiles.)* The Dakotas have a saying.

17   "No one should go far in the desert who can't sleep in

18   the shade of his arrows." You have to know the desert to

19   understand that. *(Pause)* A good quiverful of arrows is as

20   valuable as a horse. *(Pause)* Stick the arrows in the sand

21   by their points and lie with your head in the shade of

22   their feathers. *(Pause)* Remember that.

23   SUSAN: *(Smiling)* I will. *(Looks at sketch.)* I still say you made

24   the hair too ... full.

25   BEN: Ordinarily I'd give you the sketch. But I want to keep

26   it myself. Do you mind?

27   SUSAN: No.

28   BEN: *(He touches the hair on the sketch.)* There's a forest in a

29   woman's hair. A calm which isn't silence hides inside. *(He*

30   *looks at her slowly then reaches out to touch her hair.)* Why did

31   you cut it? *(A boat whistle is heard.)* The boat ... *(Pause)* Let

32   it go by.

33   SUSAN: I've got to get to California.

34   BEN: *(Caustic)* The rally ... the "big" rally. *(More softly)* Some

35   day what you're doing will seem inevitable. *(He looks at*

1   *SUSAN affectionately.)* **Marry me. We'll study Indians**
2   **together. We'll build a house ...**
3   SUSAN: *(Weakly)* **A house?**
4   BEN: **With a porch.**
5   SUSAN: *(Dreamily)* **And stone chimney ...**
6   BEN: **A home — not a squatter's cabin.**
7   SUSAN: **With baskets full of flowers hanging from the ceiling ...**
8   BEN: **A two-story house ...**
9   SUSAN: **... with shelves for books. And muslin curtains ...**
10   BEN: **Your house ... to grow old in ... yours!** *(Pause)* **You'll**
11   **win, Susan. You'll win ... and when you have the same**
12   **rights as men do, who will care about you then?**
13   SUSAN: **Oh, Ben, I'm tired ... I'm so tired ...**
14   BEN: *(Moving closer to SUSAN)* **Let me put my face in this**
15   **hair ... dark as the eclipse and scented with rain.** *(He*
16   *puts his face to her hair, then moves slowly to kiss her. After a*
17   *pause, they break apart.)*
18   SUSAN: *(Annoyed by her feelings)* **I'm happy.** *(Pause)* **Dear God,**
19   **I'm happy.** *(The boat whistle is heard.)*
20   BEN: **Tear up the boat ticket, Susan. Women will win ... It's**
21   **the ordinary course of history.**
22   SUSAN: **But I'm part of that history.** *(Pause)* **I was chosen.**
23   **And I promised.** *(Pause)* **Every day I see strings and snags**
24   **of women's hair in the brush ... all along the trail.**
25   *(Backing away from BEN and moving towards the sound of the*
26   *boat whistle)* **They say ... women's hair gets caught in the**
27   **brush. Pioneer women.** *(Pause)* **And I keep hearing their**
28   **silent voices.**
29   BEN: **Susan ... go with me ... I have arrows enough ...**
30
31
32
33
34
35

160

LITTLE VICTORIES
by Lavonne Mueller

Scene for one woman in her twenties and an older man.

See the background note to this play in the preceding selection. In this scene, Susan has been fleeing one step ahead of a federal marshal who has been trying to nab her and return her east to face charges that she voted in a polling booth. She meets the Saddle Tramp in the "kitchen" of a run-down hotel where she's taken a room for the night. He's preparing a meal for himself at the stove.

SADDLE TRAMP: You traveling all alone?

SUSAN: Yes. What line goes through Indian territory?

SADDLE TRAMP: Miles-Deadwood stage.

SUSAN: Not the kind of coach a lady would ride?

SADDLE TRAMP: Nope.

SUSAN: *(She smiles, puts a pan on her head and points to it.)* **How's this? Will it fool the Indians?**

SADDLE TRAMP: *(After a pause)* **They is savages — not morons.**

SUSAN: *(She shrugs and takes the pan off her head.)* **Any food in the Hotel de Dirt? Slice of bread? I missed supper.**

SADDLE TRAMP: **Built me some "trail stew." Ain't New York puff paste and cream fillin's.** *(He takes out a jar and empties it into the pot.)*

SUSAN: *(Pause. She holds out her hand.)* **I'm Susan.**

SADDLE TRAMP: **Double Ugly. My "front name."** *(Points to his face.)* **I was cut in two places in a fight in Crow Canyon. I give a first-class funeral ta my real name long time ago.** *(He continues stirring the stew.)* **So yer all by yerself?**

SUSAN: Yes.

SADDLE TRAMP: I know what that is ... being a cowpuncher ... alone on the range ... ridin' the fence line. Home's not where I throw my hat — but where I

161

1   spread my blanket. *(He pours her a cup of coffee.)* **Here, yodel**
2   **this.** *(Stares at her silently a few seconds.)* **Yer what we**
3   **wranglers call a loner steer ... prowlin' up and down the**
4   **outside of a dusty cattle line.** *(Pause as he tastes the stew.*
5   *He motions to the pot.)* **Go ahead, Susan.** *(Pause)* **It'll make**
6   **ya steal yer own clothes, bite off yer own nose ... watcha**
7   **waitin' for?**
8   SUSAN: *(Stares at the pot. Reluctantly she tastes the stew. She*
9   *slowly smiles.)* **Good.** *(Eats another large spoonful. He hums a*
10   *tune to himself for a moment.)*
11   SADDLE TRAMP: **I like yer laugh. It don't sound like a man's**
12   **...'n you don't try 'n soften it like some women do. I**
13   **guess we give you a lot of razzin' while back.** *(He watches*
14   *her eat.)* **You eat that much all the time?**
15   SUSAN: **I read somewhere that plenty of good food wards off**
16   **the cholera.** *(She continues eating heartily.)*
17   SADDLE TRAMP: *(After pausing to watch her eat)* **So how ya**
18   **like the West?**
19   SUSAN: **I love cowboys.**
20   SADDLE TRAMP: *(Pleased)* **Yah?**
21   SUSAN: **When I was little, I roped sheets off my mother's**
22   **clotheslines.**
23   SADDLE TRAMP: **Big ones?**
24   SUSAN: **Big as boxcars. I still love sheet-behavior of horses**
25   **when the wind blows.**
26   SADDLE TRAMP: **Well, Susan, I'll tell ya ... I have broke**
27   **horses 'n they have broke me.** *(Pause)* **But a horse once**
28   **he's yers, you ain't never gonna find a more loyal friend.**
29   *(He reaches in her soup and takes out a bone.)* **I'll jist take this**
30   **fer Plenty.**
31   SUSAN: **Your horse chews bones?**
32   SADDLE TRAMP: **Rolls 'em in her mouth like a dog.** *(Pause.)*
33   **She's old now ... 'n grayin' up around the ears. I kin loosen**
34   **her cinch 'n drop the reins on the ground 'n she stays right**
35   **next ta me.** *(Pause)* **I catch her innywhere with a biscuit.** *(Pause)*

1   She comes ta a river now ... she won't even try ta
2   swim ... jist turns on her side 'n floats across. But she's
3   the most horse I ever had.
4   SUSAN: Tell me ... Double Ugly ... what do you do when
5   your horse gets sick ... useless?
6   SADDLE TRAMP: *(After a long, reflective pause)* I feed her.
7   *(Pause)* Some people don't feel fer critters, but I do. That's
8   why I work with 'em. *(Pause)*
9   SUSAN: Does it bother you ... to think of cattle ending up
10   on a plate?
11   SADDLE TRAMP: Nope. It's the way a critter's tested before
12   he's eaten that bothers me.
13   SUSAN: *(Pausing, looking at him carefully)* I stayed with some
14   homesteaders in Calico Pass. The wife was sick ... and
15   do you know, Ugly, that they carried her right on her
16   sick-cot to the washtub to do their clothes ... 'cause
17   washing is women's work. *(Pause)*
18   SADDLE TRAMP: Don't it occur to you to blame nature fer
19   what's done to women?
20   SUSAN: Certainly not.
21   SADDLE TRAMP: A woman's body ... how it's ... formed.
22   *(Gestures around his chest.)* ... that's what is made your
23   place in life. Nature don't make mistakes. These times
24   scare me, Susan. Ya know they got them a machine fer
25   hatching eggs by artificial warmth. A machine ... ta take
26   a mother's place. *(Pause)* Now you talk about women
27   votin'. Where's it all gonna end? *(SUSAN chews silently for*
28   *a moment, then stops abruptly.)* That there's jist gravel in
29   the beans.
30   SUSAN: *(She adjusts her mouth to accommodate the gravel; stops*
31   *again.)* What's this tasty meat?
32   SADDLE TRAMP: Wolf. *(Pause. SUSAN gives out a loud wolf*
33   *howl. The SADDLE TRAMP laughs.)*
34   SUSAN: Wish the wolves around here were big enough to
35   eat marshals. *(Pause as the SADDLE TRAMP watches her eat.)*

1 **SADDLE TRAMP: I think I'd like to hear you speak, Susan.**
2 **Yep, I'd like that, all right. But I hit the trail early**
3 **tomorrow ... drivin' steer ta Fresno.**
4 **SUSAN: California?**
5 **SADDLE TRAMP: Yep.**
6 **SUSAN: Maybe ... I could get you to sign my petition before**
7 **you go.** *(SUSAN hands him a paper. He just looks at the paper.*
8 *After a second she hands him a pen.)*
9 **SADDLE TRAMP:** *(He refuses the pen, crooking his hands.)* **It**
10 **takes me time ta git the crooks outta my hands from them**
11 **bein' clamped 'round the saddle horn all day ... 'n ... well,**
12 **I got ta think on somethang serious 's this.**
13 **SUSAN: Think, then. All you want. And hear me speak in**
14 **California. 'Cause I'll be all over that state ...**
15 **SADDLE TRAMP: You know somethin' ... you don't match.**
16 *(He tenderly touches the side of her face.)* **One side of your**
17 **face is darker 'n the other.**
18 **SUSAN: That's my window-side ... I get to the station early** .
19 **... for a window seat.**
20 **SADDLE TRAMP:** *(He touches SUSAN's face again.)* **I learn from**
21 **horses to see how a person's eyes and ears work ta catch**
22 **thangs ... 'n Susan ... all of yours is workin' fine ... real**
23 **fine like a good critter's ...**
24 **SUSAN: Double Ugly, you aren't going to try and kiss me?**
25 **SADDLE TRAMP: Why ... no.**
26 **SUSAN:** *(Sighs in relief and turns away from SADDLE TRAMP.*
27 *After a pause, she twirls around to face him.)* **And why not!**
28 **Aren't I pretty enough?**
29 **SADDLE TRAMP: A sweet hardy mountain flower.**
30 **SUSAN: Then why?**
31 **SADDLE TRAMP: Loner steer don't feel what the rest of the**
32 **herd does.**
33 **SUSAN: I beg to differ with you, Ugly. These arms feel ...**
34 **these lips feel ...** *(The SADDLE TRAMP slowly backs away*
35 *from her.)* **Please ... Dougle Ugly ... cut my hair before I go.**

1   # A PERSISTENCE OF VISION
2   ## by Sandra Morris
3
4   *Scene for a black male, forty, and a woman, thirty-five.*
5
6   This play has won several state and national playwriting awards. It
7   was presented as a reading in 1988 at the John Houseman Theatre
8   Center in New York, and its first professional production was in 1990
9   by the Arena Players Repertory Theatre of Long Island. The play
10   deals with the dissolution of a marriage after a couple's child is
11   kidnapped and murdered near their northern Michigan cottage. In
12   this scene the mother, Jeanne, shares her anxieties with Adam
13   Kearney, the state police detective. The locale is Jeanne's kitchen,
14   where Kearney is sorting through some reports.
15
16   JEANNE: The radio station at Higgins Lake says we're in for
17   thunderstorms.
18   ADAM: *(Looking up)* Not for another forty-eight hours. Maybe
19   seventy-two, God willing.
20   JEANNE: Lieutenant — that last phone call. Was there . . . ?
21   ADAM: No. I would have called you. *(Pause)* The waiting's
22   awful, I know.
23   JEANNE: I've been trying to keep busy.
24   ADAM: So I've noticed. You've cleaned the cottage twice
25   since I've been here.
26   JEANNE: I'd rather go look for him myself.
27   ADAM: I understand.
28   JEANNE: Anyway, I've got Marc's room ready for when he . . .
29   when he comes home.
30   ADAM: That's good.
31   JEANNE: Lieutenant Kearney, will it disturb your work if I
32   use this end of the table?
33   ADAM: Not at all.
34   JEANNE: I was thinking I'd make soup.
35   ADAM: Sounds good. What kind?

1   **JEANNE:**   Marc likes chicken soup. I guess everybody does.
2   You do, don't you?
3   **ADAM:**   Yes, but don't feel you have to include me. I can go
4   into town and —
5   **JEANNE:**   — but that's why you're here, isn't it, Lieutenant?
6   To provide an "official presence"?
7   **ADAM:**   I'm here to find your son and to help you and your
8   husband, Mrs. Trager.
9   **JEANNE:**   The trooper they sent here last night after you
10   left spent most of the time sitting out there in his patrol
11   car. He was uncomfortable being in here with us.
12   **ADAM:**   He's young. He'll get better control of his feelings
13   when he's more experienced.
14   **JEANNE:**   And you're experienced in this kind of matter?
15   **ADAM:**   *(Reluctantly)* **Yes.**
16   **JEANNE:**   And based on your experience, Lieutenant Kearney,
17   what really are my son's chances?
18   **ADAM:**   That's a hard question, Mrs. Trager. All I can tell
19   you is — don't give up hope.
20   **JEANNE:**   Lieutenant, I *am* hoping! I'm hoping for a miracle!
21   I want to believe it was just a cruel joke and that Marc
22   will be let go somewhere — unharmed. Totally un-
23   harmed.
24   **ADAM:**   Then that's what you should hold on to.
25   **JEANNE:**   But the probability, Lieutenant! What's the
26   probability?! Fifty-fifty?! One chance in five? One in ten?
27   Tell me the truth. Please.
28   **ADAM:**   Do you really want the truth?
29   **JEANNE:**   Yes.
30   **ADAM:**   Then I'm sorry, Mrs. Trager. There's no comfort in
31   the numbers. Not when we know from the start that a
32   child has been abducted and isn't a runaway or off on a
33   lark.
34   **JEANNE:**   That's what I thought. Thank you for being honest.
35   *(JEANNE gets out vegetables for the soup and begins to cut them*

1   *up. ADAM watches her struggle to keep going.)*

2   ADAM: Look, why don't you get out of here for awhile? Go

3   for a walk.

4   JEANNE: No, I want to be here in case you hear anything.

5   ADAM: Is Mr. Trager still down at the boat shed?

6   JEANNE: Yes. Well, it helps Bucky — working with his

7   hands when he's upset.

8   ADAM: ... and you make soup.

9   JEANNE: Frankly, I ... I don't know what I'm doing. Just

10   going through the motions now.

11   ADAM: Yes, and you're doing that the hard way, too.

12   JEANNE: What do you mean?

13   ADAM: There's an easier way to do that.

14   JEANNE: Are you into cooking, Lieutenant?

15   ADAM: Not really. I just know how it's done. My grandmother

16   used to cook in one of the finest homes in St. Louis. That's

17   how I've learned what I know about cooking — watching

18   her.

19   JEANNE: Is that where you're from — St. Louis?

20   ADAM: Near there. A little place called Stanton.

21   JEANNE: Lieutenant Kearney, may I ask you a personal

22   question?

23   ADAM: Yes.

24   JEANNE: I haven't seen many black state police officers in

25   this area. Is this a promotion for you?

26   ADAM: I call it more of a test.

27   JEANNE: I see. Well, would you say that you're ... you know,

28   accepted by the other officers? I mean, do they cooperate

29   with you?

30   ADAM: *(Getting up and standing behind his chair)* You know, I

31   admire you, Mrs. Trager. You cut right through the bush,

32   don't you? The same bush your husband has been beating

33   around since I got here. Yes, I'm getting the cooperation

34   I need. And if the time comes when I don't, I'll be the first

35   one to say so.

1 JEANNE: I'm sorry. I didn't mean to offend you.
2 ADAM: *(Letting her off the hook)* **People who ask hard questions**
3 **always offend. I make my living doing it.**
4 JEANNE: *(Returning his smile)* **I seem to do it for free.** *(Pause)*
5 **You never said, Lieutenant — do you have a family?**
6 ADAM: No. I'm divorced.
7 JEANNE: I mean — do you have any children?
8 ADAM: No. My wife wouldn't stop dancing long enough to
9 have any.
10 JEANNE: Oh, she was a dancer.
11 ADAM: No. She just liked to party.
12 JEANNE: *(After a surprised pause)* **Well, she . . . she must have**
13 **been very young.**
14 ADAM: She was.
15 JEANNE: . . . and pretty.
16 ADAM: No — beautiful. *(Pause)* . . . on the outside.
17 JEANNE: I thought that's where it counts.
18 ADAM: So did I — then. *(She returns to her vegetables. He to his*
19 *paperwork. After awhile she speaks.)*
20 JEANNE: You know something, Lieutenant Kearney? You're
21 easy to talk to.
22 ADAM: That's nice to know.
23 JEANNE: And I think you're the kind of person people want
24 to confide in.
25 ADAM: I don't always let them.
26 JEANNE: Why not?
27 ADAM: Because then I feel responsible for them.
28 JEANNE: And you take your responsibilities seriously, don't
29 you?
30 ADAM: Very.
31 JEANNE: You know what I just realized? You've kept me
32 busy for at least five minutes listening to your . . . your
33 cooking tips, haven't you? Five whole minutes of not
34 remembering *why* you're really here. Am *I* one of your
35 "responsibilities" now, Lieutenant? *(ADAM gives her a faint*

168

1   *smile.)* **Thank you.**

2   ADAM: Mrs. Trager, I hope everything turns out fine for you.

3   I want to find your son and bring him home to you. But

4   whatever happens, don't let this drive a wedge between

5   you and your husband. I've seen it happen.

6   JEANNE: You know, don't you?

7   ADAM: Yes, I know.

8   JEANNE: How?

9   ADAM: Your face last night — never play poker for money

10   — I took the boy aside. He just confirmed what I

11   suspected. People we love can let us down, Mrs. Trager.

12   Most times it just pays to accept that. As for . . . well, does

13   it really matter now who let your son walk down to that

14   store?

15   JEANNE: *(In a ragged voice at last)* **Oh, I guess it doesn't. Not now.**

16   ADAM: *(Gently)* **Then tell him that.**

17

18

19

20

21

22

23

24

25

26

27

28

29

30

31

32

33

34

35

1 # WETTER THAN WATER
2 ### by Deborah Pryor
3
4 *Scene for an older man and a teenage girl.*
5
6 This dark play was first performed by the Virginia Stage Company
7 in 1986. The locale is a small island off the Louisiana coast. Frank
8 Morderoy has moved to this remote place with his wife, Hattie, in
9 order to retire. Just after they arrive, Frank is beguiled by the
10 precocious Chantel, an attractive teenager who is, however, totally
11 unscrupulous and mentally unstable. In the end she seduces Frank,
12 then helps to murder both him and Hattie. In this seriocomic scene,
13 Frank meets Chantel for the first time. She is seated at a table in
14 her father's tavern where she helps tend bar.
15
16 **CHANTEL: Hey, Speed, grab a chair, willya? You make me**
17 **feel so short.** *(She gives an exaggerated "y'all come" wave to*
18 *FRANK.)*
19 **FRANK: I really can't. I don't like to leave Hattie for too long.**
20 **She thinks I'm trying to weasel out of the unpacking —**
21 **CHANTEL:** *(She squeezes her fists and contorts her face*
22 *alarmingly.)* **Oh pleeeeeease!**
23 **FRANK:** *(He chuckles a little and sits down.)* **Well, I guess ...**
24 **CHANTEL:** *(She stares at FRANK, twists her arms and legs in*
25 *exaggerated shyness.)* **How old are you?**
26 **FRANK: You get many people out this way?**
27 **CHANTEL: How old are you?** *(FRANK doesn't answer. She*
28 *makes a megaphone out of her hands and whispers into it.)* **How**
29 **old are you?**
30 **FRANK:** *(Laughs.)* **You're a dickens. That's generally not the**
31 **sort of thing you ask people, honey.**
32 **CHANTEL:** *(Cups a hand to her ear.)* **I can hear your heart**
33 **pounding all the way over here! Must be the heat.**
34 **FRANK: You sure you're not thirsty?**
35 **CHANTEL: I just ask because I thought people went to live**

1   on islands when they were old. You don't seem old to me.

2   FRANK: I don't? Really?

3   CHANTEL: So where's Hattie? Shopping again?

4   FRANK: About how old do I seem? About how old do I look

5   to you? *(CHANTEL shrugs, smiles.)* It's funny, you saying

6   that. I think it's true about being as young as you feel.

7   Years don't really make sense. It's all . . .

8   CHANTEL: Mind over matter.

9   FRANK: Exactly. Mind over matter.

10   CHANTEL: I believe it if you believe it.

11   FRANK: *(Leans back in his chair expansively.)* So. You gonna

12   teach me all about the native ways? Turn me from a

13   tourist into a local in three easy steps?

14   CHANTEL: *(Holds up a finger.)* Some very important rules.

15   One. You may have noticed the sun. It's bad news. Maybe

16   not other places, but here it's so bright it shows you

17   everything. And you don't want to be seeing everything.

18   So get some extra dark glasses. Two, gotta keep a monster

19   gun by your bed at night. Gotta shoot 'em on sight and

20   show 'em who's boss right away. *(FRANK laughs*

21   *delightedly.)* I'm serious, Jack. It's your life I'm saving.

22   FRANK: I'm all ears.

23   CHANTEL: Three. Stick to the road. 'Cause of all the heat

24   and the color, you're liable to see things that ain't there

25   and get all off your course. Things falling apart and

26   breaking apart in the tall grass. Big flowers rearing at

27   you, poking you in the collarbone. Possums hanging

28   upside down making faces at you, trying to get you to

29   look at them. Don't — whatever you do. Dark glasses,

30   monster ammo, take the straight and narrow. Simple as

31   that. *(FRANK can't hold back his laughter.)* What? What'd I

32   say?

33   FRANK: You're an unusual kid.

34   CHANTEL: Sounds like that could maybe be an insult.

35   FRANK: It's not at all.

1   CHANTEL: So you gonna follow my expert advice?
2   FRANK: I want to live, don't I? I want to survive in this
3   dangerous country!
4   CHANTEL: He laughs. That's cute.
5   FRANK: You and your dad make a living off this place?
6   CHANTEL: Gee, Mr. Morderoy, that's generally not the sort
7   of thing you ask people.
8   FRANK: Sorry. I'll keep my nose out of it.
9   CHANTEL: It's reet, Pete, I like your nose. Hey! You wanna
10   see in my room how I can look right out at your house?
11   FRANK: Well ...
12   CHANTEL: *(She gets up and tugs at him.)* **Come on, come on,**
13   **come on, come on, come on!** *(FRANK lets himself be hauled*
14   *up, laughing.)*
15   FRANK: I guess I haven't got to rush off or anything.
16   CHANTEL: Now you're talking. You had me on tenterhooks,
17   **lemme tell ya.** *(She tugs him towards the stairs.)*
18   FRANK: Up there?
19   CHANTEL: It's where my room is. It'll be cooler.
20   FRANK: It can't be. Hot air rises.
21   CHANTEL: See? What do I know? *(FRANK enters her room and*
22   *stands on the threshhold, looking around.)*
23   FRANK: So you live here? Right over the bar. *(CHANTEL runs*
24   *to the window.)*
25   CHANTEL: There's your house, see? *(She waves down at it*
26   *cheerfully.)*
27   FRANK: *(Sniffing)* What is that?
28   CHANTEL: You gonna come all the way in the door anytime
29   soon?
30   FRANK: I smell pepper.
31   CHANTEL: For the big ole whippers we got.
32   FRANK: You have scorpions?
33   CHANTEL: We keep 'em for pets. This big. *(She measures an*
34   *absurd size.)*
35   FRANK: Geez.

172

1　CHANTEL:　*(She crooks her finger and whips it back and forth*
2　　　　*like a scorpion's stinger, coming closer and closer to FRANK.)*
3　　　　**Sometime, I'm laying awake in the dark and I can hear**
4　　　　**them along the floor. They keep armadillos for pets. They**
5　　　　**have dances and it sounds like championship bowling**
6　　　　**on TV.** *(Finally she reaches FRANK and hooks him with her*
7　　　　*finger.)* **Gotcha! Better run for help now, mister.** *(She laughs,*
8　　　　*then flounces gracelessly back on her bed, bouncing to a stop.)*
9　　　　**This is my room. This is my house.**
10　FRANK:　*(Looks out the window, squinting.)* **Hey you're right.**
11　CHANTEL:　*(Jumps up to stand with him.)* **Is she out? Can you**
12　　　　**see her?**
13　FRANK:　**Must be inside. How come you can see us but we**
14　　　　**can't see you?**
15　CHANTEL:　**I'll never get to see Hattie. Don't she ever come**
16　　　　**outside?**
17　FRANK:　**Oh sure. She's just not feeling too well.**
18　CHANTEL:　**Is she sick? What's the matter with her? She have**
19　　　　**gangrene? Is she an albino?**
20　FRANK:　**Whoa! That's some imagination you got on you. How**
21　　　　**old are you? I can't pin you down . . .**
22　CHANTEL:　**Uh-oh, the jig's up.** *(She lifts her face up to be*
23　　　　*studied.)* **You guess. I'll be whatever you say.**
24　FRANK:　**What are you, twelve, thirteen, and you got to worry**
25　　　　**about venomous animals?**
26　CHANTEL:　**Maybe Hattie could come see me like this?**
27　FRANK:　**We'll see.**
28　CHANTEL:　**Is** *she* **dying?** *(A moment's silence. FRANK laughs.)*
29　FRANK:　**No. Nobody's dying. Don't you fret about Hattie.**
30　　　　**When you get a little older, you'll find out everybody's**
31　　　　**got problems. But you can fix 'em if you want to. That's**
32　　　　**what I'm there for. To fix it all up. Don't ever say I said**
33　　　　**anything though. She's sorta sensitive.**
34　CHANTEL:　**Oh I got the deepest ears in the world. Ain't no lie**
35　　　　**too big to squeeze on in and disappear.**

1   FRANK: I wasn't lying.
2   CHANTEL: Who said you were? Just an expression. Sheesh!
3   I can tell right off the bat you're not the sort that lies. I
4   bet you would never do anything wrong, am I right?
5   FRANK: I wouldn't go that far . . .
6   CHANTEL: Nails on heads, nails on heads! I amaze myself.
7   FRANK: If you don't mind my asking, where's your mother?
8   CHANTEL: *(Shrugs.)* Pop's got this old picture of her over
9   the bar but it's creased where her face is. *(She suddenly*
10   *puts a hand on her chest, obliviously wrapped up in the rhythm*
11   *she hears.)* Crikey! Feel that sucker go! Pitty pitty bump,
12   pitty knock! Doing the jitterbug. Faster and faster!
13   FRANK: Did you lose her?
14   CHANTEL: *(Turns sharply)* I hadn't lost track. The kid never
15   loses track. I was gonna get to it in the goddamn ripeness
16   of time. Pop says she was a whore from Houma. One day
17   he hears this cute gurgling sound coming from the porch
18   and there I am still slimy with blood and my belly button
19   gnawed off. He decided to keep me. I was so fresh, I was
20   still shaped like a womb, in general.
21   FRANK: Oh, sweetheart —
22   CHANTEL: *(Brightly)* Then her insides got infected and she
23   died and Pop broke in her house and cleaned it out. That's
24   how we got the TV. *(She smiles, sits on the bed and hugs her*
25   *knees.)* So what's this trouble Hattie has? You gonna tell
26   me or do I have to ask embarrassing questions? I bet you
27   never hit her. Not even once in your whole life.
28   FRANK: I would never do that.
29   CHANTEL: See?
30   FRANK: Does your Pop hit you? *(CHANTEL smiles.)* Does he
31   hit you, honey?
32   CHANTEL: No. Sometimes he does . . . other stuff.
33   FRANK: What other stuff?
34   CHANTEL: Your clothes are so neat. Every time I seen you,
35   you got your shirt ironed and your shoes shiny.

1   Everything smooth. I bet you got fuzzy covers on your
2   john. I'll bet anything. I knew this girl once, she could
3   never look back before she flushed. I think she had fuzzy
4   covers.
5   FRANK: How'd you like to come to my house and visit?
6   CHANTEL: I'd like it a lot! I'd like it in five flavors!
7   FRANK: We'd have to ask your father.
8   CHANTEL: He'll let me have anything I want. He says I'm his
9   special girl. *(FRANK looks at her horrified a moment.)*
10   FRANK: Day after tomorrow. I'll come get you. We'll have
11   Hattie's birthday party.
12   CHANTEL: Obooy! *(She hugs FRANK roughly.)* You're my
13   best friend. I can't talk to anybody else like I talk to you.
14   Most people run away.
15   FRANK: You be looking for me, OK? I better start back before
16   it gets dark. *(He heads out the door.)*
17   CHANTEL: Mister? You're buttered on both sides and the
18   edges too.
19
20
21
22
23
24
25
26
27
28
29
30
31
32
33
34
35

175

1   **FLINT AND ROSES**
2   **by Jim Peck**
3
4   *Scene for a man in his twenties and a woman in her thirties.*
5
6   This drama was first produced in 1986 by Atlanta's Alliance Theatre,
7   and it deals with problems of coal miners and their families in the
8   Lower Midwest in 1940. A strike is in progress and Leonard Stovall,
9   a young and cunning company executive, is trying to break it by
10   working on Lucille Decker, wife of one of the miners' leaders, while
11   her husband is out. Lucille has just returned from a brief vacation
12   in Florida, when Stovall arrives at her home, and she nervously
13   invites him into the kitchen.
14
15   LUCILLE: **This is where we set. May I offer you a cup of**
16   **coffee?**
17   STOVALL: **No, thank you, Mrs. Decker.**
18   LUCILLE: **Excuse the looks of the place. I just got back from**
19   **a trip.**
20   STOVALL: **Oh?**
21   LUCILLE: **Uh-huh. Florida, the Sunshine State. Excuse this**
22   **dress. I just wear it around the house.**
23   STOVALL: **Comfort is the important thing. Did you get down**
24   **to Key West?**
25   LUCILLE: **Huh? No, I didn't go down that far. Fort**
26   **Lauderdale.**
27   STOVALL: **Ah, Fort Lauderdale. Finest beach on the east**
28   **coast. And, you were smart to go in the off season.**
29   LUCILLE: **My daughter, Sarah, had a baby, Joanna, and I**
30   **went down to help Donald, that's her husband. He paid**
31   **my way. Insisted. I was just there for two weeks. He works**
32   **at Dudley's Dry Dock and Yacht Basin. They make boats.**
33   STOVALL: **I'll say. Beautiful cabin cruisers.**
34   LUCILLE: **Me and Frankie, who you met, went down on the**
35   **train. He's my boy. He wanted to look at your car, but he**

1   won't touch it. I took him outa school but it was just two
2   weeks and I figured he wouldn't miss too much. He'll be
3   in the fifth grade. What did you want? Uh, won't you sit
4   down?
5   STOVALL: *(Sitting)* You don't mind if I smoke a cigarette, do
6   you?
7   LUCILLE: God, no. Let me get you a saucer. I don't know
8   where our ashtrays got to. Jack's been batchin' it, no
9   telling where he put our good ashtrays.
10   STOVALL: I hope you don't mind my dropping in.
11   LUCILLE: God, no. Glad to have the company, but I've not
12   had the time to bake a pie. I could warm up some beans.
13   STOVALL: Thank you just the same. Mrs. Decker, I don't
14   want to take too much of your time. I just wanted to chat
15   for a minute and maybe enlist your help.
16   LUCILLE: My help?
17   STOVALL: That's right. Did you get over to the Seminole
18   Indian village?
19   LUCILLE: Oh, yes. Well, we drove by there, but I wouldn't
20   let Donald spend the money. Nobody else pays for
21   anything when Donald's around. He's my son-in-law. It
22   looked like a very educational place.
23   STOVALL: Some of the Oceolas still live there.
24   LUCILLE: Is that right? I didn't know that.
25   STOVALL: And an old drunken Indian called Shirttail
26   Charley, a real legendary character, runs around in that
27   area.
28   LUCILLE: I heard of him.
29   STOVALL: Quite a character.
30   LUCILLE: Donald mentioned him. He's my . . . how was it I
31   could help?
32   STOVALL: *(Pause)* You know, Jack is a very influential man
33   around the Greencastle mine.
34   LUCILLE: Jack Decker is?
35   STOVALL: I've never met Jack, formally, but Mr. Laney says

177

1   he carries a lot of weight with the men. They pay
2   attention to him.
3   LUCILLE: I wouldn't know.
4   STOVALL: I'm surprised he isn't a union officer.
5   LUCILLE: Jack pays his dues, but he don't go in much for
6   meetin's.
7   STOVALL: But he serves in other ways and the men respect
8   him for it.
9   LUCILLE: He'll do his share. — Now, what he did to that
10   prizefighter, Mr. Stovall, is in the past. Jack don't pick
11   fights anymore.
12   STOVALL: I heard about that. Well, let's leave the past in the
13   past. I guess I was still in college when that happened.
14   Jack broke that gentleman's back, I heard.
15   LUCILLE: Well, he recovered. He was a scab.
16   STOVALL: All in the past. — We're in an economic bind over
17   at Greencastle, Mrs. Decker. I'm just checking with some
18   of the men and their families to see if we can work
19   together on this thing.
20   LUCILLE: Why don't you talk direct to the union officers?
21   STOVALL: Oh, we do. We do. We get together with them on a
22   regular basis. But, sometimes the rank-and-file members
23   have different ideas and we want to hear everybody's
24   side.
25   LUCILLE: You gonna talk to Jack?
26   STOVALL: As soon as I can. I was just wondering, though.
27   Maybe Jack would talk more freely with you.
28   LUCILLE: About work?
29   STOVALL: In other words, maybe you could have some
30   influence on him and then he could speak to his friends.
31   LUCILLE: They're dead set for the nickel an hour.
32   STOVALL: You know, I think I can get Mr. Laney to agree to
33   that. Eventually.
34   LUCILLE: You favor the nickel?
35   STOVALL: Oh, sure. As soon as the circumstances are right.

1   It's just that right now the margin is shaky. Five cents
2   an hour doesn't sound like much, but it adds up. We're
3   talking about a hundred and thirty men, twelve hours a
4   day, six days ... well it adds up to a healthy amount. The
5   thing is, we can't invest in modern machinery and safety
6   measures if we don't make a profit. The profit margin is
7   a delicate matter. Well, you know all this, I'm sure.
8   *(Handing her a leaflet from his briefcase)* See, from our side,
9   as I pointed out to Mr. Laney, we could shut down for a
10   year and hold our own. What grieves me is ...
11   LUCILLE: Shut down?
12   STOVALL: What grieves me is the hardship it would mean
13   for our families. A two-week or even a six-week strike is
14   one thing, but a year of unemployment, even with union
15   benefits, would be tragic.
16   LUCILLE: Shut down a year?
17   STOVALL: It wouldn't be easy on anybody. You keep house,
18   Mrs. Decker ... It's Lucille, isn't it? Do you mind if I call
19   you Lucille?
20   LUCILLE: Mrs. Decker'll do.
21   STOVALL: You keep house. Running even a modest
22   household calls for steady income. And, I have it on sound
23   authority that prices are going to skyrocket in 1941. Just
24   go right through the ceiling.
25   LUCILLE: Shut down. Mr. Stovall, nobody can take a year's
26   layoff, nor half a year.
27   STOVALL: Well, it would definitely cut down on Florida
28   vacations, wouldn't it?
29   LUCILLE: What's that mean? See, I don't understand any of
30   this nor anything about margins. And you might just as
31   well know that Jack Decker don't listen to a thing I say
32   about anything anyhow. But, him and Howard Prater,
33   next door, and the others are the ones that go down
34   underground over there at the mine, and they run the
35   cuttin' machines and load the cars and usta drive the

1   mules and get kicked clear to Sunday by the mules and
2   his daddy, Jack's, died in a coal mine fire, suffocated to
3   death down under the ground and scratched a note on the
4   mine wall with the corner of his dinner bucket "To my
5   darling son . . . " and so on, and passed out before he could
6   finish it but said in there "take good care of your mommy,
7   my boy," and his mother, Jack's, was laid up with a stroke
8   across town with her sister till she died two years ago,
9   Jack's momma, and Jack did all he could to pay her bills
10   and to keep this house running on a very delicate margin
11   and he was able to scrape up fifty dollars for extra expenses
12   for me and Frankie to go down to Florida, not for a vacation,
13   Mr. Stovall, but to help my daughter come out of the
14   hospital, and Donald paid the whole train fare and
15   wouldn't let me spend a red cent down there but I did buy
16   some presents to bring home plus take Frankie to the juice
17   bar a few times on my own, and, no, I didn't get on down
18   to Key West nor visit the Seminole Indian village although
19   my son nearly cried to go but he wouldn't ask in front of
20   Donald and I think you're a goddamn sneak to be comin'
21   around here in the daytime because you are scared silly
22   of my husband, Jack, who would not be pleased even a
23   little bit to hear you were in his house with your goddamn
24   college diploma when he's got more brains in his left thumb
25   than you got pimples on your butt which is most likely a
26   lot and if you think I'm some kinda moron and can't spot
27   a weasel when I see one then you've got some more thinkin'
28   to do, mister, because we're in this coal mine fight down
29   to the bitter end and we want our nickel-an-hour raise
30   startin' next week and not week after next and you can
31   shut us down *(Tearing up the leaflet)* for ten years but we'll
32   just see who can be the most stubborn, Mr. Leonard dumb-
33   name Stovall! Hell, we ain't movin' to Florida! Now, don't
34   say a word, not one goddamn word. Just git. *(STOVALL*
35   *leaves for front door.)* Oh, my God.

1   **FLINT AND ROSES**
2   by Jim Peck
3
4   *Scene for a man and a woman, late thirties or early forties.*
5
6   See the background note to this play in the preceding selection. In
7   this scene, Jack Decker returns home, trying to behave innocently
8   and normally after beating up and killing Leonard Stovall the night
9   before. The whole town has heard of Stovall's death but no one is
10   sure who did it. Jack tries to keep his wife from learning about his
11   involvement in the crime. He enters the kitchen carrying an old
12   framing square.
13
14   JACK: **Look here what I got. Didn't cost no seven dollars**
15   **and a little either. Old man Sonntag gave it to me for fifty**
16   **cents. — What's for supper?**
17   LUCILLE: **Nothin's for supper.**
18   JACK: **Nothin's for supper. Expect I won't make a hog outta**
19   **myself on that. How come you got on your good clothes?**
20   LUCILLE: **I haveta talk to you.**
21   JACK: **You can't do that in a housedress? Over supper?**
22   LUCILLE: **I didn't feel like fixin' supper.**
23   JACK: **I see. Wonder if I'll feel like goin' down in the mine**
24   **tomorrow. Since when did you hafta feel like fixin'**
25   **supper?**
26   LUCILLE: **Since this morning when I heard about Stovall.**
27   JACK: **People all over town heard about Stovall, and they're**
28   **eatin' supper right now.**
29   LUCILLE: **My God, Jack, he was beat to death and his neck**
30   **broke.**
31   JACK: **A man goes around showin' a wad of money he's**
32   **askin' for it. Too many people down-and-out for that.**
33   LUCILLE: **The man wasn't killed for his billfold and you**
34   **know that and I know that.**
35   JACK: **If we both know that then we both knew that before I**

181

1   ever stepped foot outta here last night.
2 LUCILLE: No. Huh-uh. No. You knew about it and I had to be
3   just like Ruthie and Howard: just shut up and play cards.
4   You went out sayin' that: just play cards, just fix supper,
5   just keep quiet and don't ask no questions, just go to bed
6   and don't bother me.
7 JACK: What the hell do you want? You want me to set up a
8   loudspeaker and tell everyone in town my business?
9 LUCILLE: I ain't everyone in town.
10 JACK: Well, I'd sooner tell everyone in town, dumbbell,
11   because if you had a solitary brain in your head you'd
12   know bein' ignorant of a few things is for your own good.
13   If you know, see, then you're a part of it. You think you
14   can get that much into your skull?
15 LUCILLE: If I know, then I'm part of it?
16 JACK: That's the way it works.
17 LUCILLE: Then go ahead.—
18 JACK: Go ahead what?
19 LUCILLE: Let me in. I am just goddamn tired of bein' in the
20   dark. And I have got my good dress on, and my suitcase
21   packed, and my pocketbook with thirteen goddamn
22   dollars in it right here beside me, and no goddamn supper
23   in sight, and I am gonna be in or I am gonna be out.
24 JACK: What's got into you?
25 LUCILLE: Nothin'. I'm sick of doin' my part and not gettin'
26   to be a member.
27 JACK: Where's Frankie?
28 LUCILLE: Out playin'.
29 JACK: *(Pause)* The boys figured ... the boys, the boys, the
30   boys, the boys ... Petey and Holland, and Howard,
31   too ... the boys figured there was no way around Stovall.
32   No way. He was determined to shut our water off.
33 LUCILLE: Uh-huh.
34 JACK: So you gotta go through him. Over him. It's a simple
35   matter. Maybe there's somethin' smarter to do, see, but

1   we're not on the smart side. They got the smart fellas,
2   the legal fellas, the college fellas, the brain boys.
3   LUCILLE: Ha! Stovall couldn't even do plain arithmetic in
4   his head when he was here.
5   JACK: Uh-huh. Anyhow, we got the boys that work with
6   their hands, so that's what we use. Our hands. And we
7   don't spend all day worryin' about what might be some
8   smarter way. So the boys, and Howard, too, figured I was
9   the one to get the sonofabitch outta the way. Don't ask
10   me why.
11   LUCILLE: It's plain why. You're the only one around with
12   the gumption.
13   JACK: I don't know. But when they say "You're the one to do
14   it," you figure nobody else is most likely gonna do it and
15   it's gotta be done. I didn't hafta do nothin'. I coulda said
16   no, and about did. But then their smart boy played the
17   wrong card.
18   LUCILLE: And you trumped him.
19   JACK: He was parked halfway down the block from that dago
20   girl's house on Water Street.
21   LUCILLE: Maria Berto.
22   JACK: That's the one. I waited there in a bush for fifteen
23   or twenty minutes, then I grabbed him just when he was
24   about to open up his car.
25   LUCILLE: That show-off car he had over here?
26   JACK: I suppose. I pulled him back to me and put my hand
27   over his goddamn face and pounded him four or five times
28   in the back to knock the wind out of his goddamn body,
29   then I turned him around and kneed him in the gut and
30   got hold of his coat and held him up while I busted his
31   ribs and his goddamn nose, and all the while he can't say
32   nothin', see, but I'm whisperin' to him, "you gonna shut
33   down the mine now, smart-ass? You gonna visit the
34   women some more?"
35   LUCILLE: The smart-ass.

1   JACK: And he's tryin' to grunt out somethin' or other and
2   he's tryin to suck in some air so's he can yell and I keep
3   whisperin' the same things to him when I whip him
4   around and slip my arm under his chin and let everything
5   get quiet.
6   LUCILLE: Uh-huh.
7   JACK: Then I just jammed his chin up and over and then
8   back the other way quick, like you snap a twig off a tree.
9   And he collapses against me, so I held him around the
10   chest for a minute and bear-squeezed him till all the air
11   was out. All of it. Then he hit the ground. — Now, you
12   tell like you're a part of it?
13   LUCILLE: Nobody saw you?
14   JACK: Naw.
15   LUCILLE: You sure?
16   JACK: I was bein' careful.
17   LUCILLE: Well, we had to stop 'em somewhere, didn't we?
18   JACK: *(Pause)* Where did you think you were headin', dressed
19   up like that?
20   LUCILLE: I was walkin' out. I don't know where to. Maybe
21   Florida.
22   JACK: On thirteen bucks?
23   LUCILLE: Maybe by thumb. I don't know.
24   JACK: Thought they didn't take in hobos down there.
25   LUCILLE: They'd hafta take in some. They'd take in us. Jack,
26   as soon as we skunk Hitler, there's gonna be a big building
27   boom down there.
28   JACK: Who's gonna skunk Hitler?
29   LUCILLE: Us and some others. The big shots down there
30   know all about it, Donald says. They're gonna build war
31   boats for awhile, then switch right over to houses.
32   JACK: Is that a fact?
33   LUCILLE: They build pretty houses down there, all different
34   colors. And the people stay so clean. Well, you seen the
35   pictures.

1   JACK: Maybe we oughta scoot down there one a these days
2   and get in on all that.
3   LUCILLE: Huh?
4   JACK: When some of this blows over.
5   LUCILLE: Move?
6   JACK: Maybe. — What are we supposed to do about supper?
7   LUCILLE: I'll bum supper off Ruthie and Howard. They'll
8   have plenty. — You mean permanent?
9   JACK: You don't think I could learn how to build houses?
10   LUCILLE: Oh, God.
11   JACK: You think some Republican like Donald's gonna
12   learn somethin' I couldn't learn?
13   LUCILLE: Are you tryin' to tease me?
14   JACK: I'll know more by breakfast time tomorrow than that
15   squirt could learn in a year.
16   LUCILLE: What about the mine, and union business?
17   JACK: There's unions everywhere. There's different kinds of
18   unions.
19   LUCILLE: Oh, my God.
20   JACK: You don't want to go?
21   LUCILLE: Hell, I'm packed and dressed.
22   JACK: They can get along without me here. And I'm damned
23   sure I can get along without them. I mean it. I've got my
24   hands dirty for the boys for the last time. I mean, all it
25   said on that wall was "take care of your mama." Be
26   damned if it said "take care of everybody in the world."
27   No. Ain't I done enough takin' care of? Hell, yes, if you
28   ask me. That's right. I ain't stickin' my neck out again.
29   If I come outta this clean.
30   LUCILLE: Jack, there ain't no way they could catch you, is
31   there? Moss was by here this afternoon.
32   JACK: He was? Again?
33   LUCILLE: Wanted to know if I remembered things the way
34   you did. I told him we played cards all evenin'.
35   JACK: Good.

1   LUCILLE: He said Stovall was robbed, too.
2   JACK: Goddamn Junior musta gone by there and picked the
3   man's pockets.
4   LUCILLE: I didn't know what to think. I know you wouldn't
5   rob anybody.
6   JACK: Well. Just set tight.
7   LUCILLE: That Junior can't be trusted.
8   JACK: Just set tight. Junior's a good egg.
9   LUCILLE: He's a no-good drunk. — You tell him and Howard
10   all you told me?
11 JACK: Naw. They know all they need to know. And nobody
12   needs to be hearin' any Florida talk either.
13 LUCILLE: I can't tell Ruthie?
14 JACK: No.
15 LUCILLE: How come?
16 JACK: None a your . . . Let's just keep it be between you and
17   me.
18 LUCILLE: You wouldn't be teasin' me on the subject of
19   Florida, would you?
20 JACK: You think I'd pass up some of that key lime pie just
21   for the sake of the boys?
22 LUCILLE: Let's go bum some supper.
23 JACK: I'll go find Frankie.
24 LUCILLE: Uh, maybe I better change clothes first. *(Exits to*
25   *the bedroom.)*
26 JACK: You shaved your legs, didn't you?
27 LUCILLE: *(Off-stage)* Nothin' wrong with that.
28 JACK: Believe I'll change my shirt first, too. *(Follows LUCILLE*
29   *into the bedroom.)*
30
31
32
33
34
35

1 # TROUBLED WATERS
2 ## by Brian Kral
3
4 *Scene for a man and a woman in their twenties.*
5
6 This play was first produced by the California Theatre Center in
7 1983, and has since been presented at the Kennedy Center's Programs
8 for Children and Youth, and on a national tour. The action is set in
9 the Florida Everglades and deals with the mandatory execution of
10 deer for the sake of ecological balance. Michael has recently found a
11 job as an Everglades Park Ranger, assisting with the execution of
12 deer in the park. His sister, Sandra, returns home from college,
13 intending to organize a protest against park policy. Knowing how
14 her brother will probably react, she conceals her real intentions from
15 Michael at this first meeting. Michael is putting on his uniform,
16 getting dressed for work, when Sandra enters. J.D. is their brother,
17 thirteen years old.
18
19 ## Scene 2
20
21 **MICHAEL:** **Sandra!**
22 **SANDRA:** **Surprise!**
23 **MICHAEL:** **What are you doing here?**
24 **SANDRA:** **It's still my home, isn't it?**
25 **MICHAEL:** **I expected you later this week.**
26 **SANDRA:** **I changed my plans and got a bus from the airport.**
27 **It was no trouble.**
28 **MICHAEL:** **It wouldn't have been any trouble to get you,**
29 **either.**
30 **SANDRA:** **I know. Where's J.D.?**
31 **MICHAEL:** **Off with a friend right now. He'll see you tonight.**
32 **SANDRA:** *(Touching his shirt)* **Is this your new uniform?**
33 **MICHAEL:** *(Finishes buttoning the cuffs.)* **Part of it.** *(Slight pause)*
34 **I was just getting ready for work.**
35 **SANDRA:** **That's fine.**

1   MICHAEL: *(Getting his shoes and socks)* **Have you got any**
2   **luggage?**
3   SANDRA: **This is it.**
4   MICHAEL: **Just one bag?**
5   SANDRA: **Why? Did you clean out my closet?**
6   MICHAEL: **Dad threatened to. But, no, your room's the way**
7   **you left it.**
8   SANDRA: **A mess, right?** *(They laugh quietly.)* **Have you heard**
9   **from Dad?**
10   MICHAEL: **Got a letter. He's doing great. They'll work**
11   **through the fall, if the weather holds up.**
12   SANDRA: **The university must be pleased.** *(Slight pause)*
13   MICHAEL: **How's school for you? Enjoying it?**
14   SANDRA: **Sure. It's exciting. There are a lot of . . . exceptional**
15   **ideas.** *(Slight pause)* **I even had a chance to horn in on**
16   **your territory a little.**
17   MICHAEL: **Oh, yeah?**
18   SANDRA: **Yeah. I took a four-credit course on wildlife**
19   **observation. It was fun!**
20   MICHAEL: *(Holding his tie)* **Great . . . You don't mind if I . . .**
21   SANDRA: **Don't worry. You have to get ready.** *(MICHAEL*
22   *begins putting on his tie.)* **And how's the life of Florida's**
23   **newest ranger?**
24   MICHAEL: **It's all right. Pretty quiet so far.**
25   SANDRA: **Really? That's not what I heard.**
26   MICHAEL: **What did you hear?**
27   SANDRA: **This thing in the Everglades, with the deer herd.**
28   **I'm sure the Park Service has got its hands full.**
29   MICHAEL: **You heard about that out there?**
30   SANDRA: **I occasionally read a newspaper, yeah — that's**
31   **why I came home early. I cancelled summer classes and**
32   **everything.**
33   MICHAEL: **Oh.** *(He finishes putting on the tie. Pause)*
34   SANDRA: **I mean, it's such a terrible thing. The idea of**
35   **sending in — what? A thousand hunters?**

1   MICHAEL: Two thousand.
2   SANDRA: Good God — *two* thousand hunters, to kill — or
3   "thin out" — those deer. I mean, I can't believe they're
4   actually going to do it.
5   MICHAEL: Well, it *is* a pretty terrible situation out there.
6   *(Struggling not to get into an argument)* But tell me about
7   this class you took. What sorta things did you do?
8   SANDRA: We did some camping. And we watched animals in
9   their natural surroundings.
10   MICHAEL: That musta been nice. Did you take any pictures?
11   SANDRA: Yes, Michael, I took some pictures. And I saw how
12   animals exist on their own. We talked a lot about
13   responsibility, and about what happens when man gets
14   in the way, but it's clear to me you'd rather not talk about
15   that.
16   MICHAEL: I just don't want to *fight* about it. There are over
17   five thousand deer in that park, and they don't have any
18   food — so what do you want us to do?
19   SANDRA: It just seems to me there must be a better solution
20   than shooting them.
21   MICHAEL: Well, we'll see. We've got till Saturday.
22   SANDRA: Is anyone trying?
23   MICHAEL: Of course they've been trying, Sandi. Everybody's
24   trying. *(Slight pause)*
25   SANDRA: Have they asked you to help?
26   MICHAEL: Sure. Rangers, game wardens — we'll all be
27   there. Doin' what we can. *(Pause)*
28   SANDRA: You'd better get going.
29   MICHAEL: Yeah. Anything I can get for you?
30   SANDRA: I think I remember where everything is. *(Slight*
31   *pause)*
32   MICHAEL: It's good to have you home. We'll talk tonight.
33   SANDRA: OK.
34
35

189

1	# TO MOSCOW
2	### by Karen Sunde
3	
4	*Scene for a man and a woman in their thirties.*
5	
6	Karen Sunde's plays have been produced internationally and Off-
7	Broadway as well as on such regional stages as Chicago's Wisdom
8	Bridge Theater, the Actor's Theatre of Louisville, and PCPA in
9	California. This play deals with the relationship between Anton
10	Chekhov and his wife, Olga Knipper, of the Moscow Art Theatre.
11	The locale is backstage at a Moscow theatre, in Olga's dressing room,
12	immediately following the successful opening of "Three Sisters."
13	Though they are already deeply in love, Anton has thus far refused
14	to propose marriage to her, for reasons explained in the scene. Due
15	to his tuberculosis, his doctor requires him to spend as much time as
16	possible in sunny Yalta, often separated from Olga, Stanislavski, and
17	the theatre company.
18	
19	*(Silence. ANTON stands looking at OLGA. She is arranging*
20	*her hair.)*
21	**ANTON: My God, but you're beautiful.** *(She looks at him in*
22	*mirror, goes on with her hair. Long pause)* **Tired?**
23	**OLGA: Yes.**
24	**ANTON:** *(Long pause)* **I'm glad to see you.** *(Pause)* **You've made**
25	**flesh out of that sphinx I wrote for you, haven't you.**
26	*(Pause)* **Stop that now, and talk to me.** *(She stops, sits*
27	*immobile.)*
28	**OLGA: I'm glad to see you too. I . . . imagined it differently.**
29	**ANTON: I know.**
30	**OLGA:** *(Pause)* **Moskvin said you were here after the third**
31	**act. I felt you here. I've been imagining it all month. If**
32	**you didn't arrive before curtain, I'd go through the whole**
33	**thing with only you in mind — your play on my tongue,**
34	**through all the aching, aching scenes, so delicious — with**
35	**you watching me, and I knowing, each living through the**

190

1 other, but still waiting, so delicious, the waiting ... a
2 great tumultuous waiting unknown to all of them,
3 between only you and me. *(Pause. He moves slowly towards*
4 *her. She turns to him. He stops.)*
5 ANTON: Olya ...
6 OLGA: *(Quickly)* But it didn't happen. *(Beat)* It's silly, but
7 when I heard you were here and I didn't see you, I
8 imagined a picture of the end. I was sure you'd be waiting
9 here when I got back, after the call. Sure of it. To surprise
10 me. I'd come running back, and you'd be here — thinking
11 I didn't expect you. It was a picture in my mind — the
12 moment when we saw each other. But it didn't happen.
13 ANTON: *(Takes her hand, raises it to his mouth, kisses her palm.)*
14 It will. *(They look at each other. He reaches for her. She gently*
15 *deflects him, moves.)*
16 OLGA: I see you have Mme. Avilov's manuscript.
17 ANTON: Yes. You know her?
18 OLGA: She was here. Seems she knows me.
19 ANTON: *(Following to embrace her)* Tell me now — were you
20 so very magnificent? Would I have leapt on to the stage
21 after you?
22 OLGA: *(Responding)* How long do you have?
23 ANTON: That depends. The doctor would only give me the
24 weekend in Moscow, but I have other plans.
25 OLGA: It hasn't been cold here.
26 ANTON: Spit it out: is the cruel theatre giving you Easter at
27 least? Or must I do battle with Konstantin. "Put out or
28 die! I must have her in the South!"
29 OLGA: He's agreed to Easter. But I won't be coming to Yalta.
30 ANTON: You must. I require it. Who else must I threaten?
31 OLGA: I can't, Anton.
32 ANTON: Can't Anton?
33 OLGA: *(Breaking away)* I can't go there again. Think a little.
34 ANTON: About what? Can't or won't? Is this a game?
35 OLGA: One you seem to be able to play. It's I that don't

191

1 understand the rules. Or are you so used to being the
2 bad boy that you recognize no rules? You can ignore your
3 sister's face. Well, I can't. I can't go creeping up staircases
4 with you in the middle of the night, and meet Masha's
5 bewildered eyes in the morning.
6 ANTON: Olya, Olya . . . *(Comes to her, kisses her. They embrace,*
7 *kissing hungrily, neck, face.)*
8 OLGA: I think you'd better announce it tonight.
9 ANTON: *(He stops. Beat)* Tonight. I have only one plan for
10 tonight. And there's no one I make announcements to
11 but you. With you there's no fuss I can't handle.
12 OLGA: Stop joking. *(Moving)* It's a joke to you, isn't it? I don't
13 believe announcements that are only made in private. I
14 don't believe you. *(They face each other, both shocked by her*
15 *words, he suddenly intense.)*
16 ANTON: You don't. What do you believe?
17 OLGA: I believe you can't bear fuss. And . . . I believe things
18 are comfortable for you just as they are. So why should
19 you risk . . . any change?
20 ANTON: Risk. *(Short laugh)* Good word. Risk. Have you
21 thought about your risk? Have you looked soberly? What
22 kind of a risk am I? I'll tell you. I'm the kind you won't
23 catch talking about it, the kind who trains his friends
24 not to talk about it either, the kind who, when he is forced
25 to think about it too seriously or too calmly takes the
26 first train to anywhere in the morning! *(Beat)* There are
27 spurts of energy, there are rising spirits. But the lungs
28 fill, the cough gets worse, and the lungs still fill, the body
29 shrinks, infection spreads, the stomach stops, the will
30 collapses. Yet, miraculously, there comes a springtime of
31 well-being. He is on the road to cure! But the young bride
32 wakes one morning in a pool of his blood. *(Silence)*
33 OLGA: It's too late for that story. You've kept me up past
34 bedtime, haven't you?
35 ANTON: Perhaps.

192

1 OLGA: Once upon a time there came the writer to the
2   actress. And he wrote her pretty scenes, and she played
3   them, oh so well. But when her mother asked her where
4   she'd been . . .? Perhaps you mistook me for something
5   out of a play — the actress-cum-whore.
6 ANTON: Olya . . . *(Reaches for her.)*
7 OLGA: Perhaps you mistook me for Lika. *(He moves swiftly to*
8   *exit, then stops at the door.)*
9 ANTON: *(Stiffly)* I never had Lika. I didn't want Lika.
10 OLGA: *(Pause. Hoarse)* Then what?
11 ANTON: I want you.
12
13
14
15
16
17
18
19
20
21
22
23
24
25
26
27
28
29
30
31
32
33
34
35

Monologs for Women

1   # THE ONLY WOMAN GENERAL
2   ### by Lavonne Mueller
3
4   This monolog was developed at the American Place Theatre Off-
5   Broadway, and was first performed in 1984 by Colleen Dewhurst.
6   The scene: a public meeting somewhere. A woman comes out in Army
7   fatigues. She has one star on her fatigue hat. She looks at the audience
8   carefully, then moves closer to them.
9
10   **A lot of people ask me what it's like being the only woman**
11   **general. Are you a token, they ask? A puppet? A crumb thrown**
12   **in the mouth of war? I assure you, I'm as much a general as**
13   **Bradley ... Ike ... Westmoreland ... or any of the others.** *(She*
14   *salutes the audience, holding the salute.)* **My name is General**
15   **Olive ... Olive for peace ... Wiggins.** *(Drops the salute abruptly.)*
16   **I'm here today to set the record straight.** *(Pause)*
17   **I started out a private in the Korean War. I was 8th Army**
18   **supply clerk in the little town of Young Dung-Po. There**
19   **weren't too many supplies in Young Dung-Po. No people**
20   **either. Even the U.S. Army pulled out — except for me. I was**
21   **a solitary outpost with only two shelves of C-ration ham and**
22   **lima beans — in case a lost patrol showed up.**
23   **I had plenty of time to sit around and think. And I came**
24   **up with this idea of designing boots with soles that leave the**
25   **footprint of Korean peasants. The idea was to help the Special**
26   **Forces behind enemy lines go undetected. I mean, who in their**
27   **right mind wanted to leave the imprint of an Army regulation**
28   **boot? I guess Special Forces agreed, and on the strength of**
29   **my invention, I made sergeant.** *(She walks to another area of the*
30   *stage.)*
31   **After I left supply, I was put on a secret project involving**
32   **the training of dogs in the small town of Chinjo. Not your**
33   **ordinary hounds either — combat dogs. I was instantly made**
34   **an officer since a lot of these mutts had seniority. I found**
35   **myself outranked by no less than fifteen old, gray, cranky,**

197

1   arthritic dogs. One fifteen-year-old was waiting to be
2   authorized a lieutenant general. Quartermaster had to
3   promote me on the spot to major so those mongrels would
4   obey me.
5   For months I lived with dogs. Dogs and the Korean
6   winter. The ground was like iron. Those winds of Manchuria
7   came whistling down the mountain peaks at me day after day.
8   I never got warm. It was lonely, too. A lot of people don't
9   realize that combat dogs aren't allowed to bark or growl. They
10   can raise their backs and point their ears up. But they can't
11   make a sound that might alert the North Korean Army. So
12   there wasn't much conversation. And you don't joke around
13   with these curs. They bit, snapped, clawed, and urinated on me.
14   After six months of dog duty, I was suddenly and
15   mercifully relieved. A senator in New York got wind of the
16   risks involved and put through a bill that made it illegal to
17   use helpless animals in combat. I was shipped back to the
18   States to head up a rumor hotline for G-2. *(She walks to another*
19   *area of the stage.)*
20   I was assigned a small office inside the windowless maze
21   of the Pentagon. *(Pause)* Rumors in the wake of Vietnam began
22   to come in by the hundreds in the early sixties. And once a
23   rumor started that a yellow baby had been born talking in
24   Saigon. "Let the Commies take over," the baby supposedly
25   said. I replied to that with stenographic-denial notes from a
26   doctor at Walter Reed. I completely dismantled the baby
27   rumor and diverted a serious crisis. I was promoted to
28   lieutenant colonel and given my first medal. This one — now
29   known as the Wiggins Cross. *(She points to a cross on her fatigues.)*
30   I immediately volunteered for Nam and was shipped to Saigon
31   in 1966. *(Pause)* I feel bad about the Vietnam war. It just never
32   had the "military sex appeal" like a lot of the others. *(She walks*
33   *to another area of the stage.)*
34   I was assigned as Public Relations Officer for the 8th
35   Special Services detachment in the little village of Cu Chi. I

1   worked out of a quonset — a tiny shed always full of ailing
2   Vietnamese — men, women, children, all in black pajamas.
3   There was me and a hundred of sick friendlies — day after
4   day. I put my hand on a little kid's head to comfort her once —
5   'cause she was bawling. That's how I lost the tip of my index
6   finger. The kid bit like a parrot. If you come to Nam, you don't
7   want to pat anybody there on the head. The Vietnamese
8   consider the head sacred. The head is for God only.
9   It was my job to help our foreign allies understand
10 instructions on the various boxes and jars of medication given
11 out freely by the Special Services. I didn't speak Vietnamese —
12 and nobody spoke English. It was my lucky break to "act out"
13 how to use a rectal suppository for the official representative
14 of the Chung government. I made full colonel after that. *(She*
15 *goes to another area of the stage.)*
16   About this time, fighting was getting fierce in Nam. So
17 General Henry Stack came over to give some of us staff officers
18 a briefing in the command post tent of 8th Army in Tay Ninh.
19 The tent was lit by a single candle. And there we were, all
20 crowded in this shadowy tent — none of us any too easy . . .
21 especially General Stack. Suddenly a shell came very close.
22 And in the near panic and scuffle, our only candle went out.
23 That's when everybody started pulling out promotion papers
24 on themselves and shoving them in front of General Stack.
25 Well . . . I figured I might as well do it too. 'Cause that old man
26 was dropping his initials on everything. Half a battalion went
27 up a grade before he lit the candle again. I was now a one-star
28 general, and anxious for real leadership. That's when the
29 Army assigned me "sniper duty" in the hills of Bong Son. *(She*
30 *goes to another area of the stage.)*
31   Now a lot of people think that the only qualification of
32 a sniper is to be able to shoot good. That's only half of it.
33 Before you can snipe, you have to keep in range of the enemy
34 without letting them know where you are. You have to be able
35 to stalk . . . get up real close before taking a shot — the way you

1   have to do when hunting animals. I was a hunter before I
2   enlisted so I know. Growing up in the wilderness of Shabona,
3   Ill-a-noise, was a real advantage that way. I hunted all the
4   time. Civilians think sniping duty is easy, but sniping's
5   strenuous work. I was alone for months. Years, actually.
6   Constantly on guard. Hour after hour ... looking. Waiting.
7   Picking off the enemy one by one.
8   The fighting got brutal just before the end of the war. I
9   saw a lot of death. I want to tell you — the wounded give off
10   the yip of a dying dog. Death is not quiet. And all those years
11   I looked out over battles from my sniper's nest ... well, it's
12   funny ... but it was always hard to tell the difference between
13   winning and losing. The landscape was the same. Same
14   ground, bushes, trees, sky. I looked real, real close ... but I
15   never could tell the difference. 'Cause nothing ... nothing
16   looked like defeat so much as victory. *(Pause)*
17   Well, I have my latest orders. The Army is parachuting
18   me into the jungles of El Salvador. *(Pause)* The unknown jungle
19   has as many directions as there are points on a compass. You
20   never know which one is a dead end. But Army orders are not
21   without logic. And no combat, however trivial, is without its
22   glory ... for General Olive ... Olive for peace ... Wiggins. *(She*
23   *salutes.)*
24
25
26
27
28
29
30
31
32
33
34
35

1 # THE GIRLHOOD OF
2 # SHAKESPEARE'S HEROINES
3 ## by Don Nigro
4
5 ## "How Many Children Had Lady Macbeth?"
6
7 *Seriocomic monolog for a female in her thirties.*
8
9 The complete play was first presented in 1988 by the Porterhouse
10 Theatre Company in Kent, Ohio, and published by Samuel French
11 in 1989. This is one of five monologs loosely based upon
12 Shakespearean themes by Don Nigro, whose work is represented
13 elsewhere in this anthology. The character, Bonnie, speaks on a bare
14 stage with a single stool. She is barefoot, dressed in blue jeans and
15 a leotard. As she begins to speak, she will take off the blue jeans and
16 begin to do gentle actor's stretches and warm-ups, using the floor and
17 the stool. As she gets more involved in her story, she will warm up
18 less, and by the last part she will be sitting on the stool, just talking
19 to us.
20
21   **Actors have always known the Scottish play is haunted,**
22 **and some of them have very definite rules about it — you must**
23 **never quote it backstage, and if you must refer to it, you never**
24 **say its title, you call it the Scottish play, or sometimes even**
25 **a *certain* Scottish play. And this curse that's on it is supposed**
26 **to account for the great number of perfectly dreadful**
27 **productions of it, although in fact most productions of most**
28 **plays are perfectly dreadful, when you come right down to it,**
29 **especially of Shakespeare. There is, you see, an unspoken**
30 **mythology perpetrated by crummy directors and producers**
31 **who think people are stupid so plays should also be stupid,**
32 **that the easier a play is to put on adequately, the better a play**
33 **is, which, if it were true, would make *Barefoot in the Park* a**
34 **much better play than *King Lear*. I think it's this cretinous**
35 **myth that's led modern playwrights to allow directors and**

201

1   producers to coax, harass, cajole, threaten and intimidate
2   them into hacking away whatever is most brave and subtle
3   and complex and different and interesting in their work,
4   leaving finally only a kind of oatmeal the director feels less
5   threatened by — the rule seems to be, if we can't make it work
6   in the first rehearsal, it's the play's fault, cut it, when of course
7   anybody who's worked on Shakespeare or Chekhov or for that
8   matter anything of value knows that it's usually those things
9   that worked so well in the first rehearsal that have grown so
10 stale and dead by the week before opening that they have to
11 be redone anyway, while those very parts of the play that
12 seemed most impossible early on, that you had to bang your
13 head against again and again, screaming and swearing and
14 crying and getting you horribly frustrated until in a fit of
15 despair or out of utter exhaustion an entirely different
16 reading from somewhere suddenly flows out of you, and it's
17 not at all what you expected but it works and turns out to be
18 the best moment in the production. But with new plays this
19 seldom gets a chance to happen, because the best parts get
20 cut in rehearsal, and that's part of the reason most
21 contemporary drama really sucks, that and greed and a lot of
22 other things I don't want to talk about right now because I
23 don't want to get too angry, I've got to go be Mariana in the
24 moated grange this evening — *Measure for Measure,* one of
25 Willy's secret best. Not such a great part, though, but I don't
26 care. I'll do Shakespeare anytime, anywhere, to my agent's
27 increasing fury and at the expense of a great many long-
28 running national dog food and deodorant commercials I might
29 have lived quite comfortably on. I've done four Mirandas,
30 three Cordelias, I just did Ophelia in New Jersey, but my
31 favorite play, for some reason, has always been the Scottish
32 play, and the role I always wanted was Lady Mac.
33   I'd been in other productions of it, playing various kinds
34 of female set decoration, an attending gentlewoman, a very
35 young and more or less naked witch, and I must confess to you,

1   all of these productions were major or minor disasters of one
2   sort or another. People got whacked or mauled in the fight
3   scenes, lights fell near people's heads, there were two bomb
4   threats, one of which, the one where I was the naked young
5   witch, I'm convinced was called in by Shakespeare himself.
6   My favorite bad production of my favorite play was the one
7   in which a certain attendant Lord was to carry on the dead
8   body of Lady Mac just as the words were spoken, The Queen,
9   my Lord, is dead. Well, this particular Lady Mac was an ex-
10 movie star who'd put on quite a bit of weight — Lady Big Mac,
11 we called her — they always come back to their roots in the
12 theatre when they get too fat for the camera — and the big
13 strong fellow whose job was to carry her dead body on-stage
14 had stepped off a platform in the dark and broken his ankle
15 shortly before his entrance, and the only other actor available
16 on the spur of the moment was a rather little fellow, but very
17 macho, who insisted he could do it, no problem. So he hoisted
18 the Amazon Lady M into his arms and staggered on-stage just
19 as the cue line, The Queen, my Lord, is dead, was spoken, lost
20 his balance, and fell over backwards with the poor dead Queen
21 on top of him. Well, the audience lost it, and then Macbeth
22 lost it, and ended up giggling his way through his tomorrow
23 and tomorrow speech, and, well, on the whole, high tragedy
24 it was not.
25   I was in another production in which one of the witches
26 fainted from the heat in the middle of her scene and fell head
27 first into the cauldron, and another in which a drunk in the
28 alley behind the theatre kept playing a terrible version of *Tea*
29 *for Two* on an accordion as loudly as possible during the
30 sleepwalking scene. This was the same production where poor
31 MacDuff developed a mental block about a rather familiar
32 Shakespearean phrase, and every night, when learning of the
33 murder of his wife and children burst out with: "What, all my
34 pretty chickens and their dam, in one swell foop?"
35   But despite all this, I continued to love the play, and still

1   longed desperately to play Lady Mac, although for a long time
2   my ingenue looks kept me from even being considered for it.
3   Finally, I got the chance. I was understudying a much older
4   woman, who obligingly ran into a door backstage just before
5   curtain and broke her nose — I was nowhere near her at the
6   time, I swear — and so I had to go on in her place. It seemed
7   like fate. I knew I was going to be terrific. I felt that I
8   understood this character, everything about her, her
9   ambition — I'm an actress, God knows I understand that —
10   her frustration — same there — her impatience with her
11   husband — I was married to a nice man who wanted me to
12   quit acting and stay home and have babies, and when he finally
13   realized I was never going to stop and take time for that, he
14   was gone. I had dared things, I had fought, I had sacrificed, I
15   had endured, and now, finally, I was getting my chance to
16   play her. It was destiny. And it went very well, I mean,
17   extremely well — I'd been waiting all my life to play this role,
18   and the audience, which had at first been disappointed it was
19   me, began to realize they were seeing something special, and
20   their resentment began to turn into appreciation, they were
21   with the play, they were lost in it, I could feel them rooting
22   for me, they were with me, it was the best performance of our
23   run, the old respected dull hag of a Lady M had been
24   transformed unexpectedly into a hot and sexy younger
25   version, that is, me, and I played the sensuality for all it was
26   worth, and an odd kind of innocence, and humor, my Lady M
27   had a sense of humor, and pathos, but she was hard as nails,
28   but she had this tenderness, it was working, everything was
29   working, the magic was there, the gods were present, old Will
30   was beaming at us, Macbeth was actually paying attention to
31   his wife for once, it was flowing, it was stunning, and then
32   came the sleepwalking scene, oh, it was going so well, it was
33   going so well, until the moron playing the Doctor, who had
34   had a couple of drinks before the show, and seemed
35   hypnotized by my boobs, tripped and knocked the candle over

1   and set my nightgown on fire.
2   I decided to try and play it, use it, pretend we had planned
3   it that way, it was part of the madness, see, and the girl playing
4   the gentlewoman was quick enough to grab the bucket we
5   had on-stage, in which I was trying to wash the bloodstains
6   off my hands, and throw it on me. The bloodstains were
7   imaginary, but, fortunately the water was not, the bucket was
8   nearly full, for some reason, and I was soaked, but, dammit,
9   this was my moment, I wasn't going to let it slip away for
10   anything, and the audience was so into it, I think they would
11   have bought it, considered it a bit of daring technical tour de
12   force on the director's part — I looked like the winner of a
13   wet nightgown contest, and that alone might have kept them
14   watching and wanting to believe, if only the gung ho assistant
15   stage manager, who had the hots for me and was about three
16   times too hyper for his job anyway, had not then run onto the
17   stage, yelled for everybody not to panic, and fire extinguished
18   me.
19   I don't know. Maybe we should have gone with *Barefoot*
20   *in the Park.* I built my whole life towards a moment when I
21   was set on fire, drenched and then covered in foam in front
22   of six hundred people. Sometimes acting is like being punished
23   for a crime you didn't commit. Oh, well. I'll get another chance,
24   some day. They usually cast her much too old, so I'll get a turn
25   or two in middle age. The problem is, I've been having this
26   odd fantasy lately. I see my children watching me play Lady
27   Macbeth. I want my children to see me do it. Isn't that crazy?
28   I don't have any children. And as the years go by, it becomes
29   increasingly unlikely that I ever will, and I miss them. I miss
30   my children. I feel like I ran off with Shakespeare and
31   abandoned them. You make choices and then there are
32   consequences, and then the consequences have consequences,
33   and for a long time you don't notice this happening, because
34   you're young and busy and have things to do and things you
35   want and no time to stop and think about it, but the

1   consequences just keep happening, every moment of your life
2   has a consequence, somewhere down the line. She didn't really
3   understand that when she made him kill the king. But
4   consequences don't care if you understand them or not, they
5   just keep happening, tomorrow and tomorrow, to the last
6   syllable of recorded time. Shakespeare knew. That son of a
7   bitch knew everything. He had children.
8   Poor babies. I wrote them out of my play. All my pretty
9   ones. In one swell foop. I guess it's a curse.

I CAN'T STOP THINKING TODAY
by Annie Evans

Stephanie should be played as a young woman in her early twenties, who is living on her own. The "City" refers to New York, where she commutes from her apartment in Brooklyn. The locale and her listener are undefined as she delivers this monolog, attempting to understand the death that morning of an old family friend, Johnny Grant.

     I can't stop thinking today. It's not like on other days I don't think. Just not like this. Not so I wish I had a remote. You know. Click off. *(Clicks her brain off with an invisible remote.)* Not so I think I'm sick. Or I disgust myself. This morning I was caught in the traffic on Flatbush. I forgot the goddamn construction and we're moving one foot at a time toward the Manhattan Bridge. I look up and there's the blimp. Not the Goodyear — the Fuji — rising into the sky. I've never seen a blimp climbing upward. They're always just there. I don't know what I thought, people climbed up ropes. Or it sort of floated upward like a hot-air balloon? So I watch this round roll of film ascending. And then I imagine it exploding, green "F"s and "I"s falling flaming from the sky and crashing about Fulton Market, and there's screaming and pandemonium. We crawled under our cars so we wouldn't get burned or crushed, but some people panic or run and are cut down by the shower of blimp and I had to tell the police and press my eyewitness account. All day it's been like this. I'm walking down Seventh. I picked up this package at Canal Street. Took the Brooklyn Bridge back. I'm actually feeling pretty good, I got a spot on the Tuesday side. I stop and look in at the antique shop. This guy stops and looks also. He's really my type. I think he's looking at the same thing I'm looking at — this lamp with a horse head as the base. Very Godfather. That's pretty neat I think, if we both liked the same thing. Then I imagined us

1   getting married. Then, I imagined him getting cancer and I
2   sit by his bedside every night. And I yell at the nurses and
3   doctors when it's time for his medication and I couldn't find
4   them, and we talk very late at night about eternity and grace
5   and then he died. I cried silently at his bedside with the moon
6   spilling through the shades. But I'm pregnant, so his story
7   wouldn't be over, and I'll raise our child alone and I'll be
8   strong.
9   The guy had the good sense to move on. Maybe he was a
10 mind reader. I'd move. It's not like I don't know why I'm doing
11 this. I know why. So why can't I stop myself? Why won't my
12 mind listen to me? I mean, this is how I mourn? I've never
13 really had the opportunity to mourn, except over dead pets.
14 I've been spared so far the inevitable. Even this is still on the
15 periphery, it still doesn't directly affect me. I'm going through
16 my day as usual. Back and forth to the City a few more times
17 than I want. I love living in Brooklyn in many ways — air,
18 grass, sky. But sometimes I feel I should walk around with a
19 suitcase. Save me a few trips. Also a portable bank machine.
20 I'm the kind who only takes out twenty dollars at a time, so I
21 need to go three times a day. God, I wish I could go about my
22 business and put my brain on record, and look at it later,
23 when I have time, when I can understand it.
24   I was on the subway just now. I've got too good a parking
25 place now to risk driving. Of course, there's congestion ahead.
26 We sit. I read the headlines of a newspaper that is open next
27 to me. A man was shot trying to stop a robbery. The subway
28 car door slams open and two guys make their way loudly
29 through the car. People watch. On guard of course. You can't
30 help it. Then, I imagine the door slamming open again. This
31 man's eyes are blazing insanity. He wants all our money. He
32 has a Saturday Night Special. People scream, fall to the ground
33 as bullets echo against the metal. A transit cop smashes in
34 from behind but the man turns too quickly. The cop goes down.
35 His gun spins towards me on the floor. I pick it up. I raise

1 myself from the floor and aim it point blank range. The
2 gunman starts to turn but I blindly pull the trigger.
3   Am I always this obsessed with death or is this an
4 exception? Did I just notice it's everywhere! The subway sign,
5 the new one by the young kid "Come to Where the Cancer Is."
6 It's printed on a dead tree. Isn't the ink the by-product of dead
7 animals or vegetables?
8   He was just a friend of the family. I hadn't seen him for
9 years. Last time was when I was still living in the City. The
10 whole Pittsburgh gang came in for the weekend. I was
11 disappointed they wanted to eat at Tavern on the Green and
12 not at like The Supreme Macaroni Factory. I felt so adult, so
13 urban guiding them through the park to Bloomingdale's.
14 Johnny Grant and I tried on hats. When I was twelve, we
15 visited Johnny's country house. He gave my brothers and me
16 a six and said go have a good time. To him, everything in the
17 world contained the possibility of fun. It's a shame he and
18 Phyllis couldn't have children. He hung her bras on the fire
19 escape on Sunday in Ocean Grove so one hundred or so senior
20 citizens would call the police. Every other word she spoke
21 was "Oh John." He brought me ducks once to my mother's
22 dismay. He danced with me at every wedding. See, I just can't
23 stop thinking today. He gave me my name. His heart stopped
24 this morning.
25
26
27
28
29
30
31
32
33
34
35

MASHA, TOO
by Karen Sunde

4   This play was first produced by The People's Light and Theatre
5   Company of Malvern, Pennsylvania, in their Short Stuff Festival in
6   1991. It deals with the relationship between the Russian writer,
7   Anton Chekhov, and his younger sister, Masha. In the following
8   monolog, Masha has just received a marriage proposal from a suitor,
9   Alexander. She wonders, though, if she is truly in love with him, and
10   he with her; and if she really wants to exchange her present life with
11   her brother for a life of her own as a married woman.

13   Oh, God, how do I know — even if tonight I know? How do I
14   know forever? Even if I can't turn away from Alexander's eyes,
15   even if I know the response he moves in me — here, and here,
16   and here *(She is feeling as though he were there, and has trouble*
17   *breathing)* — is the deepest there is ... how do I know it will
18   be there next year? And the next, and the next, until death?
19   You can't know that! How do I know this fever won't pass, and
20   I awake shivering and up to my reddened eyes in dirty
21   underwear and potato peels. While our life here is ... Why did
22   Alexander have to happen to me now? I'm not unhappy with
23   the life I have! Such triumphs — carving a life in the city, all
24   artists, Anton, all of us. Of course, I teach, that's only prudent.
25   But Anton's talent is real, he's become so important, and our
26   life ... What does Alexander want me for? A wife. And what
27   is that? Tiny hands pulling at my hem, all night sickness,
28   stoking coals, and on the next pillow ... his smile. How can I
29   know? People must do things like this not with eyes open, but
30   shut tight. They must take a breath, shut their eyes, take
31   hands, and jump ... as into a swollen cold stream on the first
32   summer day, whether the ice is all melted or not. I know
33   nothing! *(Pause)* Ooooh, stop dreaming when there's so much
34   to ... But maybe it has to be gotten straight. After all, I *am*
35   trying to figure out our lives ... Lives ... Two, three, four

1 hours, and ... Will he look different to me? Will my eye break
2 him into new colors tonight ... deeper, or clearer, or a
3 carnival sparkling, mad ...? Stop it, stop it! The time is going.
4 You aren't being practical. Or orderly. Or anything. *(Laughing*
5 *helplessly)* Orderly about moonlight? I can't, I can't. It's a
6 helpless contradiction. The pleasure floods me, my nostrils
7 expand, I quiver like a new-bridled horse. And there will be
8 moonlight. It's clear blue all day and the fourth quarter. Oh
9 yes, soft and white, smoothing the path. And he'll know. I'll
10 have answered. It will have been decided. Our lives.
11 Our ... life. *(From her vision, she breaks, astonished.)* What am I
12 dreaming? This is nonsense. I'm dreaming. It was only the
13 wind! *(Pause)* Of all the thousand summer nights ripe with
14 stars, why did it happen in autumn when ghosts walk the
15 mind, colliding in mist? It started in the game — Fortunes —
16 with the crumpled little papers, messages passed from palm
17 to palm like smudged-up, sweaty, giggling children, without
18 knowing whose you'll open. The wad came apart in my hand
19 and the most I thought of the piece that said "Will you" was
20 that it must be the first half of a question. If I'd looked up,
21 would I have seen him watching then — for a blush or a
22 shudder of surprise? Who knows. I went straight to the rest,
23 not so much engaged as annoyed that the matted softened
24 edges of the fold had let go, and raggedly split my fortune. It
25 would have to retire from the game. So it startled me, blank
26 by itself there on the lone second slip: "Marry me." Angry, that
27 a flush swept up my cheeks, my eyes darted round the table
28 more in embarrassment than in wanting to find the author.
29 He was watching. I've run it so often in my mind — him
30 watching — again and again. But later, placing my shawl from
31 behind on my shoulders, with the little squeeze he likes, a
32 sign of affection. He does it to Mama, too. Just a gentle ... But
33 he said something close to my ear, more a breath than a
34 whisper. So close I couldn't be sure it wasn't some wind in my
35 head, a suggestion put straight to my brain without actually

1   passing his lips. It said, "Will you?" I froze just an instant,
2   unsure. Does wind, does no more than breath require an
3   answer? But he drew me outside no more, no less urgent than
4   any other night. Only, he was on his way and asked no one
5   else to see him off. Only that was strange. And he didn't speak
6   of it at all — not that he was leaving for who knows how many
7   weeks, not of the wind, and not of its message. But stepping
8   on to the path I parted the mist of a world where thoughts do
9   without speech, but have the pressure of wind, and a whisper
10 belongs to no one. We had gone as far as the bridge without
11 a word when he looked full in my face and said simply, "Shall
12 I talk to Anton?" I shook my head. "Not until . . ." He knew
13 that wasn't an answer. He knew he had no more than opened
14 the subject — no more than set a whisper in my head . . . but
15 enough. How did he know? Strange, how certain he is. In play
16 we intimidate him. Well, maybe not that, but he's quiet as
17 though waiting his time, then he scores. His eyes are amused
18 and . . . full of understanding. The way he quietly, so quietly,
19 searches my face, my eyes, makes me feel so open, so still, as
20 though there's nothing else in all of this world to learn, only
21 him. *(Pause)* He's inviting me into a life.
22
23
24
25
26
27
28
29
30
31
32
33
34
35

Monologs for Men

THE GALLERY
by Chaim Potok

Asher Lev is a very famous, if notorious, young painter, who has used personal images of his family in some of his recent works on exhibition. Since he's received criticism for this, in the monolog he tries to justify what he has done. When referring to his paintings, they can be imaginatively located downstage in the audience.

Picasso said that art is a lie which makes us realize the truth. That's a ponderous thought with which to begin an evening of theatre: Art is a lie which makes us realize the truth. Of course, it follows from that remark that since theatre is a form of art, what you will see here tonight is a lie. And since it's a lie of the sort that Picasso had in mind, it will help us realize a truth. I think I know what you're asking. You're asking: What sort of truth? Well, the sort that we might sense when we come upon a cloud of butterflies, or an eagle soaring into a blue sky, or when we look with open eyes, I mean eyes that are really and truly *open* and *looking*, when we look at the mysteries all around us — the mysteries that theologians have in mind when they talk about ideas and feelings like wonder, awe, and dread. Mysteries . . . that's what it was like for me from the very beginning. A mystery. *(Pause)* My name is Asher Lev. Yes, *the* Asher Lev. You read about me in newspapers and magazines, you talk about me at your dinner affairs and cocktail parties — the notorious and legendary Asher Lev of the *Brooklyn Crucifixion. (Pause)* I'm an observant Jew. I was born in Brooklyn, the Bible belt of Judaism. The sect I was born into is the belt buckle. Now, observant Jews don't paint crucifixions. As a matter of fact, observant Jews don't paint at all — the way that I am painting. So strong words are being written and spoken about me: I am a traitor, a self-hater; I have brought shame upon my family and my people; I am a mocker of ideas that are sacred to Christians; I am a

215

1   blasphemer. *(Pause)* **Well, I am none of those things. And yet**
2   **I must confess that my accusers are not entirely wrong ... I**
3   **am, in some way, all of those things ...** *(Pause)* **Some genealogy**
4   **is necessary here. A little bit of lineage. My father's father was**
5   **a scholar and a recluse. I always pictured him with a slight**
6   **body and a huge head, eyelids swollen from lack of sleep, face**
7   **pale, lips dry, the veins showing blue along his cheeks and**
8   **temples. Shortly before he turned fifty, he became a follower**
9   **of the Russian Hasidic sect led by the Rebbe of Ladov. Very**
10   **devout people. He began to travel about the Soviet Union as**
11   **an emissary of the Rebbe. "Why did he travel so much?" I once**
12   **asked my parents. "To bring the Master of the Universe into**
13   **the world," my father said. "To find people who need help,"**
14   **my mother said.** *(Pause)* **My mother ... my mother is from a**
15   **family of leading Hasidim, members of an Eastern European**
16   **Hasidic dynasty. Great Talmudic scholars on her mother's**
17   **side; great Hasidic leaders on her father's side.** *(Pause)*
18   **So ... little Asher Lev — born in 1943 to Rivkeh and Aryeh**
19   **Lev, in the Crown Heights section of Brooklyn — little Asher**
20   **Lev was the juncture of two great family lines, the apex of a**
21   **triangle heavy with potentiality and responsibility. But he**
22   **was also born with a mystery, a gift ... He could draw. He**
23   **drew on everything. On floors, on walls, in the margins of**
24   **sacred books. His dearest companions were Eberhard and**
25   **Crayola. Washing for meals was a cosmic enterprise. My**
26   **mother encouraged me. "Draw the pretty birds, Asher," she**
27   **would say. "And the flowers. Draw the lovely flowers." My**
28   **father? My father said to me once, looking at one of my**
29   **drawings, "You have nothing better to do with your time,**
30   **Asher? You have to waste so much time with foolishness?" I**
31   **said, "It's a drawing, Papa. A drawing is not foolishness." He**
32   **looked at me in surprise. I was almost five at the time. He**
33   **thought drawing was something children did when they were**
34   **very young, and then outgrew. I would outgrow it, the way a**
35   **child outgrows the measles and the mumps. I continued to**

1 draw, but after awhile I stopped showing him my drawings.
2 *(Pause)* I did not outgrow it. *(Pause)* I should never have painted
3 those pictures. I remember. I prayed three times a day, ate
4 only kosher food, observed the Sabbath and festivals, and
5 believed that our leader — the Rebbe — is a gift to us from
6 God to help us make our lives holy. It was man's task to make
7 life holy. You see? I remember. They told me that if I wanted
8 to make life holy, I should stay in Brooklyn. I'm sorry I painted
9 those pictures, I don't know why I paint. It was a long Paris
10 winter . . . long and lonely . . . a time for thinking . . . and
11 feeling. I began thinking about my mother . . . I began to think
12 of all the years my mother stood between me and my father,
13 trying to nourish both of us, me and my father, at the same
14 time. "Show me your drawings, Asher." "Make the world
15 pretty, Asher." "Travel safely, my husband." "Go in peace and
16 return in peace, my husband." *(Pause)* Her brother was killed
17 in an accident while he was on a mission for the Rebbe. Did
18 I tell you that? I was a child, six years old. I remember there
19 was a phone call for my father, and he left the house. When
20 he came back, his face was white. He told me to go into my
21 room, he needed to talk privately with my mother. Then my
22 mother began to scream. The phone rang and rang. The
23 apartment began to fill with relatives and friends. My mother
24 kept screaming. The next day, they took my mother away to
25 a hospital. When they brought her back, she looked like a
26 skeleton. She was sick a long time. I never told you this? When
27 she recovered, my father began to travel again. She would
28 stand at the window of our apartment, looking out at the
29 parkway. She was terrified something might happen to my
30 father and he would never come back. I kept seeing that in
31 Paris: my mother standing at the window, waiting . . . I needed
32 to paint it. I remember mixing the colors; ochres, grays, dark
33 smoky alizarons, tones of Prussian and cobalt blue. I
34 remember working a long time on my mother's face. The first
35 painting didn't say what I wanted it to say. My feelings weren't

really in it. That's why I did the second one. I wanted to put
into it all the torment I felt in my mother. Do you see it? In
her mouth, the curve of her head, the arching of her body, the
clenching of her fists, the downward thrust of her legs. I
remember saying to myself, "This is for all the pain you've
suffered, Mama. This is for all the torment of your past and
future years. For the unspeakable mystery that brings good
fathers and sons into this world and lets a mother watch them
tear at each other's throats. For the love I have for you, for
all the things about you that I remember, and for all the things
I should remember and have forgotten." *(Pause)* That's why I
painted those pictures. Do I have to show them? On the other
hand, if I don't show them, the act of art is incomplete. It's
cowardice not to show them. You don't think they're too
strong? I think they're too — they dominate the wall, the
room — too much. I should have muted them. I can still do it.
There's still time. Do you have any paints here? I can get some
paints outside. They're too raw. They're ... not ready. It won't
be a success if the critics tear me to pieces. I'm worried. Those
paintings are going to hurt people ... I can't let them hurt
people ... These are people I love.

SUNDAY SERMON
by David Henry Hwang

Comic monolog for a male actor, indeterminate age.

David Henry Hwang is one of the United States' most prolific and successful new playwrights. One scene from his play, "The Dance and the Railroad" appears earlier in this volume. This monolog, first written in 1982 and widely-performed since then, reveals his comic talents at their satirical best. Though it dates from the Reagan-Bush era, the single political reference can be easily updated; and its theme is timeless because the twisted "gospel" which it conveys is still being preached and will always find a receptive audience. It is easily performed on a bare stage, but the properties indicated are probably essential.

(A PASTOR comes up to a pulpit. Over the loudspeakers a congregation is heard singing "Onward, Christian Soldiers." Music stops.)
    You may be seated. *(Pause)* **We thank the choir for that inspiring and enthusiastic rendition. Their choice of anthem seems particularly appropriate in view of today's sermon topic: "How to Spread the Gospel in the Event of Nuclear War." I know there are people who would rather we shy away from the tough decisions every Christian must make once the bombs hit the ground. I do not count myself or you among them. Many of us have been conditioned to stereotype a nuclear holocaust as a bad thing. This is simply narrow-minded. A nuclear war can be a great tragedy or a great opportunity, a vehicle for Satan or for the soldiers of righteousness. If we don't reap the harvest of such an event, you can be sure that scores of Satan's little workers will be out sowing the seeds of evil, out amongst the maimed and wounded, enslaving them to illicit drugs, performing abortions, teaching evolution, and encouraging positive portrayals of homosexuals on our television networks! We can**

1   refuse to prepare now, but what will we think when we are
2   sitting in our bomb shelter, ineffective while a disciple of
3   Satan turns our fellow shelterees to moral decay and perverse
4   cult practices? What will we feel as one by one, they become
5   Mormons or Christian Scientists? We will think only, "I should
6   have prepared when there was still time." The first thing the
7   post-holocaust disciple must do is distinguish between the
8   living and the dead. In some cases, this will be simple, as
9   perhaps half the population will be instantaneously
10   vaporized. Others, however, may be simply disfigured beyond
11   recognition. Don't let this discourage you. Here is a field of
12   souls ripe for the saving. It has been said that there are no
13   atheists in foxholes; well, I suggest there would be no agnostics
14   after a nuclear attack. That co-worker at the office — the one
15   who flaunts his tarts around your desk and calls you "Jesus
16   freak!" — he'll be singing a different tune when his face melts,
17   you can be sure of that! This is the perfect time for you to
18   loosen your tie, carry his dismembered trunk over to a quiet
19   spot, and have that "special" talk.
20   What good is the *opportunity*, though, if you are
21   unprepared to witness? That's why each of you should take
22   our Friday night evangelism training classes and get copies
23   of this little booklet: "The Four Spiritual Laws." This breaks
24   the process of salvation down into four easily recited steps,
25   such as, "One, God loves you and has a wonderful plan for
26   your life." Delbert Jennings, after only three Friday night
27   classes, recited all four laws and the salvation prayer in only
28   one minute, forty-two seconds! Using them, he has already
29   converted three football players and a rock 'n roll singer! And
30   time will be of the essence after a nuclear explosion, especially
31   since most sources of medical care will have been destroyed.
32   So learn the laws and carry this little book at all times,
33   especially when U.S.-Soviet relations seem to be "heating up."
34   After the initial explosion, you and the other survivors will
35   likely want to go underground to escape the effects of radiation

1   fallout. Shelters are easily made. Here I will demonstrate what
2   an official of the Reagan administration recently said we must
3   do to combat the long-term effects of a nuclear war. *(He unveils*
4   *an aquarium filled with dirt.)* It will be a simple matter to dig a
5   hole *(He does so)*, get inside *(He takes out plastic dolls and dumps*
6   *them in the hole)*, and cover the top with leaves and twigs *(He*
7   *does so)*. There! Now we're protected! And doesn't that look
8   comfy! Brothers and sisters, what an opportunity to witness
9   this will be! How many times have you tried to spread the
10 good news only to be told: "I don't have time" or "I have to
11 go"? Well, now you have the perfect rejoinders to these oft-
12 used lines of Satan. *(He sticks his fingers through the leaves and*
13 *manipulates the dolls, also doing their voices.)*
14   *(Woman's voice)* "I don't have the time."
15   *(Man's voice)* "Why, Jill, don't you realize that we'll have
16 to stay down here some twenty years until the radiation
17 reaches an acceptable level? Now, let's list the sins you've
18 committed since puberty."
19   *(Woman's voice)* "But I have to go."
20   *(Man's voice)* "All right. But you'll die a slow and painful
21 death, with nausea, internal bleeding, and skin falling off.
22 Rather than face such agony, let's discuss the Christian view
23 of a woman's role."
24   Ah! What a difference a nuclear war will make to us, the
25 soul-winners! And after twenty or thirty years have passed
26 and you emerge from your shelter with your now God-fearing
27 and obedient wife, you will find a world waiting to be re-made.
28 No more houses of prostitution, no more ERA, no more drugs,
29 no more Kurt Vonnegut! Gone will be gun-control laws,
30 homosexual housing ordinances, busing, and teenage free
31 clinics! And we will be able to start once again, hand in hand,
32 to re-create the world envisioned by the founding fathers: a
33 nation of free men, mule and woman by their side, working
34 the land with their hands and organizing television boycotts!
35 When we look at it this way, is a nuclear war all that bad? This

1   **world has become filthy, corrupt, and sinful. Let us wipe it**
2   **out and begin again! Thank you.**
3
4
5
6
7
8
9
10
11
12
13
14
15
16
17
18
19
20
21
22
23
24
25
26
27
28
29
30
31
32
33
34
35

LLOYD'S PRAYER
by Kevin Kling

The character is an evangelist, the setting is a church or tent meeting, revival-style. "Bobby" is an effective prop underneath the sheet in his cage, and he may be created as the character describes, or mimed entirely.

Brothers and sisters, a miracle! I see among you disbelief. I see among you the doubter's stare: what is this man saying? A miracle in our times? Ha! This man is crazy, this man is insane, this man is a product of the sixties. And to you people I say walk away — you can walk away. You can be on your merry way. Make like a big old widebody 747 and hippity-hop down the bunny trail. Well, goodbye, adios, qu'est-ce que sera, sera. I got got got no time for you. For I have a miracle to tell. Now, under this sheet is a miracle. I said, under this sheet is a living, breathing miracle in our times. That's right! Brothers and sisters, how many among you are lonely? Let's see the hands, come on, I know you're out there. How many? That's right. How many feel at times the world is against them, that the world has singled them out for some unknown reason and has them stuck on the spin cycle? And how many know loss and pain? Come on, let's see those hands. And who has wanted to scream out, why me? And how many feel empty like there's a big old gerbil living inside you chewing up any happiness that tries to get in, a bottomless pit inside a pit that swallows any happiness that may come your way? We all have these feelings, we all know pain, we all know that gerbil. Some more than others, but all at one time or another. Brothers and sisters, I want to introduce you to Little Bobby. It's all right, Ma'am. Look upon him. Have you ever seen a more despicable creature? Look, brothers and sisters! I know it's hard to look. Yes, that's right, he's all real, all live. Eats, sleeps, and drinks just like you or me. So what makes Little Bobby here so different?

1 Why does he seem so hideous, so disgusting? Is it the hair
2 covering ninety-five — that's right, ninety-five — per cent of
3 his body? I think not. Is it his stooped posture? His dull stare?
4 His gaping mouth? What? I'll tell you what, the reason Little
5 Bobby scares us. The reason Little Bobby give us the heebie-
6 jeebies. The reason Little Bobby has those lizards running up
7 and down your spines is because when we look at Little Bobby
8 we are looking in a mirror. That's right. That's what you're
9 looking at. And you. And you and you and you. So stare and
10 stare hard 'cause it ain't gonna change. Not today, not
11 tomorrow, and not in a week. No sirree, Little Bobby is here
12 to stay. Now I hear you askin', "Well, I don't wanna be Little
13 Bobby." Well, that's too bad 'cause you are. "But there's got
14 to be somethin' I can do?" Nope, not a thing. "What if I'm rich?"
15 Too bad, Mister Vanderbilt. "Then I'll get drunk." We all gotta
16 wake up some time. "I give up! If I can't save myself, how can
17 I help the Little Bobby in that cage?" What? You want to help
18 Little Bobby? "That's right." Why, look there! Your posture
19 just improved. You're walkin' straight and tall! And, why,
20 you're breathin' through your nose again! I can hear it makin'
21 the faintest of whistlin' noises, like runnin' in corduroys. Why,
22 you're lookin' much better indeed! Isn't that somethin'! All
23 you did was offer to help a fellow human and you ended up
24 helpin' yourself. A miracle! Hallelujah! You see, brothers and
25 sisters, apathy is like . . . a meatball that falls off your plate.
26 At first you think, well, it's just a little spot on my shirt. But
27 then that meatball starts to rolling. And before you know it,
28 you got some sauce on your tie and then your jacket, then
29 your pants, your shoe, the carpet, and that meatball just keeps
30 on a-rolling till it's mucked-up everything you own! The devil
31 is just such a meatball, and he works just as fast. Just as
32 efficient and twice as destructive. See, he already knows the
33 path to wickedness. He's not some rogue meatball scampering
34 aimlessly about your lives. He has a course, a *plan* he has. He
35 is out to get you! And he knows where you are weak and he'll

1 attack there — *Bam! Bam! Bam!* — till he has you, and by then
2 Little Bobby will look like Miss America compared to you.
3 "Well then, Brother Lloyd, how do I keep that meatball on my
4 plate?" It's the easiest thing in the world! But you gotta act
5 now because once it falls off there's no catching it. God wants
6 to help but he can't do it alone. He needs cooperation.
7 Cooperation. That means you helping him keep that meatball
8 of a devil in check. You can't be watching that meatball all
9 the time, you got spaghetti to eat! And God knows that. He
10 doesn't need your help all the time — just when an
11 opportunity presents itself. Now is such an opportunity. Little
12 Bobby needs your help. We all see his predicament: the boy
13 must be kept in a cage. He is wild and untamed. Any of us
14 could have been born into this way of life, but God in his
15 mercy spared us and gave the burden to Bobby. How can we
16 repay Little Bobby, this child of the Beast? I have taken it
17 upon myself to try to bring him to the Lord. It's not easy, folks.
18 Bobby can't even say grace at the supper table. But I'll bring
19 him around even if it's the last thing I ever do. It won't be
20 easy. I have time for little else these days. Folks, I hate to do
21 this, but I'm askin' — not for me, mind you, but for Little
22 Bobby. Can you find it in your hearts to spare whatever you
23 can to help Bobby find the Lord? Won't you become a partner
24 with me in my crusade for Bobby? His meatball is off the plate
25 and rolling fast and I'll be one poor excuse for a brother if I
26 don't stick out my foot and stop it. Give what you can, and
27 remember when you help Bobby you're really helpin'
28 yourselves! Thank you! And Hallelujah!
29
30
31
32
33
34
35

ANTON, HIMSELF
by Karen Sunde

This play was originally commissioned by Actors Theatre of Louisville
and produced in their Classics in Context Festival in 1989. It was
also performed in Yalta and at the Moscow Art Theatre in Moscow,
1990. It deals with the early years of the famous Russian playwright,
Anton Chekhov, who has already contracted tuberculosis. In this
scene his first full-length play, "The Seagull," has just flopped in
Moscow, and he has returned to his estate in Melikovo to continue
his life as a country doctor and writer of short stories.

**You think I'm a coward. Hiding. Whining. Sniffling. You
don't have any idea. I can *will* myself to deal with anything.
And have. But this is ... An artist is very public ... I mean,
the artist may be private. Many are, extremely. But his work
is ... completely exposed. And trying to be a *theatre*
artist ... you're just asking to be ... How much more
"exposed" can you be? You gather a crowd on purpose and
say "on this night at this hour for your pleasure and edification
I will expose myself." So the whole world is free, to come and
treat me as it will. Isn't it unsound psychologically — to desire
public approval so much that you're willing to risk public
humiliation? This desire must be born of profound self-hatred!**
*(He virtually spits this last, then holds bitterly. When the pause ends,
we realize that he has not been able to shake his last thought.)* **What
is particularly insane is that the qualities of personality most
needed to produce a fine theatre artist — emotional range,
sensitivity, expressiveness — are those least suited to combat
public humiliation. *(Pause)* In the beginning it was just fun. I
scribbled out stories. Of course, the grandest fun were the
charades: to play a prank in some wild costume, titillate the
guests, scandalize the neighborhood. Then — the moment
someone actually bought a story and paid me for it — the
whole thing metamorphosed into a back-hours industry: so**

1　many kopeks a line, speed and volume the essence, such and
2　such subjects preferred, such and such a tone, avoid what the
3　censor will cut. *(Laughs at himself, then stops short at a memory.)*
4　When Grigorovich wrote me, I was ashamed. Great old man
5　of letters — the story he so much admired I'd whipped off in
6　one sitting ... in the bathhouse. Little "smelt"; literary
7　excrement appearing in papers I called "Filth of the Day." But
8　art? Miniature tales, calendar jokes, dramatic sketches,
9　telegrams, reviews, imaginary letters, articles, aphorisms,
10　caricature captions, picture ideas. After all that, the little
11　plays, the one-act farces sliced easily off my loaf. I could write
12　a hundred a year. Subjects sprout out of me like oil from the
13　soil of Baku. And it's fine to write plays as a sport, to go for
14　your take as a fisher approaches the net — with expectation
15　... then delighted surprise at the catch. But these *long*
16　plays ... How did I ever trick myself into ... Everyone speaks
17　about plays as though it were easy to write them! *(Worked up*
18　*again)* To write a good play takes a certain talent. To write a
19　poor play then change it into a good one — to take a new focus,
20　cross out, add, insert monologs, revive the dead and bury the
21　living — takes far more talent. It's like buying an old soldier's
22　pants and trying to make a dress coat out of them. *(Finally,*
23　*nearly bawling it out)* I *know* "The Seagull" is a mess! It's
24　comedy ... but I couldn't keep to the form. I began it forte
25　and wound up pianissimo, used practically no action, lots of
26　talk about writing, and tons of love. I'm clearly *not* a
27　playwright. *(Animated tussle with himself)* Then why not take it
28　like a man? I did! I behaved perfectly! Exactly as a wooer who
29　makes a proposal, is refused, and quietly leaves. And the
30　panic? That's not my affair. I can't be held ... It's really very
31　simple. I expected the worst from the start. And right off the
32　leading lady backed out, had to be replaced. We lost three
33　rehearsals over that. And *then* ... they didn't know their lines,
34　they did too much "acting," and everywhere I felt ... hovering
35　malice. I considered staying away. As the house filled I counted

227

1   off the blondes and brunettes: hostile, hostile, hostile, coldly
2   indifferent. But that's only if they'd been a real audience, and
3   they weren't. It was a benefit. And there's nothing worse. It's
4   better to play to two, three people, or no one. No one at all is
5   better than an audience that *didn't* come to see your play.
6   They came for farce, to cheer the comedienne Levkevya —
7   who wasn't even on the stage. The performance began and
8   my heart died at the restlessness. But at first they held. Then,
9   as expectation built to the play within the play and Nina
10   appeared ... (the one enchanting actress I had) ... with the
11   moon behind her, beginning her solemn incantation: "Men,
12   lions, eagles and quails ..." they burst out laughing. And they
13   whistled. Then booed. *(He begins to cough.)* Complete nightmare.
14   The actors were in a panic. Critics buzzed with glee. *(Overcomes*
15   *the coughing. Quiet)* I stood, like stone, unable to remember
16   where I was. It is one thing to undergo an agony — but to have
17   *advertised* yourself — to have sold *tickets* to it?! To die, to
18   disappear, to be nobody ... nobody. *(Pause)* By the second act
19   cacophony swamped the whole. With actors playing their most
20   tender scenes the audience whooped and guffawed, turned
21   their backs on the stage, chattered to friends behind. So I left.
22   But did *not* flee. I sat rationally composed in Levkevya's
23   dressing room until the end. And then I walked the streets. I
24   can't answer for anyone else. If they went frantically looking,
25   it's their affair. They should have known. Next morning I
26   packed, wrote letters, and left. Yes, on the early train. Yes,
27   even though it wasn't express. Twenty-two hours to Moscow?
28   Fine. I'll sleep and dream of fame, bliss, tomorrow ...
29   Melikovo — no actors, producers, audience, papers. Bliss. I
30   didn't even squeak, I simply left. Potapenko came. I let him
31   see me off. Only because he hadn't seen the play. I wouldn't
32   talk to anyone who had. Yes, not even Masha. Potapenko
33   hadn't come because Lika had been there. And he's the third-
34   rate writer who ruined Lika. Potapenko came. And I joked.
35   *(He coughs, fumbles for a handkerchief, which becomes red-stained,*

1 *hurriedly refolds and conceals it.)* **Pain is strange. You can hold**
2 **it in but it twists your face. Dignity. When you're stripped**
3 **bare it's dignity you reach for. It may be the last pole of**
4 **civilization. But no doubt I slander the animals in saying so.**
5 **Dignity. Self-preservation precludes sharing the pain, letting**
6 ***any* other presume you are so far hurt that he may dare step**
7 **in the boat with you. To meet one who witnessed your**
8 **humiliation is to suffer it again. The only way to minimize is**
9 **to avoid.** *(Sprightly, mischievous)* **And at the station are there**
10 **newspapers on the platform? Look — the newsboy's sweet-**
11 **natured face, but in his hands poison. Poisonous reviews. And**
12 **everyone, coming or going just this minute read them.** *(Brief*
13 *choking, caught immediately)* **If, as an artist you are working at**
14 **peak, pushing the limits of what you've done before . . . you**
15 **are wide open. You cannot richly connect with what lies under**
16 **the conscious mind and remain protected. So when work is**
17 **done with*out* care, its negative reception is a matter of fortune**
18 **only. But when an artist unveils his developing essence . . . one**
19 **hostile word will wither his center of being.** *(Silence)* **Masha**
20 **came on the train directly after me. Worried, no doubt, that**
21 **I'd hang myself. Nevertheless, today I am well, I am working.**
22 **But my heart is tin. I feel nothing for my plays but disgust.**
23 **Never — not if I live seven hundred *years* will I write another**
24 **one.**
25
26
27
28
29
30
31
32
33
34
35

RESOURCE TEXTS

I. Anthologies of Monologs and Scenes

Bard, Messaline, and Newhouse, eds. *And What Are You Going to Do for Us Now?* Toronto: Simon & Pierre, 1987. Selections from more than forty of Canada's award-winning plays.

Bert, Norman, ed. *The Scenebook for Actors*. Colorado Springs: Meriwether, 1990. Some of the playwrights include David Mamet, Harold Pinter, Oliver Goldsmith, Eugene Ionesco.

Cartwright, Mason W., ed. *Monologues from Chekhov*. Toluca Lake, California: Dramaline, 1987. Short and long selections from "Uncle Vanya," "The Seagull," "Three Sisters," and "The Cherry Orchard."

Champagne, Leonora, ed. *Out From Under: Texts by Women Performance Artists*. New York: Theatre Communications Group, 1990. Not audition material in short formats, but extended pieces for scene work or performance.

Dent, Karen. *The Soaps — Scene Stealing Scenes for Actors*. Colorado Springs: Meriwether, 1989. Written by a New York scriptwriter for the soaps, this collection contains pieces from three to ten minutes.

Earley, Michael, and Keil, Philippa, eds. *Soliloquy! The Shakespeare Monologues*. 2 vols. New York: Applause, 1986. These two volumes contain over 175 pieces for men and women of all ages, and tips for acting Shakespeare.

_____. *Classic American Monologues*. 2 vols. New York: Applause, 1987. Useful mainly as a class text since many of the selections are "signature" pieces done by famous actors, many from famous films.

_____. *Solo! The Best Monologues of the 80's*. 2 vols. New York: Applause, 1987. More than 150 selections here, for men and women.

Ellis, Roger, ed. *Competition Monologues*. Lanham, MD: University Press of America, 1988. Forty-four monologs, 30-60 seconds, from recent plays produced by American regional theatres. The only anthology limited exclusively to characters 18-35 years old, recommended as a supplement to university and professional-level acting classes. Contains a 14-page introduction on preparation of monologs.

_____. *Competition Monologues II*. Lanham, MD: University Press of America, 1990. Forty-nine monologs, 1-2 minutes, from recent contemporary plays produced by American regional theatres. The only anthology limited exclusively to characters 18-35 years old, recommended as a supplement to university and professional-level acting classes. Contains a 14-page introduction on preparation of monologs.

Friedman, Ginger, ed. *The Perfect Monologue*. New York: Penguin, 1990.

Grumbach, Jane, and Emerson, Robert, eds. *Monologues: Men*. 2 vols. New York: Drama Book Specialists, 1976.

_____. *Monologues: Women*. 2 vols. New York: Drama Book Specialists, 1976.

Handman, Wynn, ed. *Modern American Scenes for Student Actors*. New York: Bantam, 1978.

Harrington, Laura, ed. *100 Monologues: An Audition Sourcebook From New Dramatists*. New York: Mentor, 1989. The New Dramatists organization in New York is one of the country's most famous theatres for producing staged readings & productions by new American playwrights.

Karshner, Roger, ed. *Monologues From the Classics*. Toluca Lake, California: Dramaline, 1986. A very good selection from Shakespeare, Marlowe, and others.

_____. *Shakespeare's Monologues They Haven't Heard*. Toluca Lake, California: Dramaline, 1987. As the title suggests, many unusual pieces here, although by now "they" will probably have heard them.

Karton, Joshua, ed. *Film Scenes for Actors*. New York: Bantam, 1983 and 1987. 2 vols.

Keil, Carl, ed. *Soliloquy! The Elizabethan and Jacobean Monologues*. New York: Applause, 1987. 2 vols. Over 50 speeches from the period, with helpful notes. Separate volumes for men and women.

Kluger, Garry Michael. *Original Audition Scenes for Actors*. Colorado Springs; Meriwether, 1987. These short scenes were written by a professional media actor, and designed for film/TV auditioning. Comic, dramatic, and monolog material.

Lane, Eric, and Shengold, Nina, eds. *The Actor's Book of Scenes From New Plays*. New York: Penguin, 1988.

Lawrence, Eddie and Robards, Jason. *57 Original Auditions for Actors.* Colorado Springs: Meriwether, 1983. Two-minute monologs by type-characters, this is a workbook for the professional and non-professional.

Michaels, Ian, ed. *Monologues From Oscar Wilde.* Toluca Lake, California: Dramaline, 1988.

_____. *Monologues from George Bernard Shaw.* Toluca Lake, California: Dramaline, 1988. These volumes contain short and long selections from these authors.

Pike, Frank, and Dunn, Thomas G., eds. *Scenes and Monologues from the New American Theater.* New York: Mentor, 1988. Contains commercial hits and previously unpublished works. Helpful reference material on playwrights' agents and how to obtain new, relatively unknown plays.

Rudnicki, Stefan, ed. *Classical Monologues.* New York: Drama Book Specialists, 1979-82. 4 vols. An excellent body of material, but limited exclusively to Renaissance authors.

_____. *The Actor's Book of Class Monologues.* New York: Penguin, 1988.

Schulman, Michael, and Mekler, Eva, eds. *Contemporary Scenes for Student Actors.* New York: Penguin, 1980. The first 14 pages of introduction is one of the most succinct and valuable approaches to scene acting that can be found anywhere.

_____. *The Actor's Scenebook, Volume II.* New York: Bantam, 1988. Scenes and monologs here, with an introductory section on creating characters.

Schulman, Nina, and Mekler, Pam, eds. *The Actor's Scenebook from the Best of Broadway, Off-Broadway, and London's West End Theatre.* New York: Bantam, 1984.

Shengold, Nina, ed. *The Actor's Book of Contemporary Stage Monologues.* New York: Penguin, 1988. More than 150 selections for men and women. Provocative interviews with Swoozie Kurtz, Christopher Durang, Lanford Wilson, and Tina Howe.

Smith, Marisa, and Graham, Kristin, eds. *Monologues from Literature: A Sourcebook for Actors.* New York: Fawcett-Columbine, 1990. An excellent sourcebook of 200 selections, many of them suitable for high school forensics competition.

Smith, Marisa, and Schewel, Amy, eds. *The Actor's Book of Movie Monologues.* New York: Penguin, 1986. More than 100 monologs here, with an "afterword" containing tips by casting directors.

Stoller, Sigmund A., ed. *TV Scenes for Actors.* Colorado Springs: Meriwether, 1989. This anthology contains twenty-six of the best scenes from suspense and character dramas of the "golden years" of TV acting.

II. Handbooks on Audition Technique and Scene Work

Anton, William. *Auditioning for the Actor.* Leucadia, California, Theatre Arts, 1989.

Craig, David. *On Performing: A Handbook for Actors, Dancers, Singers on the Musical Stage.* New York; McGraw-Hill, 1988. America's foremost musical theatre coach delivers his advice to actors at all levels of experience. Interviews with nine successful performers and a brief history of the American musical theatre.

Black, David. *The Actor's Auditioning.* New York: Vintage, 1990.

Blu, Susan, and Mellin, Molly Ann. *A Guide to Commercial Voice-Over Excellence.* New York: Focal, 1989.

Ellis, Roger. *A Student Actor's Audition Handbook.* Chicago: Nelson-Hall, 1986. The definitive text for actors preparing their own material for stage and musical auditions. Recommended as a class text for teachers and coaches at the university or professional level. Also contains chapters on resumés, types of auditions, interviews, and selecting material.

Hunt, Gordon. *How to Audition.* New York: Harper & Row, 1977. A popular book, though the interviews are now dated. Recently re-issued in paperback.

Shurtleff, Michael. *Audition.* New York: Walker, 1980. Probably the single best-selling text on auditioning, although the Shurtleff "method" needs to be taught by an experienced coach.

Silver, Fred. *Auditioning for the Musical Theatre.* New York: Penguin, 1988. Sensible pointers on everything from what to wear to what to sing. Contains a valuable section of 130 possible audition songs.

III. Books on Acting As a Career

Callan, K. *The New York Agent Book*. Los Angeles: Sweden, 1988 (distributed by Broadway Press, New York). Tips from New York's top agents based on extensive interviews. For beginning and experienced actors.

——————. *An Actor's Workbook*. Los Angeles: Sweden, 1988 (distributed by Broadway Press, New York). Inside tips from Hollywood executives and casting agents. Valuable discussions of how to evaluate your career and your present agent. Step-by-step procedure for finding the right agent.

——————. *How to Sell Yourself As an Actor from New York to Los Angeles (and Everywhere In Between)*. Los Angeles: Sweden, 1988. A practical discussion of many aspects of an acting career. The author tends to regard any work between the coasts as amateurish, but despite this provincial attitude the book is valuable reading for actors just out of school.

Charles, Jill. *The Actor's Picture Resumé Book*. Dorset, VT: Theater Directories, 1991. Excellent description of materials required for "making the rounds," with up-to-date professional samples of photos and how to create your portfolio for the stage, film, or television.

Cohen, Robert. *Acting Professionally*. 3rd ed. Palo Alto: Mayfield, 1990. The most straightforward, accurate, and honest description of the business from one who's in it.

Colyer, Carlton. *The Art of Acting*. Colorado Springs: Meriwether Publishing, 1989. Basic exercises to multidimensional performances. Written by a professional actor who has performed with many of the greatest names of the American stage. Full of practical ideas for growth.

Katz, Judith. *The Business of Show Business*. New York: Harper & Row, 1981. A highly motivational and readable book that lays out all the options for young actors. Takes the "mystique" out of the profession.

Logan, Tom. *How to Act and Eat at the Same Time*. Washington, D.C.: Communications, 1982. A "must" reading for young professionals.

——————. *Acting in the Million-Dollar Minute: The Art and Business of Performing in TV Commercials*. Washington, D.C.: Communications, 1984. Indispensable reading for anyone considering this aspect of the profession.

McNoughton, Robert and Bruce. *Act Now: An Actor's Guide for Breaking In.* Hollywood: Global, 1982. An outstanding, up-to-date perspective on stage and film acting, dealing especially with young actors.

Rogers, Lynne and Henry, Marie. *How to Be a Working Actor.* New York: Evans, 1986. Step-by-step procedures for getting yourself established. A very businesslike approach to marketing yourself, from two successful women who learned it from the ground up.

CREDITS

The Scarlet Letter is reprinted courtesy of the adaptor, Frank Bessell, Artistic Director of the Berkshire Public Theatre, 30 Union St., P.O. Box 860, Pittsfield, MA 01202.

Welcome Home is reprinted courtesy of the author, Kathryn Schultz-Miller, c/o the Artreach Touring Theatre, 3074 Madison Ave., Cincinnati, OH 45209.

The Geography of Luck is reprinted by special permission of Marlane Meyer's agent, Peregrine Whittlesey, 345 E. 80th St., #31F, New York, NY 10028.

A Persistence of Vision is reprinted courtesy of the author, Sandra Morris, 5925 Cedar Knoll Dr., Brighton, MI 48116.

Diesel Moon is reprinted by special permission of Robert Auletta's agent, Helen Merrill Ltd., 435 W. 23rd St., #1A, New York, NY 10011.

Frankenstein: The Real Story is reprinted courtesy of the author, Gail Erwin, 1753 So. 106th St., Omaha, NE 68124.

White Man Dancing is reprinted by special permission of Stephen Metcalfe's agent, Mary Meagher, The Gersh Agency, 130 W. 42nd St., New York, NY 10036.

This One Thing I Do is reprinted by special permission of Claire Braz-Valentine & Michael Griggs' agent, Samuel French, Inc., 45 W. 25th St., New York, NY 10010.

Five Scenes From Life, by Alan Brody. Copyright 1989 by Alan Brody. Reprinted by permission of the author.

> CAUTION: Professionals and amateurs are hereby warned that FIVE SCENES FROM LIFE is subject to a royalty. It is fully protected by copyright. Inquiries and permission must be secured from the author's agent, Graham Agency, 311 W. 43rd St., New York, NY 10036.

Roots in Water. Copyright 1990 by Richard Nelson. All rights reserved.

> WARNING: Professionals and amateurs are hereby warned that ROOTS IN WATER is under copyright and is subject to a royalty. All inquiries regarding rights should be addressed to the author's agent in writing, William Morris Agency, Inc., 1350 Avenue of the Americas, New York, NY 10019, Attention: Peter Franklin.

For Her and *I Can't Stop Thinking Today* are reprinted by special permission of Annie Evans' agent, Mary Meagher, The Gersh Agency, 130 W. 42nd St., New York, NY 10036.

Signs of Life is reprinted by permission of the author, Debbie Baley, Perseverance Theatre, 914 3rd St., Douglas, AK 99824.

Zara Spook and Other Lures is reprinted by special permission of Joan Ackermann's agent, Mary Harden, Bret Adams Ltd., 448 W. 44th St., New York, NY 10036.

Tables and Chairs is reprinted by permission of the author, Stanley Rutherford, Box 50, Camp Meeker, CA 95419.

The Only Woman General and *Little Victories* are reprinted by permission of the author, Lavonne Mueller, Dept. of Theatre Arts, University of Iowa, Iowa City, IA 52242.

Gleaning/Rebusca is reprinted by permission of the author, Caridad Svich, c/o

mond's agent, Helen Merrill, Helen Merrill Ltd., 435 W. 23rd St., #1A, New York, NY 10011.

Wetter Than Water is reprinted by special permission with Deborah Pryor's agent, William Craver, Writers and Artists Agency, 19 W. 44th St., #1000, New York, NY 10036-5901.

Flint and Roses is reprinted by special permission of Jim Peck's agent, Mitch Douglas, ICM Inc., 40 W. 57th St., New York, NY 10019.

To Moscow is reprinted by special permission of the author, Karen Sunde, 23 Leroy St., #8, New York, NY 10014.

Anton, Himself was originally commissioned by Actors Theatre of Louisville, and first published in "Moscow Art Theatre," a monograph. It is reprinted here by special permission of the author, Karen Sunde, 23 Leroy St., #8, New York, NY 10014.

Masha, Too was commissioned and originally produced by The People's Light and Theatre Company, Danny S. Fruchter, Producing Director. It is reprinted here by special permission of the author, Karen Sunde, 23 Leroy St., #8, New York, NY 10014.

Cinderella Waltz and *The Girlhood of Shakespeare's Heroines* are reprinted by special permission of the author's agent, Charles R. Van Nostrand, Samuel French, Inc., 45 W. 25th St., New York, NY 10010. Copyright © 1978, 1984, 1987 by Don Nigro. Reprinted by permission of Samuel French, Inc.

About the Editor

Roger Ellis is a theatre teacher and director living in Michigan. He earned his M.A. in Theatre from the University of Santa Clara, and his Ph.D. in Dramatic Art from the University of California at Berkeley. He trained as an actor under Carlo Mazzone-Clementi of Dell'Arte, Michael Shurtleff, Robert Goldsby of the Berkeley Repertory Theatre, and James Roose-Evans of Great Britain's National Theatre. He has also spent nine seasons as an actor-director with repertory, summer stock, festival and dinner theatres in California and Michigan; and frequently conducts workshops in the Great Lakes region on acting and auditioning skills. He has authored or edited ten books for the stage, including anthologies, critical texts and auditioning handbooks. In 1992 he initiated an ethnic theatre program at Grand Valley State University in Michigan, creating guest artist residencies and presenting new American plays dealing with cultural diversity; and he has been director of the university's Shakespeare Festival since 1993. He is currently the president of the Theatre Alliance of Michigan, and a Professor of Theatre Arts at Grand Valley State University.

A NEW ANTHOLOGY OF WORLD DRAMA

with historical introductions
to each play by

DR. NORMAN A. BERT

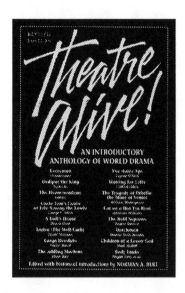

A major new anthology of world drama from many cultures. Sixteen famous plays by leading international playwrights including: **Children of a Lesser God** — *Medoff*, **Largo Desolato** — *Havel*, **The Hairy Ape** — *O'Neill*, **Cat on a Hot Tin Roof** — *Williams*, **The Bald Soprano** — *Ionesco*, **Izutsu** — *Motokiyo*, **Waiting for Lefty** — *Odets*, **A Doll's House** — *Ibsen*, **The Adding Machine** — *Rice*, **The Hypochondriac** — *Molière*, **Uncle Tom's Cabin** — *Aiken*, **Oedipus the King** — *Sophocles*, **Dutchman** — *Baraka*, **Everyman** — *Anonymous*, **The Tragedy of Othello** — *Shakespeare* and **Body Leaks** — *Terry*. All major periods of theatre from classical to contemporary 20th century. A well-researched introduction precedes each script offering fascinating historical orientation. Recommended as an exceptional text for theatre classes. It presents the entire globe of theatre history — "where we've been and where we're going." ISBN 1-56608-008-8

Paperback book (848 pages)

Order Form

Meriwether Publishing Ltd.
P.O. Box 7710
Colorado Springs, CO 80933-7710
Telephone: (719) 594-4422
Website: www.meriwetherpublishing.com

Please send me the following books:

_____	**Scenes and Monologs from the Best New Plays #BK-B140** **edited by Roger Ellis** *An anthology of new American plays*	**$15.95**
_____	**Audition Monologs for Student Actors #BK-B232** **edited by Roger Ellis** *Selections from contemporary plays*	**$15.95**
_____	**Multicultural Theatre #BK-B205** **edited by Roger Ellis** *Scenes and monologs by multicultural writers*	**$15.95**
_____	**Multicultural Theatre II #BK-B223** **edited by Roger Ellis** *Contemporary Hispanic, Asian and African-American plays*	**$15.95**
_____	**International Plays for Young Audiences #BK-B240** **edited by Roger Ellis** *Contemporary works by leading playwrights*	**$16.95**
_____	**Plays for Young Audiences by Max Bush #BK-B131** **edited by Roger Ellis** *An anthology of widely produced plays for youth*	**$16.95**
_____	**The Theatre Audition Book #BK-B224** **by Gerald Lee Ratliff** *Playing monologs from contemporary, modern, period and classical plays*	**$16.95**

These and other fine Meriwether Publishing books are available at your local bookstore or direct from the publisher. Prices subject to change without notice. Check our website or call for current prices.

Name: _____

Organization name: _____

Address: _____

City: _____ State: _____

Zip: _____ Phone: _____

❑ **Check enclosed**

❑ **Visa / MasterCard / Discover #** _____

Expiration

Signature: _____ *date:* _____

(required for credit card orders)

Colorado residents: Please add 3% sales tax.
Shipping: Include $2.75 for the first book and 50¢ for each additional book ordered.

❑ *Please send me a copy of your complete catalog of books and plays.*

Order Form

Meriwether Publishing Ltd.
P.O. Box 7710
Colorado Springs, CO 80933-7710
Telephone: (719) 594-4422
Website: www.meriwetherpublishing.com

Please send me the following books:

_____ **Scenes and Monologs from the Best** $15.95
New Plays #BK-B140
edited by Roger Ellis
An anthology of new American plays

_____ **Audition Monologs for Student** $15.95
Actors #BK-B232
edited by Roger Ellis
Selections from contemporary plays

_____ **Multicultural Theatre #BK-B205** $15.95
edited by Roger Ellis
Scenes and monologs by multicultural writers

_____ **Multicultural Theatre II #BK-B223** $15.95
edited by Roger Ellis
Contemporary Hispanic, Asian and African-American plays

_____ **International Plays for Young** $16.95
Audiences #BK-B240
edited by Roger Ellis
Contemporary works by leading playwrights

_____ **Plays for Young Audiences by Max Bush** $16.95
#BK-B131
edited by Roger Ellis
An anthology of widely produced plays for youth

_____ **The Theatre Audition Book #BK-B224** $16.95
by Gerald Lee Ratliff
Playing monologs from contemporary, modern,
period and classical plays

These and other fine Meriwether Publishing books are available at
your local bookstore or direct from the publisher. Prices subject to
change without notice. Check our website or call for current prices.

Name: _____

Organization name: _____

Address: _____

City: _____ State: _____

Zip: _____ Phone: _____

❏ **Check enclosed**

❏ **Visa / MasterCard / Discover #** _____

                                           Expiration
Signature: _____ *date:* _____

        (required for credit card orders)

Colorado residents: Please add 3% sales tax.
Shipping: Include $2.75 for the first book and 50¢ for each additional book ordered.

❏ *Please send me a copy of your complete catalog of books and plays.*